A LIFE OF LOVE FOR THE PROPHET MUḤAMMAD (PBUH)

A Biography of Shaikh Muḥammad Al-Muḥammad Al-Kasnazān

Louay Fatoohi

SAFIS PUBLISHING
Birmingham – UK

Published in the United Kingdom by
Safis Publishing Limited, Birmingham, UK.
www.safispub.com

ISBN 978-1-906342-41-8 (paperback)
978-1-906342-42-5 (ebook)

First Edition

Version Identifier: 22033001

Cover image: A representation of a dream encounter of Shaikh Muḥammad al-Muḥammad with the Prophet Muḥammad (PBUH) inside his noble shrine in late 2015 or early 2016, which is described in Chapter twenty-three. The photo of the Shaikh is from a session of odes of praise at the takya in Amman on 11 January 2019.

The Author

Louay Fatoohi was born in Baghdad, Iraq, in 1961. He and his wife migrated to the UK in 1992. He lives in Birmingham, England. He obtained a BSc in physics from Baghdad University, Iraq, in 1984 and a PhD in astronomy from Durham University, UK, in 1998.

Originally from a Christian family, Louay reverted to Islam in his early twenties. He is one of the caliphs (representatives) of Ṭarīqa Kasnazāniyya. In addition to being his faith of choice and way of life, Islam is for him a subject of deep intellectual interest. He is interested in Qur'anic and Islamic studies in general, but his main areas of research are as follows:

- The comparative study of history in the Qur'an, Jewish and Christian scriptures, and independent historical sources
- Sufism
- The history of the Qur'anic text and revelation
- Qur'anic exegesis

Louay is a prolific author who has published over twenty-five books in English and Arabic in Islamic studies. He has also published over twenty research papers on cosmology, applied historical astronomy, and the Islamic calendar.

Contents

Allah (high is He) is present and sees and witnesses what happens. He is the King of Kings, "His is the creation and the command" (al-A'rāf 7:54). Allah is eternal; Allah is alive and never dies, "To Allah we belong and to Him we will return" (al-Baqara 2:156); "every soul will taste death" (Āl 'Imrān 3:185). Every day, we come closer to death because every day brings the appointed time closer. We have to take advantage of life and dedicate it to obeying Allah (exalted and high is He). No one lives forever.

Think well and have faith in Allah (high is He), obey His commandments, and refrain from what He ordered you not to do. Your Ṭarīqa guides you to the closeness of Allah. Always hold yourselves to account, exchange advice and guidance, and love each other in Allah's cause. Remember Him often and often read prayers on our Master the Messenger (PBUH). May Allah bless you. Allāhumma ṣallī 'alā sayyidinā Muḥammadi 'l-waṣfi wal-waḥyi war-risālati wal-ḥikmati wa'alā 'ālihi wa-ṣaḥbihi wa-sallim taslīmā. "Our Lord! Give us good in this world and good in the hereafter and protect us from the torment of the Fire!" (al-Baqara 2:201).

Shaikh Muḥammad al-Muḥammad al-Kasnazān
(*Sermon*, 2 April 2000)

Preface: Sources and Documentation

This book is mainly extracted from my detailed biography of Shaikh Muḥammad al-Muḥammad al-Kasnazān. I should introduce that book first before talking about the current derivative work.

The first Arabic edition of my detailed biography of our Master (may Allah sanctify his secret), *Shaikh Muḥammad al-Muḥammad al-Kasnazān al-Ḥusaynī: A Life in the Footsteps of the Best of Lives*, was published in October 2018. A revised second edition followed in May 2019. As the English translation of the biography was about to be completed, on 4 July 2020, Allah chose our noble Shaikh to be with Him, in the company of the Prophets, the truthful, the martyrs, and the righteous. After serving as the Shaikh of Ṭarīqa of his great-grandfather, the Prophet Muḥammad (PBUH), for forty-two years, he was succeeded by the man he had chosen decades earlier to take over after him, his eldest son, Shaikh Shamduddīn Muḥammad Nahro al-Kasnazān. Less than two months later, the English translation of the biography was published at the end of August 2020.

I compiled the material of the biography from a variety of sources. I took the thinking and opinions of our Shaikh directly from him. I confined my sources in this case to his public sermons that I was fortunate enough to attend or obtain video or audio recordings of, his speeches and conversations in private sessions that he was generous enough to give me the opportunity to attend, and his published writings. When quoting from his sermons, I converted the wording from the Iraqi dialect to standard Arabic and edited them, carefully preserving the original meaning without any change.

I have taken the details of our Shaikh's life, as well as the history of the Kasnazānī Shaikhs before him, from two main sources, in addition to him: first, his relatives and followers who accompanied him in the various stages of his life, before and after assuming the Shaikhdom; second, his sermons, conversations, and writings. I would like to particularly thank Shaikh Sāmān Maʿrūf, who is married to one of our Shaikh's sisters and whose sister was married to our Shaikh; caliph Yāsīn

Ṣūfī ʿAbd Allah, who accompanied our Shaikh closely and knew him since his childhood and was a dervish from the time of his father and predecessor, Shaikh ʿAbd al-Karīm al-Kasnazān. I am also greatly indebted to caliph ʿImād ʿAbd al-Ṣamad who, in addition to providing me with some of the material of the book, facilitated the collection of other material. My wife, Dr Shetha al-Dargazelli, contributed immensely valuable corrections and comments on drafts of the book.

I carefully examined the historical details that I did not get directly from the Shaikh. He instructed me to be particularly careful when examining accounts of supernatural feats of the Shaikhs of Ṭarīqa, to spot and discard false reports and to investigate and verify any inaccuracies in reports of real events. He asked me to check with him or with Shaikh Sāmān if need be. Many events are decades old, and human memory often forgets some details over time or even changes them inadvertently. Additionally, the narrators of some events did not witness them but conveyed what they had heard. I compiled and scrutinised these narratives with care, something that I was helped with by the multiplicity of sources. I did not include narratives where I could not feel confident in their authenticity and accuracy. At times, I could not verify certain details of a particular event, so I documented the details that I determined to be accurate and ignored the rest.

While listening to my interviewees talking about the history of our Shaikh during the compilation of the material for the book, the following majestic line of poetry would appear in my head now and then:

> Never I sat to talk to people
> but you were the subject of my speech with my conversants.

The martyr al-Hallāj here describes the complete engrossment with the love of Allah (mighty and sublime is He) that took over his mind, heart, and senses such that he could no longer talk about anyone other than his Beloved. Talking about the Shaikhs of Ṭarīqa and their lives is a form of remembering Allah. What distinguished them and made them the centre of attention is the life of piety and worship that every one of them led. In addition, they dedicated their lives to guiding those who seek nearness to Allah and urging and showing them how to be a source of good for themselves and others.

Nearness to Allah grants every Shaikh of Ṭarīqa great, special blessings that are manifested in countless supernatural wonders. These "karāmas", as they are known, are the ink with which a large part of the Shaikh's life is written. Karāmas play a major role in the Shaikh's life, surrounding him even before becoming a Shaikh. Some karāmas point to him even before his birth, confirming his selection by Allah for that spiritual leadership. Accordingly, wonders permeated all stages of the life of Shaikh Muḥammad al-Muḥammad al-Kasnazān. It is only natural, then, that his biography is imbued with supernatural feats.

As there are countless karāmas and they continue to occur all the time, no book can compile more than a tiny number of them. I have only mentioned wonders that have explanatory functions in their respective contexts. The life of our Shaikh cannot be sufficiently covered without referring to the history, legacy, and karāmas of the Shaikhs of Ṭarīqa Kasnazāniyya who preceded him. I have, however, quoted only a small part of this blessed history, as required by the subjects and objectives of the book.

I wrote the biography in a unique way. It introduced the life of the honourable Shaikh in the context of explaining the Sufi method to get close to Allah, and it expounded Sufism in the course of narrating his life story. Said differently, the book explained Sufism through our Shaikh's life and, at the same time, recounted his life events through an introduction to Sufism, which represents the spiritual side of Islam. Many who are interested in the life of the Shaikh would also be interested in an introduction to Sufi concepts and practices, in particular, if they are not familiar with Sufism. This integrated introduction to both the life of a Sufi Shaikh and his thought is possible because his life embodies his beliefs.

Some readers, however, would rather read the biography of our Shaikh and his Sufi thought separately so that they can concentrate on one of them at a time. I, therefore, decided to extract two middle-sized books from the large-volume biography: one focuses on the biography of the Shaikh and the second introduces Sufism according to Ṭarīqa 'Aliyya Qādiriyya Kasnazāniyya (Ṭarīqa Kasnazāniyya). I did my best to avoid any repetition between the two books other than the minimal amount that I considered necessary to appear in both books. To ensure the two books covered all the topics of the sourcebook, I worked on them at the same time. I also had to restructure and rewrite the source material. I have also taken this opportunity to add to both books additional materials that I did not include in the sourcebook.

I substantively abbreviated the two chapters on the Shaikh's involvement in the Kurdish movement and the persecution of Ṭarīqa by the Iraqi regime in the 1990s. Details of various events in these chapters were necessary to cover in the original book to serve as a reference for historians, but much of this information is of little interest to those who are not specifically concerned with the details of these two periods. The two abbreviated chapters in this book document what is relevant from these two periods to the life of the Shaikh and Ṭarīqa.

I decided to write these two books in Arabic first and then translate them into English. The first book, *Ḥayātun wa fanā'un fī ḥubbi al-Nabī Muḥammad (PBUH): sīrat al-sayyid al-Shaikh Muḥammad al-Muḥammad al-Kasnazān*, which focuses on the biography of the Shaikh, came out in November 2020. The second, which explains the Sufi path according to Ṭarīqa Kasnazāniyya, was published one month later, under the title *al-Taṣawwuf fī al-Ṭarīqa al-ʿAliyya al-Qādiriyya al-Kasnazāniyya: manhajun taṭbiqiyyun lil-jānib al-ruḥī lil-Islām*. The present volume is the English translation of the biography book.

Allah willing, we guide the nation with proper guidance, in line with how the Messenger guided the nation. We enjoin virtue and forbid vice. We enjoin brotherhood, love, worship, and equality. We enjoin taking each other for a brother and having love for each other. We enjoin good deeds. We enjoin what Allah (mighty and glorified is He) sent down in the Qur'an on the honourable beloved (PBUH) to enjoin to the Islamic nation. We enjoin what Allah (mighty and glorified is He) enjoined, that is, the instructions in the Book and the Sunna. This is our work. This is our Ṭarīqa.

Shaikh Muḥammad al-Muḥammad al-Kasnazān
(*Sermon*, 7 February 2013)

Introduction: Structure and Contents

I have structured this book to follow the life of the Shaikh in chronological order as much as possible. I have compiled in this biography information about the various stages of his life and all of its aspects. This should give the reader a reasonably complete picture of his life, with its many challenges, sufferings, and achievements; events that brought happiness and others that filled the heart with sadness.

This biography is not confined to the history of Shaikh Muḥammad al-Muḥammad after becoming the Master at the age of forty, but it also follows the different stages of his earlier life. I have also covered events that predated his birth that are relevant to studying his life. One thing that this biography shows is the fundamental changes that happened to his character, personality, behaviour, and interests after assuming the Shaikhdom. After a life occupied by worldly interests in which Ṭarīqa played a small role, as he was the son of the Master of Ṭarīqa and one of its dervishes, becoming its Shaikh made Ṭarīqa his first concern and calling people to Allah his main activity and the main driver of his behaviour.

This is a brief overview of the contents of the book. **Chapter one** introduces our Shaikh's noble pedigree, which goes back to the Messenger of Allah, Muḥammad (PBUH), from both parental sides. It also follows the history of the Barzinjī family in the north of Iraq to which he belongs. The chapter further presents the Shaikhs of Ṭarīqa Kasnazāniyya.

Chapter two recounts how our Shaikh's parents got married. It also talks about the special love and care that Shaikh Ḥusayn, our Shaikh's uncle and the Shaikh of Ṭarīqa at the time, had for his infant nephew. **Chapter three** discusses the spiritual home environment in which the Shaikh was brought up. The chapter focuses on his mother, Ḥafṣa, and her role as the wife of the Master of Ṭarīqa. We learn about his father, Shaikh ʿAbd al-Karīm, more in later chapters.

Our Shaikh's religious studies and schooling are explained in **Chapter four. Chapter five** discusses briefly his role in defending the rights of the Kurdish people in the north of Iraq in the first half of the 1960s. His marriage and children are introduced in **Chapter six.**

Becoming a Shaikh of Ṭarīqa is an act of divine election through the Prophet (PBUH), not self-appointment or a majority decision by a group of people. **Chapter seven** explains the selection of Shaikh Muḥammad al-Muḥammad for the future Shaikhdom of Ṭarīqa. **Chapter eight** recounts how he became the Shaikh after the passing of his predecessor. Our Shaikh performed "khalwa" (seclusion) on three different occasions after assuming the Shaikhdom. This is the subject of **Chapter nine.**

His decision in the early 1980s to move the headquarters of Ṭarīqa from Kirkuk to the capital, Baghdad, led to an unprecedented number of people becoming dervishes of Ṭarīqa Kasnazāniyya. This is discussed in **Chapter ten. Chapter eleven** introduces Shaikh Muḥammad al-Muḥammad's exceptional preaching efforts. **Chapter twelve** details the substantial changes that he made to the dhikrs of Ṭarīqa. The Shaikh loved worshipping Allah and would spend most of the day and night performing dhikr. **Chapter thirteen** discusses his worshipping practices.

In 1990, the Shaikh proposed a new Islamic lunar calendar that celebrates the birth of the Prophet Muḥammad (PBUH), which he called the "Muhammadī" calendar. He followed it in 1994 with an equivalent solar calendar called the "Muhammadī Shamsī" calendar. These calendars are the subject of **Chapter fourteen. Chapter fifteen** talks about the love the Shaikh had for visiting and renovating holy places. Listening to odes of praise of the Prophet (PBUH) and the Shaikhs is much loved by Sufis, and so was the case with our Shaikh. This is explained in **Chapter sixteen.**

Chapter seventeen focuses on the political persecution that Ṭarīqa Kasnazāniyya faced in Iraq, which forced the Shaikh to emigrate from Baghdad and eventually from Iraqi. Since his childhood, he was fond of reading and, after becoming the Shaikh of Ṭarīqa, he regularly urged dervishes to never stop learning and seeking knowledge. This is discussed in **Chapter eighteen.** His choice of his eldest son to succeed him as the Shaikh of Ṭarīqa is the subject of **Chapter nineteen.**

The Shaikhs of Ṭarīqa emulate the traits of the Prophet (PBUH). **Chapter twenty** presents some of our Shaikh's noble manners. The

Shaikhdom of Ṭarīqa is a position of leadership. **Chapter twenty-one** discusses some of his leadership qualities.

Chapter twenty-two introduces his various hobbies and interests that had not been discussed in earlier chapters. **Chapter twenty-three** recounts his last illness and departure to the spirit world.

Appendix A is a compilation of major events and dates in the life of the Shaikh, listed in chronological order.

Our actions and our movements are all by the spiritual influence of the Messenger (PBUH), the people of the Prophetic household, al-Karrār (Imām ʿAlī), Imām Ḥusayn, our Master al-Gaylāni, and our Master Shāh al-Kasnazān, may Allah sanctify their secrets. We walk with their spiritual influence, their power, their blessing, and their supervision.

Shaikh Muḥammad al-Muḥammad al-Kasnazān
(*Sermon*, 7 January 2010)

1

Prophetic Lineage and Eminent Shaikhs

The lineage of sayyid[1] Shaikh Muḥammad al-Muḥammad al-Kasnazān traces back to the Prophet Muḥammad (PBUH) on both his father's and mother's side. Descending from the Prophet (PBUH) has great significance, as illustrated in this ḥadīth:

> Indeed, I am leaving among you that which, if you hold fast to, you shall not go astray after me. One of them is greater than the other: Allah's Book, which is a rope extending from the sky to the earth, and my family, the people of my household. They shall not split until they meet me at the basin, so look after how you deal with them after me".[2]

This ḥadīth has a clear instruction: following Allah and the Prophet (PBUH) means to follow the Qur'an and the Prophetic household. The latter does not refer to all those who are related to the Prophet (PBUH) by blood. Rather, it means that those who are nearest Him, most active in preaching and calling to His way, and the inheritors of most of the Prophet's (PBUH) spiritual states have been and will be from his progeny. Indeed, history shows that the most successful and effective callers to Allah's way have been from the Prophetic household. The above ḥadīth explains this verse, "Allah intends only to remove from you the impurity [of sin], O people of the [Prophet's] household, and to purify you with [extensive] purification" (al-Āḥzāb 33:33).

---

[1] "Sayyid" (feminine "sayyid"), which means "master" (feminine "lady"), is an honourary title that is used for the desendants of the Prophet (PBUH).

[2] Al-Tirmidhī, *Al-Jāmi' al-kabīr*, VI, no. 3788, p. 125. This ḥadīth is known as the ḥadīth of "'itra" or "thaqalayn", because one or both of these words occur in some of its versions. "'Itra" means "descendants", "relatives", and "clan", but in this ḥadīth it expressly refers to the descendants of the Prophet (PBUH). The word "thaqalayn" is the dual form of "thaqal", which means "something immensely valuable and important". It refers in this ḥadīth to "the Qur'an" and the "descendants of the Prophet (PBUH)".

Some accounts suggest that the Prophet (PBUH) said the above words a few months before his passing from this world. According to the way it is narrated in *Saḥiḥ Muslim*, before stating the ḥadīth, the Messenger (PBUH) said, "I am only a man who is about to receive my Lord's messenger [i.e. the Angel of Death]",[3] which confirms that the ḥadīth was stated just before he departed from this world. This compilation of ḥadīths also mentions that the Prophet (PBUH) delivered the sermon at the brook of Khumm, which means that it is likely the same sermon in which Imam ʿAlī's authority over the Muslims was declared, "O Allah! Whoever I have been a Master to, then ʿAlī is his Master too. O Allah! Befriend those who befriend him and be enemy to those who take him for an enemy; support those who support him and forsake those who forsake him".[4] It is evident from the ḥadīth that it was a "final will", meaning that it is likely one of the last major instructions he issued. This, in turn, confirms its importance and clarifies its meaning and significance.

Shaikh Muḥammad al-Muḥammad al-Kasnazān descended from a family from northern Iraq known as "Barzinjī" after sayyid ʿĪsā al-Barzinjī. Persecution forced many descendants of the Messenger of Allah (PBUH) to emigrate from his homeland of the Arabian Peninsula. This emigration was apparently harmful to the emigrants but, on a deeper level, it was actually a source of mercy for the inhabitants of the destination areas as the emigrants guided them to the way of their great forefather (PBUH).

One of these descendants, Yūsuf, emigrated north to the city of Hamadān, in northwestern present-day Iran, so he acquired the title of "al-Hamadānī". Sayyid Yūsuf al-Hamadānī was a scholar, a Sufi, and an ascetic, and he was well versed in Islamic jurisprudence. As a result of his piety and knowledge, thousands of people gathered around him to learn about Sufism and other religious sciences. He was known as "the Shooting Star of Religion".

To avoid any confusion, we should clarify that the Yūsuf al-Hamadānī we are referring to is not Shaikh Abū Yaʿqūb Yūsuf al-Hamadānī, who was a contemporary of Shaikh ʿAbd al-Qādir al-

---

[3] Muslim, *Ṣaḥīḥ*, IV, no. 2408, p. 1873.

[4] Aḥmad b. Ḥanbal, *Musnad al-Imām Aḥmad b. Ḥanbal*, I, no. 950-951, p. 262-263.

Gaylānī. When Shaikh ʿAbd al-Qādir visited Abū Yaʿqūb, the latter said to him, "It's as if I see you [in the future] in Baghdad, sitting on the preaching chair, addressing the public, saying, 'this foot of mine is on the neck of every walī'. It's as if I see the walīs in your time bowing their necks out of reverence for you".[5] Sayyid Yūsuf al-Hamadānī, on the other hand, came about two centuries after Shaikh ʿAbd al-Qādir.

Yūsuf al-Hamadānī was the son of sayyid Muḥammad al-Manṣūr; son of sayyid ʿAbd al-ʿAzīz; son of sayyid ʿAbd Allah; son of sayyid Ismāʿīl al-Muḥaddath; son of Imām Mūsā al-Kāẓim; son of Imām Jaʿfar al-Ṣādiq; son of Imām Muḥammad al-Bāqir; son of Imām ʿAlī Zayn al-ʿĀbidīn; son of Imām al-Ḥusayn; son of Imām ʿAlī Ibn Abī Ṭālib (may Allah ennoble his face) and sayyida Fāṭima al-Zahrāʾ, the daughter of the Seal of Prophets and Messengers, Muḥammad (PBUH).[6]

Sayyid Yūsuf had a son named Bābā ʿAlī, who became a prominent scholar and Sufi and had three sons: Mūsā, ʿĪsā, and Muḥammad. The three brothers went to perform the pilgrimage and to visit the Messenger (PBUH). Returning via Iraq, they headed north until they reached the area that later became known as "Barzinja", where they decided to stay for some time. One night, ʿĪsā saw the Prophet (PBUH) order him to permanently settle in the area and build a mosque there. His elder brother, Mūsā, stayed with him, while their younger brother, Muḥammad, returned to Hamadān, before settling in Afghanistan.

Sayyid Mūsā and sayyid ʿĪsā carried out the Prophet's (PBUH) order to build a mosque and reside in the area. They dedicated themselves to the service of Islam, preaching to people. Sayyid Mūsā married the daughter of a well-known Shaikh there. A short while afterwards, he was preaching in a nearby area when he was assassinated by an extremist group of the Nuṣayriyya sect.[7] Sayyid ʿĪsā brought back his brother's corpse and buried him in Barzinja. He married his widow, Fāṭima, and Allah blessed them with twelve children. Sayyid Mūsā did not have any children, so all Barzinjī sayyids, including our Shaikh's family, are descendants of sayyid ʿĪsā. The shrines of sayyids ʿĪsā and

---

[5] Al-Haytamī, *Al-Fatāwā al-ḥadīthiyya*, 316.

[6] One source in which the early ancestors of our Shaikh are listed is Al-Najafī, *Baḥr al-ansāb*, 62.

[7] Nuṣayriyya is another name for the "ʿAlawīs" or "Alawites".

Mūsā exist today close to the mosque they built.[8]

The history of the Barzinjī sayyids, in general, shows that they inherited an indescribable blessing from their forefather (PBUH). We see this in the great number of walīs that have come from this blessed lineage and in their countless karāmas. Their offspring are found all over the world. Shaikh Muḥammad al-Muḥammad al-Kasnazān describes his forefather sayyid ʿĪsā al-Barzinjī as the "Reviver of the Family and Religion".

Sayyid ʿĪsā al-Barzinjī was also known by the title "Nūr Bakhsh", which means "Giver of Light", because light would appear on the face of anyone who took the pledge from him. The Messenger (PBUH) kissed him just above his forehead, so he would drape his turban just above his forehead so that the light would not affect the beholder's sight.

Shaikh Muḥammad al-Muḥammad descended from the Barzinjī family through its Kasnazānī branch. The great-grandfather of this blessed family was Shaikh ʿAbd al-Karīm Shāh al-Kasnazān (1824-1902), from whom it derives its name. He was the son of sayyid Ḥusayn; son of sayyid Ḥasan; son of sayyid ʿAbd al-Karīm al-Khāwī; son of sayyid Ismāʿīl al-Wilyānī; son of sayyid Muḥammad an-Nūdīhī (who is known as "the Red Sulphur"); son of sayyid Bābā ʿAlī al-Wandarīna; son of sayyid Bābā Rasūl al-Kabīr; son of sayyid ʿAbd al-Sayyid al-Thānī; son of sayyid ʿAbd al-Rasūl; son of sayyid Qalandar; son of sayyid ʿAbd al-Sayyid; son of sayyid ʿĪsā al-Aḥdab; son of sayyid Ḥusayn; son of sayyid Bāyazīd; son of sayyid ʿAbd al-Karīm al-Awwal; son of sayyid ʿĪsā al-Barzinjī.

Shaikh ʿAbd al-Karīm acquired the title "Kasnazān" after going for a retreat in a cave on Mount Sagarma in northern Iraq. Shaikh ʿAbd al-Qādir al-Gaylānī had gone into seclusion in that cave 750 years earlier, which is why it was locally known by the Kurdish name "Gaylān Āwā", which means "Gaylān's Shelter". Shaikh ʿAbd al-Karīm was instructed to go into his retreat by his uncle and the Master of Ṭarīqa Qādiriyya at the time, Shaikh ʿAbd al-Qādir Qāzān Qāya. He remained in

---

[8] Al-Mudarris, *ʿUlamāʾunā fī-khidmat al-ʿilm wal-dīn*, 421-422. There are several different narratives in various sources about how sayyids ʿĪsā and Mūsā settled down in Barzinja, such as the version by Edmonds, *Kurds, Turks and Arabs*, 68-71.

consecutive seclusions for two years during which his family lost all contact with him and could not find him. This absence earned him the Kurdish title "Kasnazān", which means "no one knows", as no one knew his fate. When someone would inquire about what happened to him, the reply would be "Kasnazān". The Sufi explanation of this title, however, is to be found in these words of the Shaikh later in his life, "Allah has granted me a network of secrets that no one knows of, save Allah and his Prophet (PBUH)". These secrets that no one has knowledge of are the explanation of the unique title "Kasnazān".

Three years after coming out of his retreat, Shaikh ʿAbd al-Karīm moved to live in an area called "Karbchna". His followers went to live with him there, turning a place that had only two or three houses into a relatively large village. He lived there for the rest of his life. Karbchna became the home village of the Shaikhs of the Kasnazānī family.

Shaikh ʿAbd al-Karīm Shāh al-Kasnazān became the Master of the Qādirī Ṭarīqa. His great life of piety drew him very close to Allah. He became a renewer (*mujaddid*) of the practice of Islam. During his time, Ṭarīqa entered a new phase and became known as "Ṭarīqa ʿAliyya Qādiriyya Kasnazāniyya". Its name is derived from the names of three of its greatest Masters, Imām ʿAlī Ibn Abī Ṭālib, Shaikh ʿAbd al-Qādir al-Gaylānī, and Shaikh ʿAbd al-Karīm Shāh al-Kasnazān.

Ṭarīqa Kasnazāniyya, as it is abbreviated, has a continuous, unbroken chain of Shaikhs, meaning it has always had a living Shaikh: every Shaikh was given the Masterdom of Ṭarīqa by hand by his predecessor. This blessed Ṭarīqa goes back to the Prophet Muḥammad (PBUH), who bequeathed his spiritual knowledge to the Master of Ṭarīqa after him, Imām ʿAlī Ibn Abī Ṭālib (may Allah ennoble his face). Imām ʿAlī passed Ṭarīqa through two branches.

Our Master calls the first "the Golden Branch" because it comprises Shaikhs from the Prophetic household. It begins with Imām Ḥusayn, who passed it to Imām ʿAlī Zayn al-ʿAbidīn, to Imām Muḥammad al-Bāqir, to Imām Jaʿfar al-Ṣādiq, to Imām Mūsa al-Kāẓim, to Imām ʿAlī al-Riḍā.

Imām ʿAlī bequeathed Ṭarīqa through a second route to Shaikh Ḥasan al-Baṣrī, who passed it to Shaikh Ḥabīb al-ʿAjamī, to Shaikh Dāwūd al-Ṭāʾī. The two branches of Ṭarīqa Kasnazāniyya meet at Shaikh Maʿrūf al-Karkhī, who inherited the Shaikhdom of Ṭarīqa from his two Masters, Imām ʿAlī al-Riḍā and Shaikh Dāwūd al-Ṭāʾī.

The unbroken chain of Ṭarīqa Kasnazāniyya Shaikhs continues from Shaikh Maʿrūf al-Karkhī to Shaikh Sarī al-Saqaṭī, to Shaikh Junayd al-Baghdādī, to Shaikh Abū Bakr al-Shiblī, to Shaikh ʿAbd al-Wāḥid al-Yamānī, to Shaikh Abū Faraj al-Ṭarsūsī, to Shaikh ʿAlī al-Hagārī, to Shaikh Abū Saʿīd al-Makhzūmī, to Shaikh ʿAbd al-Qādir al-Gaylānī, to Shaikh ʿAbd al-Razzāq al-Gaylānī, to Shaikh Dāwūd al-Ṭḥānī, to Shaikh Muḥammad Gharībullah, to Shaikh ʿAbd al-Fattāḥ al-Sayyāḥ, to Shaikh Muḥammad Qāsim, to Shaikh Muḥammad Ṣādiq, to Shaikh Ḥusayn al-Baḥrānī, to Shaikh Aḥmad al-Aḥsāʾī, to Shaikh Ismāʿīl al-Wilyānī, to Shaikh Muḥyī al-Dīn Karkūk, to Shaikh ʿAbd al-Ṣamad Galazarda, to Shaikh Ḥusayn Qāzānqāya, to Shaikh ʿAbd al-Qādir Qāzānqāya, to Shaikh ʿAbd al-Karīm Shāh al-Kasnazān, may Allah sanctify the secrets of them all.

Shāh al-Kasnazān was succeeded in 1902 by his youngest son, ʿAbd al-Qādir (1867-1922). Shaikh ʿAbd al-Qādir was forced to leave Karbchna in the middle of 1919 and emigrate to western Iran, having fought and urged people to fight against the British army that occupied Iraq and reached the north. He was only fifty-five years old when he died. His son and the Master of Ṭarīqa after him, Ḥusayn, returned his body to Karbchna and buried him next to his father, Shāh al-Kasnazān.

Shaikh Ḥusayn (1888-1939) was renowned for his spiritual exercises, leading a life of unparalleled asceticism. He departed this world at only fifty-two years old, leaving as his successor his brother, ʿAbd al-Karīm (1912-1978), the father of Shaikh Muḥammad al-Muḥammad. For more details on the life of each of the Kasnazānī Shaikhs, see our book *Sufism in Ṭarīqa ʿAliyya Qādiriyya Kasnazāniyya: A Practical Guide for the Spiritual Path of Islam.*

Shaikh Muḥammad al-Muḥammad's mother, Ḥafṣa, also traces her lineage back to the Prophet (PBUH) on her mother's side and her father's side. She was the daughter of sayyid ʿAbd al-Qādir Gulanabar, son of sayyid Muḥammad Ṣāliḥ, son of sayyid ʿAbd al-Qādir Qāzānqāya, son of sayyid Ḥusayn Qāzānqāya, son of sayyid Maḥmūd Klīsa, son of sayyid Ismāʿīl al-Wilyānī, the sixth great-grandfather of Shaikh Muḥammad al-Muḥammad al-Kasnazān on his father's side.

Sayyida Ḥafṣa's father, sayyid ʿAbd al-Qādir, was a caliph of Shāh al-Kasnazān. Although he was sometimes called "Guptapa" after the village he resided in, in the district of Sangāw, he was known as "Gulanabar", which means "bulletproof". One day, Shāh al-Kasnazān placed his blessed hand on sayyid ʿAbd al-Qādir's back and told him that bullets would not kill him. He entered many battles, including against the Russians, who invaded northern Iraq via Iran at the beginning of World War I, and later against the British. Despite having slight traces of bullets on his body, he did not die because of any of those shots. He lived to be approximately ninety years old. Sayyida Ḥafṣa recounted that when her father would return from fighting the Russians, he would undo the belt on his Kurdish clothes, and bullets that hit him without harming him would fall from the belt. This was so well known that even a staff member of the British administration in Iraq at the time mentioned that sayyid ʿAbd al-Qādir was famed for being "bulletproof".[9]

One related miracle of Shāh al-Kasnazān is that some people asked him to give them something similar to the "gula bard"—an amulet that made a person bulletproof—that the renowned walī Kāka Aḥmad al-Shaikh used to give. Shāh al-Kasnazān tore off a piece of the fur rug he was sitting on with his hand and said, "This is a gula bard for you". He did not need to make a special amulet for protection against bullets, as a small piece of the fur he was sitting on was enough to do the job.

A while after Shāh al-Kasnazān passed away and his relatives had inherited his personal belongings, no one knew where the rug had ended up or who had it. One night, our Shaikh's niece dreamt that a piece of Shāh al-Kasnazān's rug and another piece of the belongings of Shaikh ʿAbd al-Qādir Kasnazān were inside a pillow that was in the possession of her paternal aunt. Upon waking up, she opened the pillow and found what she had seen in the dream. This rug was given to our Shaikh who used to present small pieces of it to some dervishes for blessings.

Thus, Shaikh Muḥammad al-Muḥammad descended from the bloodline of Imām Ḥusayn from both parents who belonged to the Kasnazānī branch of the Barzinjī family. One aspect of the blessings of this noble ancestry is that his father and ten of his ancestors on his father's side were also Masters of Ṭarīqa Kasnazāniyya: his father, Shaikh

---

[9] Edmonds, *Kurds, Turks and Arabs*, 340-341.

ʿAbd al-Karīm al-Kasnazān; his grandfather, Shaikh ʿAbd al-Qādir al-Kasnazān; and his great-grandfather, Shaikh ʿAbd al-Karīm Shāh al-Kasnazān. Another Master of Ṭarīqa is Shaikh Ismāʿīl al-Wilyānī, the first person to bring Ṭarīqa Qādiriyya to Iraqi Kurdistan. Then there are the six Imāms: Mūsā al-Kāẓim, Jaʿfar al-Ṣādiq, Muḥammad al-Bāqir, ʿAlī Zayn al-ʿĀbidīn, Ḥusayn, and ʿAlī Ibn Abī Ṭālib (peace be upon them all). Two of our Shaikh's ancestors from his mother's side, Shaikh Ḥusayn Qāzānqāya and his son, Shaikh ʿAbd al-Qādir, were also Masters of Ṭarīqa.

The seeker wants things, and Allah (exalted and high is He), the Messenger, and the Shaikhs also want things from the seeker. They want him to apply the Muḥammadan Shariah and then apply the states, sayings, and deeds of the Messenger to himself. If a person does not benefit himself, how could he benefit others? A seeker must apply Ṭarīqa first himself, then have his family, wife, and children to do likewise. If he can, he should also get others—such as friends, relatives, and acquaintances—to apply it.

Shaikh Muḥammad al-Muḥammad al-Kasnazān
(*Sermon*, 5 December 2012)

2

A Birth of Good News

Sayyida Ḥafṣa Gulanabar was chosen as Shaikh ʿAbd al-Karīm's wife by divine decree. Her brother, Musṭafā, was a childhood friend of Shaikh Ḥusayn and they remained very close. The two friends also fought together against the British army in northern Iraq. Musṭafā had offered Shaikh Ḥusayn his sister, Ḥafṣa, in marriage but the Shaikh did not want to marry again.

About two years after returning to Karbchna from his emigration to Iran, Shaikh Ḥusayn spoke to Musṭafā about marrying the young woman to his brother, ʿAbd al-Karīm. Shaikh Musṭafā consented to this great honour. Sultan Ḥusayn called for his brother, who at the time was no older than thirteen. When the child heard his elder brother the Shaikh of Ṭarīqa's decision, he began to cry and ran away, as children are wont to do. Sultan Ḥusayn told him that he had his reasons that the young boy could not yet understand for wanting this marriage to take place. He knew that the marriage of his brother, who would be the Shaikh of Ṭarīqa after him, to the young woman would produce Shaikh ʿAbd al-Karīm's successor to the Masterdom of Ṭarīqa. The young woman was five years older than Shaikh ʿAbd al-Karīm, which was contrary to the prevalent tradition of having an older husband and younger wife. This confirms that there must have been a subtle purpose behind their marriage.

Shaikh ʿAbd al-Karīm married sayyida Ḥafṣa early in his youth. They had their first son, Ḥusayn, in 1927, and in 1937, the first of their four daughters, ʿĀʾishā, was born. Then, at dawn on Friday 15 April 1938, Allah gifted them with their third child and the secret behind their marriage.

Sayyida Shamsa (may Allah have mercy on her), Shaikh Ḥusayn's daughter, related what happened on the blessed night our Shaikh was born. At the time, she was ten years old. When Shaikh Ḥusayn learned that the wife of his brother, ʿAbd al-Karīm, went into labour at night, he kept walking back and forth between the house's entrance and patio, reciting "Yā Hū, Yā Hū", waiting for the newborn's delivery. He calmed down and sat only when he was told of the delivery at dawn.[1] That our Shaikh was not the first child of Shaikh ʿAbd al-Karīm and sayyida Ḥafṣa highlights the exceptional nature of Sultan[2] Ḥusayn's interest in the newborn.

It was Sultan Ḥusayn who named his nephew "Muḥammad", following the prevalent tradition of the Shaikh of Ṭarīqa naming newborns. About eighty years later, specifically in 2016, the Messenger (PBUH) blessed our Shaikh's name with his, with him now being called "Muḥammad al-Muḥammad".

When Sultan Ḥusayn sent for the newborn, a number of his children, some of whom were very young, were in his assembly. When he extended his hand to greet the swaddled newborn, an aged dervish told him that this would make his children jealous. The Shaikh took the child, placed him on his lap, and began praising him, saying, "This is the reviver of religion, this will benefit religion, this will live a long life".

Shaikh Ḥusayn must have seen a future Shaikh of Ṭarīqa in his nephew, just as his father and the Master of Ṭarīqa before him had said about him a quarter of a century earlier. When Shaikh ʿAbd al-Qādir was informed of the birth of his son, ʿAbd al-Karīm, he asked that the newborn be brought to him. When the baby was placed before him, the Shaikh moved his cane above the child to and fro and said, "What Allah wills, what Allah wills. Allah (exalted and high is He) will guide many Arabs at the hands of the son of this man to the true path". Indeed, in Shaikh Muḥammad al-Muḥammad's time, especially after he moved the central takya to Baghdad in 1982 and he permanently moved from Kirkuk to live there, a vast number of Arabs took the Ṭarīqa's pledge.

When Shaikh Muḥammad al-Muḥammad was two to three months old, he became so ill that his parents thought that he might not survive. They took him to his uncle, Sultan Ḥusayn, who had been in a

---

[1] Shaikh Muḥammad al-Muḥammad al-Kasnazān, *sermon*, 10 February 2016.

[2] The title "Sultan" is used for the Kasnazānī Shaikhs because they are heirs of Shaikh ʿAbd al-Qādir al-Gaylānī, who was known as the "Sultan of walīs".

continuous retreat, isolated from people and the world. Aware that Allah had decreed a tremendous spiritual role for the child, the Shaikh reassured them and told them not to worry about their baby for he had guardians protecting him.

One event that embodies Sultan Ḥusayn's exceptional love for his nephew took place when the ascetic was on his deathbed, hours before his departure from this world. Shaikh ʿAbd al-Karīm and his wife were sitting close to him, weeping over his imminent departure from this world. When Shaikh Ḥusayn, who was lying on the bed, saw their child, who was less than a year old and in the company of a guardian, he motioned for the baby to be brought to him. He held him on his chest and began kissing him and sniffing his neck as if he could smell the pleasant fragrance of Ṭarīqa the baby was destined to take care of forty years later. Those present were further overwhelmed by emotion when they witnessed the moving scene. Shaikh ʿAbd al-Karīm lifted the child off the chest of Shaikh Ḥusayn, upon whom asceticism and seclusion over the years had taken their toll, to avoid any discomfort the baby's weight would cause. This was the last good omen from Sultan Ḥusayn before his passing about the lofty status that the young Muḥammad al-Muḥammad would have in the future.

Shaikh ʿAbd al-Karīm al-Kasnazān would not sleep at night. After leaving his assembly with the dervishes, he would perform the night prayer and remain in a state of dhikr until he would complete the morning prayer, the Sunna prayer, and his other devotions. Then, he would sleep. Even when he was extremely ill, he would continue to recite the Qur'an.

Shaikh Muḥammad al-Muḥammad al-Kasnazān
(*Sermon*, 24 September 2016)

3

Upbringing in a Spiritual Household

Shaikh Muḥammad al-Muḥammad was brought up in a household in which the remembrance of Allah never stopped and the call to piety and good deeds could be heard all the time. His father was the Master of Ṭarīqa, having succeeded Shaikh Ḥusayn when our Shaikh was less than one year old. His mother was an exceptionally devout woman who dedicated herself to helping the Shaikh of Ṭarīqa.

Shaikh 'Abd al-Karīm was the primary influence on our Shaikh. The latter learned the best traits and virtues from his Master, and this influence shaped his personality and behaviour tremendously. He loved his father immensely and deeply revered him, so much so that he could not bring himself to sit in his father's presence until he was asked to do so. He often avoided sitting in his assembly even after the Shaikh asked him to do so. He would not approach the Shaikh unless he had been summoned by him or he needed to ask for his thoughts and instructions on a certain matter.

As was the case with all of Shaikh 'Abd al-Karīm's family, our Shaikh would refer to his father as "Shaikh". While his biological father, Shaikh 'Abd al-Karīm was his spiritual father in the spirit world before that. The seeker's soul is connected to his Shaikh's soul from the day Allah created souls. Despite the significance and sanctity of a paternal relationship, the seeker's relationship to his Shaikh has a greater effect on his life. Generation by generation, this blessed family inherited respect and reverence for the Shaikh. For example, the family of our Master only referred to him as "Shaikh". His children would only stand in his presence, except for Shaikh Nahro, who our Shaikh insisted should sit in his assembly, often because he needed him close to him because he was his General Deputy.

Our Shaikh's spiritual relationship with Shaikh 'Abd al-Karīm was unique; it was not merely a relationship of a disciple with his Shaikh. Rather, it was also a relationship of a Shaikh of Ṭarīqa in the making with his teacher and the present Master. Just as our Shaikh had immense love for his father, Shaikh ʿAbd al-Karīm had an exceptional love for our Shaikh, as we shall see later. Our Shaikh recalled that when he was less than ten years old, he used to accompany Shaikh ʿAbd al-Karīm in his daily visits to the farm of Shāh al-Kasnazān, behind Karbchna, as he oversaw farming work. The Shaikh would perform the afternoon prayer and the afternoon dhikr, and at times the sunset prayer as well, before returning.[1] At night, our Shaikh would not sleep until his father came home after the conclusion of his night gathering with the dervishes. He would then sleep on his father's leg. When Shaikh ʿAbd al-Karīm would travel for preaching, our Shaikh would fall ill until his father came back because of his love for and attachment to him.[2]

Sayyida Ḥafṣa was a little girl of no more than two or three years old when her mother, sayyida Khadīja, passed away. Her father put her under the care of her maternal uncle, Shaikh ʿAbd al-Karīm Qādir Karam, while she was still young. While in the care of her uncle, she learned the Qur'an under Mullā Muḥyī al-Dīn, who was the family's cleric. After marrying Shaikh ʿAbd al-Karīm, she completed her studies under the wife of the great Āzhar Shaikh ʿAbd al-Ḥalīm Maḥmūd when the couple visited Sultan Ḥusayn and stayed in Karbchna for a while. Shaikh ʿAbd al-Karīm also studied the Qur'an under Shaikh ʿAbd al-Ḥalīm. The latter completed his university studies in Egypt and became a scholar in 1932. He joined the Āzhar mission at the Sorbonne University, France, at the end of 1937 and stayed there until he received his doctorate in 1940. Since Sultan Ḥusayn departed this life in early 1939, we can date Shaikh ʿAbd al-Ḥalīm's visit to Karbchna to some time between 1932 and 1937. His decision to pursue a doctorate in Islamic Sufism, specifically on the renowned Sufi Ḥārith Ibn Asad al-Muḥāsibī (AH 243), points to the influence the time he spent with Shaikh Ḥusayn al-Kasnazān had on him. ʿAbd al-Halīm Maḥmūd became the Shaikh of al-Āzhar in 1973, holding this position until his

[1] Shaikh Muḥammad al-Muḥammad al-Kasnazān, *sermon*, 11 August 2019.

[2] Shaikh Muḥammad al-Muḥammad al-Kasnazān, *sermon*, 1 May 2018.

passing in 1978.[3]

Sayyida Ḥafṣa was an exceptionally devout woman who was always in a state of dhikr and constantly maintained her ablution. Our Shaikh reiterated that he only saw her doing three things: praying, reciting the Qur'an, and reading either dhikrs or the book *Dalā'il al-Khayrāt*, which is a compilation of various formulas of prayers upon the Prophet (PBUH). She never suckled her children without being in a state of ablution. This was also the case of Sultan Ḥusayn's wife with her children. Sayyida Ḥafṣa and Shaikh ʿAbd al-Karīm also had three other daughters, Kāfiya, Ḥalīma, and Salmā.

Early in 1956, their eldest son, Ḥusayn, died from an incurable disease, at just twenty-nine years old. From then on until she passed away in 1992, Sayyida Ḥafṣa was in a constant state of spiritual retreat. She became vegetarian, she would not eat fat or oil, and she would not go near gravy or rice. She even forbade herself from eating certain kinds of fruit, such as oranges or sugary fruit. She refrained from eating all the foods that her deceased son used to enjoy. Most of the time, she only ate thin bread with soup.

As was the case with the wives of the Messenger (PBUH), a Shaikh's wife plays an important role in helping him fulfil his duties in service to Allah's way. A Shaikh's life has special demands that his wife is well suited to tend to, such as ensuring the conditions of cleanliness, purity, and permissibility of his drink, food, belongings, and places of sitting, worshipping, and sleeping; knowing what foods the Shaikh can and cannot eat; and preparing the Shaikh's food while in a state of ablution. A Shaikh maintains a tremendous level of pious restraint, so his wife, as well as all who help in and manage his household, must care for that.

The Shaikh of Ṭarīqa's wife bears part of his burden on her shoulders. His household is not an ordinary home. Rather, it is one of Allah's homes, established in service to all who travel on the path to Allah. It is an open-doored takya that people from all over constantly flock to for different needs. Hence, the housework is managed around the clock. A Shaikh's house is one of those that Allah (exalted and high is He) describes in His noble Book, "In homes that Allah has ordered to be raised and that His name be mentioned therein; exalting Him

[3] ʿAbd al-Raḥmān, *Shuyūkh al-azhar*, 5, 15-16.

within them in the morning and the evenings [are] men whom neither commerce nor sale distracts from the remembrance of Allah and performance of prayer and giving of charity" (al-Nūr 24:36-37). While the Shaikh is responsible for all affairs of Ṭarīqa and its dervishes, his wife helps manage the affairs of this house of dhikr. This includes supervising the preparation of food for guests, who come and go at any time, and ensuring the takya is well kept. Sayyida Ḥafṣa was an exemplary wife who spent her life helping Shaikh ʿAbd al-Karīm serve Ṭarīqa and its dervishes.

In the same way that there are male caliphs in the takya who are responsible for preaching to men, there are female caliphs in the women's part of the takya who teach females. Sayyida Ḥafṣa often sat in there to receive visitors, give them the pledge, listen to their needs, and advise them, as she was very knowledgeable in religious matters. She would also bless water and give to those in need and/or would pray for them. She had a special room where she would receive those with private needs that could not be addressed in front of other women. The Shaikh of Ṭarīqa's wife helps him in serving Ṭarīqa and its dervishes. Sayyida Ḥafṣa carried out this duty in the best possible way and was a real help to Shaikh ʿAbd al-Karīm. She continued to serve Ṭarīqa and its female disciples after Shaikh ʿAbd al-Karīm's passing and the succession of her son, Shaikh Muḥammad al-Muḥammad, as Shaikh of Ṭarīqa. Our Shaikh's wife, Kažāl, assumed those responsibilities after Sayyida Ḥafṣa's death.

Sayyida Ḥafṣa was a walī whose karāmas were witnessed by many people. During her burial ceremony, attendees noticed that her foot was sticking out of her shroud. Before they could touch the foot to push it back inside, she pulled it in as if she were still alive.

She had a special standing with Shaikh ʿAbd al-Karīm, who listened to her opinions on things. The following is an incident that reveals her special status with the Master of Ṭarīqa. One night in 1973 or 1974, some dervishes went to preach in a remote area near ʿẒaym in the Diyālā governorate. They demonstrated some feats of darbāsha, which are performed to show the spiritual power of Ṭarīqa.[4] At one point, a caliph named Qāsim recklessly inserted a sword inside a dervish's belly.

[4] For more on darbāsha, see Fatoohi, *Shaikh Muhammad al-Muhammad*, 122-125.

This caused a bigger and deeper wound than usual, so much so that some of the dervish's internal organs came out. The caliph tied the dervish's belly with a large bandage, asking the Shaikhs for spiritual support to help the man recover. Contrary to what usually happens to those who practice feats of darbāsha, the preaching and dhikr ended and the wounded dervish did not recover. Disturbed and concerned by what had happened, the caliph decided to take the injured dervish to the Shaikh in Kirkuk.

At the time, in that remote area, there were no taxis, so they had to wait until dawn when a dump truck came to deliver building plaster material to a resident of the area. The driver agreed to transport the wounded dervish and placed him in the back of the truck. The truck was far from being as clean as it needed to be for someone with a wound, not to mention one as serious as that. Since most of the roads in that area were unpaved at the time, the injured dervish was constantly jostled by bumps on the road.

At about six in the morning, they arrived at the takya. The dervish was unconscious but breathing. Any doctor would have asserted that even though the dervish was still alive, he would not live much longer and that it would be useless to attempt to treat him given the seriousness of the injury. Shaikh ʿAbd al-Karīm sent for our Shaikh, who was resting at home. When he came, he found Shaikh ʿAbd al-Karīm very angry, pointing to the dervish lying on the ground with his internal organs out. The purpose of practising darbāsha is not to expose the body to the most serious danger but rather to provide sufficient proof to onlookers that since the dervish did not suffer what the body would naturally suffer in such feats, Ṭarīqa must have spiritual power. The more dangerous the act, the greater the spiritual energy needed to protect the dervish. Dervishes are not supposed to try the most daring feats.

In his anger at the caliph's recklessness, Shaikh ʿAbd al-Karīm refused to intervene. He told those present to take the injured dervish to the hospital and to take the caliph to the police. At that moment, sayyida Ḥafṣa reproached Shaikh ʿAbd al-Karīm and reminded him that as the Master, he remained responsible for the welfare of the dervish, even if the caliph had made a mistake. Besides, the wounded dervish was now in his house, so he could not abandon him and send him to the hospital.

Likewise, the caliph could not be sent to the police. Shaikh ʿAbd al-Karīm calmed down, listened to his wife's request, and backed down from his decision.

At the Shaikh's request, a dervish opened the bandage. It had dried and was stuck to the wound as a result of the amount of blood and secretions that had leaked out, as well as the length of time the wound had remained untreated. The afflicted area was contaminated with plaster during transport. With the help of two other dervishes, a third forcefully pushed the stiff, swollen bowels back into the wounded dervish's belly using a headwrap as a bandage that they wrapped around his belly. They did this with no medical knowledge, using their bare hands and without sterilisation. This would be extremely dangerous in normal circumstances because it would contaminate the body's internal organs. This circumstance, however, was supernatural because it involved the spiritual intervention of the Shaikhs. Shaikh ʿAbd al-Karīm instructed the dervishes to put dust from Shāh al-Kasnazān's shrine on the wounds and place the injured dervish in the middle of a circle of dhikr. The dhikr was performed by those who were in the takya at the time, around seven, including Shaikh Muḥammad al-Muḥammad.

During the dhikr, the injured dervish's face began to gradually gain colour and he began to regain consciousness. After the dhikr ended, Shaikh ʿAbd al-Karīm asked that the dervish be left alone to sleep. Our Shaikh returned to his house and the rest of the dervishes went their separate ways. After about six hours, the dervish woke up feeling hungry. He asked for soup. After eating, he felt the need to use the facilities. Medically speaking, bowel movement indicates the proper functioning of the intestinal organs. The dervish made a complete recovery.

This incident of Shaikh ʿAbd al-Karīm complying with sayyida Ḥafṣa's suggestion reminds us of situations where wives of the Messenger (PBUH) helped him by sharing their views on certain issues that he took on board. One example can be drawn from events that took place at the Treaty of Ḥudaybiyya. After the Messenger (PBUH) and the polytheists agreed to the treaty's terms and wrote them down, he instructed his Companions to proceed with the necessary slaughtering of sacrifices and shaving of their heads to perform the lesser pilgrimage. Some Companions objected because they thought that the treaty's terms were not in the Muslims' best interest. They did not carry out the Prophet's (PBUH) command even though he repeated it three times. When he went home, he told his wife, Umm Salamā, about what happened. She suggested, "O Prophet of Allah, do you like it [i.e. the treaty]? Go, and don't say a word to any of them until you slaughter your goat and call your barber to shave your head". He came out and did not speak to anyone. He slaughtered his goat and had his head shaved. This reminded the Companions that the actions of the Messenger (PBUH) are driven by divine decrees, there was wisdom behind them, even if that wisdom escaped them, and that he could not disobey Allah's command, even if it was disapproved by those near and dear to him. One by one, the Companions began to slaughter their animals and shave their heads.[5]

Naturally, sayyida Ḥafṣa also had a special standing with her son, Shaikh Muḥammad al-Muḥammad. We see evidence of this in another karāma involving a dervish who was injured while performing a feat of darbāsha that took place on a winter day in the mid-1980s, during the Masterdom of Shaikh Muḥammad al-Muḥammad. The dervish was brought from Mosul to the central takya in Baghdad. He was wrapped in a blanket that was full of dried blood by the time they reached the central takya, as it takes more than five hours to get to Baghdad from Mosul. Shaikh Muḥammad al-Muḥammad was very angry with what this dervish had done and did not want to intervene to cure him. Sayyida Ḥafṣa reminded her son of the similar incident that had occurred during his father's time and asked him to help the dervish. He instructed dervishes to recite a poem composed in the Iraqi dialect in praise of Sultan Ḥusayn al-Kasnazān, *niʿmaen Abū Ṭāhir yā rāʿī al-shāra.* The word "niʿmaen" is a word of praise; "Abū Ṭāhir" is a title of Sultan Ḥusayn, where "Abū" means father and "Ṭāhir" is the name of his eldest son; "rāʿī al-shāra" means "of the sign", meaning the one who leaves a sign when he spiritually intervenes, such as answering a seeker's request for aid. Lowering his head during the ode's recitation, the Shaikh gently struck the dervish's leg with his blessed foot, at which point the dervish moved. The dervish was then taken to the hospital where he was given a large amount of blood. The doctors in the hospital could not

[5] Al-Bukhārī, *Al-Jāmiʿ al-ṣaḥīḥ*, II, no. 2644, p. 119.

understand how this person was still alive!

In September 1992 in Baghdad, sayyida Ḥafṣa passed away and was buried near the Kirkuk takya in the Shaikh Muḥyī al-Dīn Karkūk cemetery, named after one of the Masters of Ṭarīqa Kasnazāniyya. Our Shaikh's wife, sayyida Każāl, assumed sayyida Ḥafṣa's responsibilities in the takya.

Shaikh Muḥammad al-Muḥammad had the best upbringing, under the care of a father who was a Shaikh of Ṭarīqa and an excellent educator, and a devout mother who spent her life helping her husband serve Ṭarīqa and seekers of nearness to Allah. He was nurtured with an Islamic upbringing that gave him the best qualities and traits. When Allah wants to make someone a means of guidance, He chooses for him to be raised by those who will nurture and educate him to be brought up according to His plan.

We do not instruct a seeker to abandon knowledge, because it is through knowledge he worships his Lord. Knowledge makes the person understand the act of worship because knowledge is light, "Are those who know equal to those who do not know?" (al-Zumar 39:9). We instruct the disciple to perform righteous deeds. We instruct the disciple to study, to read, to go to school, to learn, to become educated, and to worship. How beautiful it is when a seeker is well-educated!

Shaikh Muḥammad al-Muḥammad al-Kasnazān
(*Sermon*, 29 January 2010)

4

Religious and Academic Education

Shaikh Muḥammad al-Muḥammad inherited his forefathers' love for learning in general and for studying the sciences of Sharia in particular. As a child, he entered Karbchna's religious school, which was founded by Shāh al-Kasnazān. There, he studied under prominent scholars and jurists, such as Mullā Kāka Aḥmad Sayf al-Dīn, the encyclopaedic scholar who authored many books and studied several disciplines, including history, sociology, mathematics, and physics. In his diaries, this scholar mentions that he decided to go to teach at Karbchna's religious school because the spiritual influence of the Karbchna Shaikhs gave him a tremendous ability to serve students. Our Shaikh also studied under Mullā Sa'īd Zamnākū, who authored an entire Qur'anic exegesis, and Mullā 'Alī Musṭafā, also known as "'Alī Laylān".

Ḥusayn, who was about eleven years older than our Shaikh, cared for his younger brother, especially since their father was busy managing the Ṭarīqa's affairs. He preferred that his brother join a secular school and study Medicine, instead of continuing his education in a religious school. At the time, secular schools accepted graduates from religious schools, as long as they passed a special exam. Ḥusayn hired a private teacher, Karīm Zindī (may Allah have mercy on him), to teach his twelve-year-old brother the subjects that are taught in secular schools, such as history, science, English, and mathematics, to prepare him for the admission exam. Zindī taught our Shaikh for four years.

Our Shaikh passed the exam in Kirkuk and was accepted into the sixth grade. He then completed secondary education at a school located near the historic Kirkuk Citadel. Shaikh 'Abd al-Karīm would leave Karbchna with his family during the winter and reside in the takya within the Citadel. In the latter half of the 1940s, Shaikh 'Abd al-Karīm bought a tract of land in the Citadel on which he founded the first takya in Kirkuk that had a residence for the Shaikh. When Sultan Ḥusayn would visit Kirkuk, he used to live in a takya in the Citadel, which was run by one of his caliphs. It was near the land where Shaikh ʿAbd al-Karīm later built a takya,

During his years of study in Kirkuk, our Shaikh would stay in the takya to continue his studies when Shaikh ʿAbd al-Karīm returned to Karbchna or went to the village of Hawmārāmān in Qaradāgh in Sulaymāniyya. Shaikh ʿAbd al-Karīm rotated his place of residence between Kirkuk, Hawmārāmān, and Karbchna.

Shaikh Muḥammad al-Muḥammad completed secondary education and entered high school, which at the time took two years to complete. Towards the end of 1954, his brother, Ḥusayn, became ill with a disease that doctors failed to diagnose. His condition gradually worsened until he became bedridden. After his second operation at the al-Imām Hospital in Baghdad, it became clear that he had cancer. The disease prevented him from helping his father, so Shaikh Muḥammad al-Muḥammad was forced to abandon his studies to be close to his father and his ailing brother. In early 1956, Shaikh Ḥusayn passed away in the Kirkuk Citadel takya.

The death of his brother made our Shaikh abandon any thought of resuming his studies as he was needed to be in the service of his father. He had to take on the responsibility of managing the many social and tribal relations and overseeing his father's farms. His father bought him a Jeep for transport for his new responsibilities. Since childhood, our Shaikh was active and full of energy and enjoyed taking on responsibilities.

In 1956, he had to perform compulsory military service, but he only stayed in the army for about forty days. He took the option then of paying the set amount of money in lieu of performing mandatory military service.

After he abandoned his secular studies and returned to Karbchna, he enrolled at the local religious school once again and received certification as a religious scholar from Mullā ʿAbd Allah Muḥammad ʿAzīz al-Karbchnī (may Allah have mercy on him). The latter was one of Shaikh ʿAbd al-Karīm's caliphs and washed his noble body after his death. The political developments after the military coup that overthrew the monarchy in 1958 and his interest in defending the rights of the Kurdish minority in Iraq led to the migration of our Shaikh with his father to the village of Būbān in Penjwin in Sulaymāniyya on the Iraqi-

Iranian border in early 1959. At the beginning of 1961, he joined the armed Kurdish movement, which he remained part of for six years. We will read about this period in the next chapter. He could no longer continue his studies, which required stability, dedication, and persistence.

Our Shaikh's love for education is seen in his attempt to go to university when he was about forty years old. He took permission from Shaikh 'Abd al-Karīm to study at al-Āzhar University. At the end of 1977, he travelled to Cairo and stayed there for forty-two days. He obtained an initial certificate from al-Āzhar that would allow him to continue as an external student. He planned to live in Kirkuk and travel to the university every year for the necessary exams. About two months after his return, in early February 1978, Shaikh 'Abd al-Karīm passed away. Upon succeeding his father as the Master of Ṭarīqa, he was forced to completely abandon any thoughts of completing his studies.

Being forced to terminate his academic studies did not stop the Shaikh from self-educating through reading, which was his main hobby. We will discuss this in more detail in Chapter eighteen.

We are called "The Messenger's nation", so what is the difference between a Shī'ī and a Sunnī? A Kurd and an Arab? A Persian and anyone else? We are all the Messenger's nation. There is no difference between an Arab and a non-Arab, except in piety[1], "Indeed, the noblest of you in the sight of Allah is the most righteous of you" (al-Ḥujurāt 49:13).

Shaikh Muḥammad al-Muḥammad al-Kasnazān
(*Sermon*, 2 November 2013)

---

[1] The Prophet (PBUH) said in his Farewell sermon, "O people, your Lord is one and your father Adam is one. There is no superiority for an Arab over a foreigner, nor for a foreigner over an Arab, and neither for a white-skinned person over a black-skinned, nor for a black-skinned over a white-skinned, except by piety: 'Indeed, the most noble of you in the sight of Allah is the most pious of you' (al-Ḥujurāt 49:13)". See Al-Bayhaqī, *Shu'ab al-'Īmān*, IV, no. 5137, p. 289.

5

Political and Military Activity with the Kurdish Movement

The Messenger (PBUH) loved worshipping and being alone with his Lord even before the Qur'an was revealed, but he was never cut off from society. He combined worshipping Allah alone and having a fully integrated social life. He was a mecca for those who wanted to trust something and was truthful in dealing with people. He was known as "the truthful, trustworthy one". After the revelation of the Qur'an, his worship took a new dimension, which was calling people to Allah. The need to defend and spread his message caused him to combine his role as a prophet and messenger of Allah to people with leading the Muslims politically and militarily and protecting them.

As was the case with the Prophet (PBUH), the responsibilities of the spiritual leadership of Ṭarīqa and the extensive worshipping of the Shaikhs did not keep them away from people. They lived in the heart of society, enjoining people to do good and forbidding evil, changing what displeases Allah by hand, tongue, and heart, following the ḥadīth, "If anyone sees an evil, let him change it with his hand; if he is not able to do so, then [let him change it] with his tongue; and if he is not able to do so, then with his heart—and that is the weakest of faith".[1] For instance, Imām ʿAlī Ibn Abī Ṭālib had an unparalleled record of carrying out armed jihad with the Prophet (PBUH) against the polytheists who wanted to deprive the Muslims of their right to choose their religion, as well as after the death of the Messenger in defence of the great principles of Islam against those who wanted to undermine them under the name of Islam. Likewise, Imām Ḥusayn displayed one of the finest acts of self-sacrifice when he confronted those who betrayed the will of the Prophet (PBUH) and tried to exploit Islam for personal gain.

---

[1] Muslim, *Ṣaḥīḥ*, I, no. 49, p. 69.

The Greatest Ghawth, Shaikh ʿAbd al-Qādir al-Gaylānī, also considered serving society, which included standing against injustice and aggression, as part of his duty to serve people and call them to God. He distanced himself from rulers and people of power in order to be completely free and independent in guiding people, unlike clerics who chose to be instruments in the hands of the powerful in return for worldly gain. Yet he did not hesitate to intervene in politics when the public's best interest so required. In AH 541 (1146 CE), the Abbasid caliph al-Muqtafī li-ʾAmri Allah appointed Yaḥyā Ibn Saʿīd, known as Ibn Marjam, as a judge. He was unjust and accepted bribes but no one could confront or stop him. Shaikh ʿAbd al-Qādir took advantage of al-Muqtafī's presence in the mosque one day and addressed him from the pulpit, "You have put the worst tyrant in charge of the Muslims. What will you say tomorrow, before the Lord of the peoples?" The caliph dismissed that unjust judge.[2]

Similarly, the Shaikh's school in Baghdad was a preparation centre for Muslims fighting against the Crusaders, as he was a contemporary of the political and military leaders ʿImād al-Dīn Zinkī and his son, Nūr al-Dīn Zinkī.[3] The success of the Abbasid caliphate in restoring its authority and power after its decline in the Seljuk period, including the resurgence of the Abbasid ministry office, contributed to the victories of Nūr al-Dīn Zinkī and Saladin al-Āyyūbī against the Crusaders. The Qādiri school and its great Master also played a big role in raising the awareness of and mobilising the public.[4] Shaikh ʿAbd al-ʿAzīz, one of Shaikh ʿAbd al-Qādir's sons, fought against the Crusaders. He took part in Saladin's conquest of Ashkelon in AH 583 (1187 CE), then he went to Jerusalem.[5]

The Kasnazānī Shaikhs fought foreign invaders and aggressors and emigrated when they needed to, just as their grand Master (PBUH) emigrated and fought before them. Shaikh ʿAbd al-Qādir Kasnazān released a fatwa that called for armed jihad against the Russian forces that invaded Iranian, then Iraqi, lands at the beginning of World War I,

---

[2] Al-Tādifī, *Qalāʾid al-jawāhir*, 6.

[3] Al-Gaylānī, *Hākathā ẓahara jīl ṣalāḥ al-dīn*, 170, 249-255.

[4] Al-Ṣallābī, *Al-Dawla al-zangiyya*, 640.

[5] Al-Tādifī, *Qalāʾid al-jawāhir*, 43; Al-Gaylānī, *Al-Shaikh ʿAbd al-Qādir*, 273.

massacring and abusing many women, children, and elderly people and mutilating their bodies. As Shaikh ʿAbd al-Qādir al-Gaylānī urged his sons to fight the occupation of the Crusaders, Shaikh ʿAbd al-Qādir Kasnazān instructed his son and the Shaikh of Ṭarīqa after him, Ḥusayn, to fight the foreign occupiers of the Muslim land in Kurdistan. He assembled an army and placed Shaikh Ḥusayn as its commander. This army teamed up with another force and entered into a fierce battle against the Russian army. After a few days of fighting, the small number of lightly armed Muslim fighters defeated the large Russian army, which was heavily armed with various kinds of weapons, causing many deaths and taking prisoners.[6]

Shaikh ʿAbd al-Qādir al-Kasnazān also declared jihad against the British occupation in Iraq. On 22 May 1919, Shaikh Ḥusayn led one of the two forces that drew the British into an ambush between the villages of Karbchna and Kchan. The Muslim fighters killed some of the invaders and captured others. They also disarmed the convoy and seized the cash it carried and their horses.[7] Less than a month after their defeat at the Battle of Sangāw, the British mobilized a large army to retaliate and regain control of the areas they lost. The large difference in the number of troops favoured the invaders, who chased the Muslim fighters and went to Karbchna and burned it down. Shaikh ʿAbd al-Qādir and his family, including Shaikh Ḥusayn, had to migrate to Iran. The Shaikh died there about three years later. Shaikh Ḥusayn brought his father's coffin to Karbchna and later, in the second half of 1923, he permanently returned from Iran to settle there. The anger of the British administration in Iraq at Shaikh ʿAbd al-Qādir can be seen in the description of him by one of its high-ranking officials as a "turbulent and dangerous agitator".[8]

Shaikh Muḥammad al-Muḥammad became involved in the Kurdish movement in northern Iraq in 1959. In early February, Shaikh ʿAbd al-Karīm had to leave Karbchna to live in the village of Būbān in the Iraqi city of Penjwin, northeast of Karbchna, on the Iraqi-Iranian border.

---

[6] Al-Kasnazān, "Al-Mujāhid al-Akbar".

[7] Ḥamdā, *Al-Kurd wa Kurdistan* 72-73; Bell, *Review of the civil administration of Mesopotamia*, 64-65.

[8] Edmonds, *Kurds, Turks and Arabs*, 356.

Naturally, our Shaikh accompanied his father. This migration was triggered by the chaos that spread with the unmanaged implementation of the Agrarian Reform Law that was introduced by the first government after the bloody removal of the monarchy in July 1958. This nationwide law failed to take into account the specifics of the situation in Kurdistan, whose agricultural lands depended mainly on rain rather than irrigation. This further exacerbated the Kurds' feeling of the violation of their national rights. The disagreement between the tribal and political leadership of the Kurds and the Iraqi government continued to escalate until it developed into armed confrontation.

Our Shaikh entered politics after the migration of Shaikh ʿAbd al-Karīm. In addition to being the son of a Shaikh of Ṭarīqa, his rise to prominence was helped by his wide network of contacts and his influential personality. He was treated like a tribal chief despite his young age. He possessed leadership qualities, including bravery that made him fear no one and nothing, and he earned the trust of others. He always had a military force under his command to protect the takya from aghas and other people of power and influence who might be tempted to harm Ṭarīqa. He also provided support to the oppressed, some of whom sought refuge in the takya in Būbān.

Brigadier General ʿAbd al-Karīm Qāsim, who led the military coup against the monarchy and became prime minister, knew Shaikh ʿAbd al-Karīm; he and officers in his regiment had visited him in the early 1950s. In 1960, he heard that Shaikh ʿAbd al-Karīm had moved to Penjwin because of the developments caused by the misapplication of the Agrarian Reform Law and the way he was dealing with Kurdish national rights. He sought to mend the situation and please the Shaikh, so he sent one of his advisers, who was a Kurd, to invite the Shaikh to Baghdad to meet him in person. The Shaikh thanked the envoy for the invitation but he graciously declined it. Instead, he sent Shaikh Muḥammad al-Muḥammad as his representative, with a small delegation. Qāsim's generosity with the delegation did not solve the fundamental issue that caused Shaikh ʿAbd al-Karīm to leave Karbchna. Also, his exceptional treatment of his representatives did not reflect a change in his policies in dealing with the Kurdish problem. The relations and trust between the government and the Kurdish movement continued to deteriorate.

In the latter half of 1961, in the presence of Shaikh ʿAbd al-Karīm, under his auspices, and with his religious backing, tribal chieftains assembled and swore on a muṣḥaf to work together and not to betray one another or the cause. It must be noted that the support of Shaikhs ʿAbd al-Karīm and Muḥammad al-Muḥammad for the Kurdish movement to have the national rights of the Kurds acknowledged was given within the framework of the unity of Iraq. The Kasnazānī Shaikhs always stood against any proposal to divide Iraq, whether on national, sectarian, or any other grounds. Shrines of Shaikhs of Ṭarīqa Kasnazāniyya bless Iraq from north to south and east to west. Our Shaikhs have rejected any action that would create borders between these holy shrines.

As the situation between the government and the Kurds worsened, the army upped its activity in the region and started preparation for fighting. Some tribal fighters started cutting off roads for the army. On 7 September 1961, Shaikh Muḥammad al-Muḥammad led an armed force that attacked and occupied a police station on the road between Penjwin and Darbandikhān, seizing its weapons to secure the supply route between the two areas. This was one of the first military operations of the Kurdish revolution. Our Shaikh played a significant role in the Kurdish movement for several years until the struggle against the government for the national rights of the Kurds turned into an inner conflict between the two wings of the Kurdish movement, the Kurdistan Democratic Party (KDP) and the tribal side. This led him to lose his enthusiasm for military action. In the middle of 1966, his increased disillusionment with the Kurdish movement evolved into a decision to retire from armed action. Readers who are interested in detailed information on the history of Shaikh Muḥammad al-Muḥammad in the Kurdish movement may consult the relevant chapter in our comprehensive biography of him.[9]

During his years of military action, our Shaikh was exposed to many dangers, yet divine care kept all harm away from him. He mentions that during one battle, the army shelled them with artillery from a mountaintop in Ṭūz Khūrmātū. He felt what he thought was dust caused by the shelling hitting his body now and then. When he looked

[9] Fatoohi, *Shaikh Muhammad al-Muhammad*, 165–207.

closer, he saw that what felt like dust was, in fact, shell fragments. Shaikh ʿAbd al-Karīm would reassure our Shaikh's mother and his family about his welfare during his years of involvement in the Kurdish movement, saying, "He will not be killed. I will not let any harm come his way".[10]

On 11 March 1974, the Iraqi government announced the implementation of the autonomy accord that it had struck with the Kurdish leadership four years earlier. But the implementation was unilateral because the Kurds demanded the recognition of Kirkuk as part of the autonomous region, which the government rejected. The government sought the help of Kurdish leaders, including well-known figures who had a history with the Kurdish movement, that saw in the autonomy agreement a real opportunity for the Kurds to obtain their national rights within the unity of Iraq. It sought practical support from these individuals for the accord. Shaikh Muḥammad al-Muḥammad was one of these leading figures, becoming a member of the Legislative Council of the Autonomous Region in its second cycle in 1977. He put his membership of the council on hold, however, after Shaikh ʿAbd al-Karīm's death, to dedicate himself to Ṭarīqa. Assuming the Shaikhdom of Ṭarīqa marked a radical turning point in all aspects of his life.

Shaikh Muḥammad al-Muḥammad struggled for human rights and against injustice, just like the Shaikhs of Ṭarīqa Kasnazāniyya before him: his grandfather, Shaikh ʿAbd al-Qādir; his uncle, Shaikh Ḥusayn; and his father, Shaikh ʿAbd al-Karīm. Those six years of jihad (1961-1966) played a significant role in building his character and shaping his development. They were a phase in the formation of a spiritual Master for whom Allah had decreed greatness.

---

[10] Shaikh Muḥammad al-Muḥammad al-Kasnazān, *sermon*, 18 June 2018.

Shaikh Nahro is my heart; he is my liver. He is your servant—a servant of your Ṭarīqa. I, my children, and everything we own are in the service to Ṭarīqa. We are servants to your Ṭarīqa. We are all soldiers of the Messenger (PBUH), soldiers of Sharia because it is our foundation.

Shaikh Muḥammad al-Muḥammad al-Kasnazān
(*Sermon*, 2006)

6

Family Life

Towards the end of 1957, Shaikh Muḥammad al-Muḥammad married his paternal uncle's daughter. At the time, he lived in Karbchna. This marriage, which resulted in a son, who later died, and a daughter called Sardasht, was not destined to last. Our Shaikh's involvement in 1961 in political and military activities, in defence of Kurdish national rights, made reconciling his new commitments and his family responsibilities impossible. His work for the Kurdish movement required him to not have a fixed address and to be in a state of constant movement. He divorced his wife that year.

A few years after he retired from the Kurdish movement, he decided to remarry. Out of the love he had for his mother and the confidence he had in her judgement, he let her choose his wife, if Shaikh ʿAbd al-Karīm would bless her selection. She chose a young woman named Kažāl from a well-known family that is related to our Shaikh's family. She is the daughter of Shaikh Maʿrūf, son of Shaikh ʿAbd al-Karīm Qādir Karam, a maternal uncle of sayyida Ḥafṣa who took care of his niece as a little girl after her mother's death.

There was a strong relationship between the two families, even when Shaikh ʿAbd al-Karīm's family lived in Karbchna and Penjwin before they settled in Kirkuk, where sayyida Kažāl's family lived. Sayyida Ḥafṣa had a lot of love for her cousin and milk-brother, Maʿrūf, who was also a close friend of her son, Ḥusayn, and later became Shaikh ʿAbd al-Karīm's lawyer for issues related to farmland in Sangāw. The Shaikh of Ṭarīqa also had a lot of love for him. In 1959, the Iraqi authorities sentenced Shaikh Maʿrūf to death for political reasons. The sentence was carried out in 1963.

Shaikh Muḥammad al-Muḥammad married sayyida Kažāl in early 1969. At the time, he lived in Hawmarāmān, Qaradāgh. He used to move between Hawmarāmān and Kirkuk, where Shaikh ʿAbd al-Karīm lived. In 1971, he permanently moved to Kirkuk, next to his father's house. He later built an additional parlour in front of his house to receive guests.

He was blessed with his eldest son, Nahro, on 12 December 1969. After about a year and a half, Ghāndī was born. Our Shaikh's two eldest sons were named after the eminent leaders of the Indian independence movement, Mahatma Gandhi, who led India to independence in 1947, and Jawaharlal Nehru, Gandhi's political successor and the first prime minister of independent India. Our Shaikh's choosing of these two names reflects his admiration for these two leaders and what they did for their people. The word "Nahro" in Kurdish also means "small river".

Our Shaikh always wanted to have many children. In 1972, when he only had Nahro and Ghāndī, a dervish named Maḥmūd Gulāl, who had "ḥāl", said to him, "Would you be satisfied with seven? I guarantee that you will have seven sons". Indeed, our Shaikh had five more sons, so that is seven in total! In 1973, he had Malās, whose name means "prepared" and "vigilant" in Kurdish. It is also the name of the highest mountain in Karbchna. He next had Bresh, whose name is that of a mountain summit near Karbchna. He then had ʿAmmār, Junayd, and, finally in 1983, ʿAbd al-Karīm. As we have mentioned, our Shaikh had a daughter, Sardasht, from his first marriage.

Let's stop here to quickly define the concept of "ḥāl", which is often encountered in Sufi literature. This term refers to various spiritual states that transcend the material world that Allah bestows upon some of his servants. This is done through the Messenger (PBUH), who passes them down to the present Shaikh of Ṭarīqa, who grants them to whichever seeker he wants. Ḥāl is not earned by the dervish but, rather, it is granted by the Shaikh. It is a spiritual power that takes different forms. It may last momentarily, such as an incident, feeling, or experience that happens to the dervish, or be a continuous matter. Some ḥāls are particular spiritual powers that the Shaikh gives a disciple to help with the needs of Ṭarīqa. In this case, the person of ḥāl would have certain roles in Ṭarīqa. The effects of ḥāl sometimes appear in the form of karāmas that occur at the hands of those who have it. Such ḥāls are ranks gifted by the Shaikh to the seekers. Just as the Shaikh is the one who grants a seeker any particular ḥāl, he may change it to another ḥāl, the same way he may also withdraw it from the seeker if he no longer qualifies for that responsibility.

Like any children of a Shaikh who are brought up in the centre of Ṭarīqa, our Shaikh's children, as noted earlier, treated him first and foremost as the Shaikh of Ṭarīqa and second as their biological father. They referred to him only as "Shaikh", did not sit in his assembly unless they had to do so, and did not speak before him, unless he spoke to them or when they had something to tell him.

Just as he asked the seekers to serve Ṭarīqa and selflessly devote themselves to calling people to the way of the Messenger (PBUH), our Shaikh demanded the same sincerity and sacrifice of his children. He directly taught them Ṭarīqa's etiquettes and also appointed those who educated them in this regard. This was the practice of all Shaikhs. For example, Shaikh ʿAbd al-Qādir al-Kasnazān gave one of his elder cousins, Shihāb, the responsibility of educating his children about Ṭarīqa. He would say to him, "Teach the children to be close to the takya and the dervishes. The cobbler teaches his son his craft from an early age". Whether his children were working in business, politics, or any other field, our Shaikh would ask them to put themselves at the service of Ṭarīqa. This is one of his sayings in this regard in a sermon to dervishes:

> My only concern is preaching. Everything I have is in service to you. Even my children are at your service, in service to Ṭarıqa. My soul is in service to you and Ṭarīqa. I am a servant to Ṭarīqa and its dervishes. I am proud of this title because my forefathers referred to themselves in writing as "Servant of the Poor".[1]

The Arabic term that here is translated as "the poor", is "fuqarāʾ", the plural of "faqīr". The latter literally means "poor person", but this term is figuratively used for those who seek nearness to Allah, i.e. the followers of Ṭarīqa. Here, our Master was referring to the fact that every Kasnazānī Shaikh called himself "Servant of the Poor" and some of htem sealed their letters with this title.

In the same way that our Shaikh urged disciples to attain the greatest degree of knowledge they possibly can, he made sure that each of his sons obtained at least a university degree. Despite his huge amount of Ṭarīqa work, he followed his children's progress in their studies since their youth. When his youngest child, ʿAbd al-Karīm, was a small boy,

---

[1] Shaikh Muḥammad al-Muḥammad al-Kasnazān, *sermon*, 22 December 2005.

he did not like going to school, and at times would manage to stay at home. When our Shaikh would see him in the house when school was still in session, he would ask someone to take him to school, even if there was not much time left in the school day. He also appointed a close relative to follow up on the details of their studies closely.

All of his sons obtained a basic university degree. Shaikh Nahro obtained a bachelor's in Accounting, then completed his doctorate in Islamic History; Ghāndī holds a BA in Law and an MA in Media; Malās holds a BA and an MA in Architecture; Bresh holds a bachelor's degree in Dentistry; ʿAmmār holds a bachelor's degree in Medicine; Junayd holds a bachelor's degree in Pharmacology; and ʿAbd al-Karīm holds a bachelor's degree in Medicine. He let his sons choose whatever fields they wanted to study, but he particularly liked Medicine because medicinal fields provide a great service to people. He described it as a form of worship. His preference influenced his sons, with medical fields dominating their choices of study.

As we mentioned earlier, a Shaikh's wife helps her husband in managing the affairs of the takya. After the death of our Shaikh's mother, these tasks were passed down to sayyida Kažāl. One beautiful attribute that she has is that she never gets angry, even in the most difficult and irritating circumstances. She is a very humble woman who receives female visitors to the takya, looks after their needs, and makes sure that they are cared for and treated generously during their visit.

Assuming Shaikhdom is, according to the people of Ṭarīqa, a heavenly selection—a heavenly designation—that takes place by the command of Allah (blessed and exalted is He) and the command of His Messenger, our Master, the Seal of Prophets and Messengers, Muḥammad (PBUH).

Shaikh Muḥammad al-Muḥammad al-Kasnazān
(*Al-Ṭarīqa al-'Alīyya al-Qādiriyya al-Kasnazāniyya*, p. 161)

7

Being Chosen for the Shaikhdom of Ṭarīqa

As is the case with all Masters of Ṭarīqa, Shaikh Muḥammad al-Muḥammad was appointed to the Shaikhdom of Ṭarīqa by divine decree and communication by the Messenger (PBUH). There are innumerable karāmas and spiritual unveilings that illustrate that Allah chose him for the Shaikhdom of Ṭarīqa, including some that occurred before his birth. We already saw, in Chapter two, Shaikh ʿAbd al-Qādir's revelation when his son, ʿAbd al-Karīm, was being swaddled—that is, twenty-six years before the birth of our Shaikh— that Allah will guide many Arabs at the hands of the son of Shaikh ʿAbd al-Karīm.

In the 1950s, a walī and disciple of Ṭarīqa Kasnazāniyya saw a vision that prophesied that event. Ṣāliḥ Muḥammad Amīn (may Allah have mercy on him) saw Shaikhs taking the Ṭarīqa's banners from northern Iraq to Baghdad in the centre of the country. He implored them to keep the Ṭarīqa's banners in the north but they only left a small banner and took the rest south. In 1973 or 1974, Shaikh ʿAbd al-Karīm revealed that the Shaikhs' gaze and the Ṭarīqa's blessing were oriented towards the Arabs in the south. In 1975, Shaikh ʿAbd al-Karīm was in Karbchna overseeing renovations of the roof of the shrines' hall and the mosque when the walī Aḥmad Muḥammad Amīn (may Allah have mercy on him) spoke to the Shaikh about seeing in ḥāl something similar to what his brother, Ṣāliḥ, saw two decades earlier. He saw the Ṭarīqa's banners, canes, and prayer rugs being loaded into a car to transport them to the south. He tried to prevent this, but he only succeeded in taking some of the canes. As we will see in Chapter ten, in the early 1980s, Shaikh Muḥammad al-Muḥammad moved the central takya from Kirkuk to Baghdad. This resulted in a considerable amount of the Arab population of Iraq becoming followers of Ṭarīqa Kasnazāniyya.

Naturally, the future Shaikh of Ṭarīqa receives indications and experiences that tell him that Allah has destined an important future for him. In the spring of 1957, when he was nineteen years old, Shaikh Muḥammad al-Muḥammad would sit on a small hill in the morning, overseeing the planting of rice in the farmland that he had in Hawmarāmān, Qaradāgh. He used to take advantage of his time alone to memorize the Qur'an. One night, he was sitting on his bed, reclining on cushions between his back and the wall, facing the Ka'ba, so he was facing towards Karbchna, where Shaikh 'Abd al-Karīm lived. He was reciting the chapter of Yāsīn from the Qur'an when he closed his eyes. He saw a white light like the moon approaching him from afar. The whiteness of the light was indescribably beautiful and like no white he had ever seen. He realised that it was the Messenger (PBUH), who is described as a light in the Qur'an, "There has come to you from Allah a light and a clear Book" (al-Mā'ida 5:15). The light continued to approach him until it entered his eyes, mouth, ears, nose, neck—all over his body. The light caused a unique sense of delight, and it was so dense that he could feel it moving through his body. After the Prophetic light had entered his body, he felt as if his body was not there anymore. He was overcome with a spiritual state of crying accompanied by a feeling of pleasure that he had never experienced.[1]

Shaikh 'Abd al-Karīm had hinted to individual dervishes in private that "Kāka Muḥammad", which is how he used to refer to our Shaikh, would succeed him as Shaikh of Ṭarīqa. Still, for many long years, our Shaikh's role in serving Ṭarīqa remained limited to meeting the takya's needs and helping disciples with their worldly needs. He did not have any role in the spiritual matters of Ṭarīqa or its dervishes. That began to change when Shaikh 'Abd al-Karīm decided to perform the pilgrimage to Mecca in 1971. In that year, the pilgrimage was at the beginning of February. Shaikh 'Abd al-Karīm gave our Shaikh the Ṭarīqa's pledge by hand and appointed him as his General Deputy, meaning his successor for the spiritual, not only worldly, matters of Ṭarīqa. Our Shaikh asked his Master to give him permission to practise all spiritual sciences, and the Shaikh granted him his request. Before his trip, the Shaikh informed the dervishes who visited him in Kirkuk that Kāka Muḥammad was his

---

[1] Shaikh Muḥammad al-Muḥammad al-Kasnazān, *sermon*, 10 February 2016; 22 September 2016.

General Deputy and that he would take his place while he was away. One thing he told them was, "As of today, you do not know the real Kāka Muḥammad. The day will come, however, when you, and everyone in the world, will know his reality". Our Shaikh stayed in the takya, representing his Master while he was on his pilgrimage.

Shaikh ʿAbd al-Karīm would attend the dhikr circles on Monday and Thursday nights in the central takya in Kirkuk, so this became one of his General Deputy's tasks in the absence of the Master. One night, the winter cold was brutal, as usual, but it was hot inside the takya because it was filled with dervishes and because of the heating system. Our Shaikh was standing in front of the takya's open door, covering a part of its opening. When the disciples were chanting the first dhikr that is accompanied by drums, "Ḥayy Allāh, Ḥayy Allāh", he felt a cool breeze enter from outside, touch his body, and enter the centre of the dhikr circle. The breeze had a unique fragrance, similar to that of a damask rose, which our Shaikh recognised as the Messenger's (PBUH) special scent. This pleasant fragrance remained for days on the left side of his body, where the Prophetic breeze had touched him.

Shaikh ʿAbd al-Karīm had a special love for Shaikh Muḥammad al-Muḥammad that was unlike his love for anyone else. The Shaikh would always ask about his whereabouts and what he was doing when he was not around. He would also pass on to his son the most precious and beautiful gifts he received. This was not a result of the usual love and care that a father gives his son. Rather, this love and care were both unique and special because they were those of a Shaikh of Ṭarīqa for his successor, for the Muḥammadan inheritor after him. Our Shaikh reciprocated this special spiritual love for his Master.

The same situation was repeated in Shaikh Muḥammad al-Muḥammad's love and attention for his General Deputy, Shaikh Nahro. He loved and cared for all of his children, but what he felt for Shaikh Nahro was unique. It was not a result of his being the eldest of his children but rather because he was his General Deputy, whom our Shaikh had announced would succeed him as the Master of Ṭarīqa. Anyone who had witnessed the relationship between Shaikh ʿAbd al-Karīm and Shaikh Muḥammad al-Muḥammad recognised that the relationship between Shaikh Muḥammad al-Muḥammad and Shaikh Nahro was of that same kind of unique spiritual bond. To me personally, it appeared that our Shaikh loved only the Prophet (PBUH) more than Shaikh Nahro.

Those who possess ḥāls are often spiritually attracted to the future Shaikh of Ṭarīqa even before he assumes its Shaikhdom. Dervishes who experienced spiritual unveilings knew that Shaikh Muḥammad al-Muḥammad would succeed his father, even before Shaikh 'Abd al-Karīm announced it. In the early 1960s, about fifteen years before our Shaikh became the Master of Ṭarīqa, a dervish named Majīd from Khurmāl, Sulaymāniyya, who had ḥāl, said that a day would come when dervishes of "King Muḥammad", as he liked to refer to Shaikh Muḥammad al-Muḥammad, would come to visit him by plane. At the time, dervishes would exclusively travel by land to visit Shaikh 'Abd al-Karīm, as air travel was not common. He also said that the majority of "King Muḥammad's" future dervishes would be bareheaded. He said this at a time when the majority of people, including disciples, whether Arab or Kurdish, would cover their heads.

Also in the 1960s, when our Shaikh was still involved in the Kurdish movement, he met an aged female dervish in the company of her grandsons. When he greeted her, the elderly woman returned the greeting and added, referring to her grandsons, "These are your dervishes". This happened a few years before Shaikh 'Abd al-Karīm appointed him as his Deputy. There are many examples of similar unveilings. The Messenger (PBUH) also told some dervishes that Shaikh Muḥammad al-Muḥammad would succeed his father as Shaikh of Ṭarīqa.

Three or four years before Shaikh Muḥammad al-Muḥammad became the Master of Ṭarīqa, three accomplished disciples—Uncle Ḥusayn, 'Alī Fshān, and Ibrāhīm Galālī—would sometimes leave Shaikh 'Abd al-Karīm's assembly and stand at the door of our Shaikh's assembly hall. Our Shaikh would be annoyed, sometimes to the point of being upset, and ask them to go to Shaikh 'Abd al-Karīm's assembly, as he was the Shaikh of Ṭarīqa, to whom they were spiritually linked. Also, he did not like anyone to remind him that Shaikh 'Abd al-Karīm would one day pass away. The dervishes would reply that they liked to be near his assembly. One day in 1973 or 1974, Uncle Ḥusayn and 'Alī Fshān made a crown out of metal wires and, along with Ibrāhīm Galālī, brought it to our Shaikh's assembly. When he saw them carrying it, he understood what they intended to do and became upset. He asked them to leave, which they did only after placing the crown in his assembly hall.

As the present Shaikh of Ṭarīqa's death and the advent of the new Shaikh draw near, dervishes who possess ḥāls begin to sense this imminent change. Where there was once only love for the present Shaikh, love for the next Shaikh begins to grow in their hearts, so they start feeling drawn to him. About five or six months before Shaikh 'Abd al-Karīm's departure, our Shaikh noticed an increase in dervishes with ḥāls who would come close to him. He was anxious about this because he knew what it meant. They began, for instance, to come to his assembly after Shaikh Abd al-Karīm left his assembly and went to his private room for worship. Our Shaikh would try his best to dismiss them, but their inclination towards him was not their choice. It was, rather, a divine intervention as Allah directed their hearts towards the person whom He had chosen to succeed the present Shaikh. This supernatural intervention is necessary because, otherwise, a dervish's heart cannot love any other Master besides his present one.

The intervention of the Prophet (PBUH) and the Shaikhs of Ṭarīqa in moving the dervishes' hearts is demonstrated in visions and spiritual experiences that reveal to dervishes the future Shaikh's imminent assumption of the Shaikhdom and attract their hearts to him. A few months before Shaikh 'Abd al-Karīm's departure, for example, Aḥmad Muḥammad Amīn visited our Shaikh and told him about a vision he had seen. He saw the honourable Messenger (PBUH) take one of two outfits from a bundle of clothes and give it to our Shaikh. About two months later, another walī and caliph, called Ḥājj Mullā 'Abd Allah, visited our Shaikh and told him that he saw the Messenger (PBUH) ask for a cane then give it to our Shaikh. Visions and spiritual unveilings like these confirmed to our Shaikh the imminence of his Master's passing and his assumption of the Shaikhdom. A dream of the Prophet (PBUH) is always a true dream because he (PBUH) said, "Whoever sees me [in a dream] then, indeed, he has seen the truth, as Satan cannot appear in my form",[2] and, "Whoever sees me in a dream has really seen me, as Satan cannot impersonate me".[3]

---

[2] Al-Bukhārī, *Al-Jāmi' al-ṣaḥīḥ*, III, no. 6749, p. 603.

[3] Ibid., I, no. 109, p. 82.

Karāmas and spiritual indications confirming that Shaikh Muḥammad al-Muḥammad was destined for the Ṭarīqa's Masterdom continued to happen. They included our Shaikh taking the pledge directly from the Prophet (PBUH). Less than two months before Shaikh ʿAbd al-Karīm's death, our Shaikh was blessed with meeting the Messenger of Allah (PBUH) in a dream. He (PBUH) was sitting with his back reclined against the side of Shaikh Ḥusayn's head in his shrine in Karbchna. He was facing the Kaʿba, almost in the direction of Kirkuk, where Shaikh ʿAbd al-Karīm lived. He had a light beard and seemed sad. As soon as our Shaikh saw him, he rushed towards him and fell to his knees before him. With complete subservience and submission, he extended his hand balled into a fist. His clenched fist met the Messenger's (PBUH). His fist seemed like a child's fist in comparison to the Prophet's (PBUH).[4] His joy in meeting the Messenger (PBUH) was mixed with apprehension over what the vision indicated. When he told his Master about the dream, Shaikh ʿAbd al-Karīm did not say a single word. They both understood what the dream meant: Shaikh ʿAbd al-Karīm would soon be leaving this world and the Shaikhdom would be transferred to our Shaikh. This taking of the pledge at the Prophet's (PBUH) hand explains our Master's words about his noble palm, "Whoever touched this palm has touched the Prophet's (PBUH) palm".

Sultan Ḥusayn also visited Shaikh Muḥammad al-Muḥammad in a vision and placed his nephew's hand in his and gave him the succession of Ṭarīqa. Shaikh ʿAbd al-Karīm then gave the Ṭarīqa's succession to our Shaikh by hand. Progressively, he gave him all the permissions and spiritual Sufi matters he had from the Shaikhs of Ṭarīqa. These included the permission to write supplications that Kāka Aḥmad al-Shaikh gave to Shāh al-Kasnazān, even though Kasnazānī Shaikhs only used them in exceptional cases. Our Shaikh would sometimes give certain caliphs special supplications to use temporarily while on preaching tours, to cure specific diseases, for example. Ṭarīqa Kasnazāniyya's daily and perennial dhikrs have enormous spiritual power. By consistently performing them, a dervish can obtain various karāmas, spiritual

[4] Shaikh Muḥammad al-Muḥammad al-Kasnazān, *sermon*, 10 February 2016; Al-Kasnazān, *Al-Ṭarīqa al-ʿaliyya al-qādiriyya al-kasnazāniyya*, 163-164.

rewards, and whatever he needs. Shaikh ʿAbd al-Karīm also handed to our Shaikh the responsibility of the takya and told him that his time was up.

The notification came once more during Shaikh ʿAbd al-Karīm's last visit to the shrines of the Shaikhs in Karbchna. Our Shaikh came from Kirkuk to visit him after a few days. When Shaikh ʿAbd al-Karīm decided to return to Kirkuk, he went to visit the shrines as usual before leaving. This visit, however, was not like the previous ones. He came out of the hall of the shrines and sat on a chair near the door with a joyous expression. He went on to address the large crowd of caliphs and disciples that were present:

> My children! My dervishes! From this day forth, sayyid Shaikh Muḥammad is your Shaikh. This is our Master's order. Whoever obeys him has obeyed us, and whoever loves him has loved us. Whoever disobeys him has disobeyed us.

He turned towards the shrines and said:

> I am saying my farewell to you now. This is my last visit to you. This is your deputy whom you have entrusted.[5]

While crying, our Shaikh took his Master's hand and kissed it, saying, "You are in good health. You have broken our hearts". Those present were overwhelmed by the gravity, majesty, and sadness of the situation. After returning from Karbchna, Shaikh ʿAbd al-Karīm entrusted his son and General Deputy with the administration of Ṭarīqa's takyas. He passed away about two months later, and Shaikh Muḥammad al-Muḥammad succeeded him. Before his demise, Shaikh ʿAbd al-Karīm also made final farewell trips to the holy shrines in Baghdad, Karbala, and Najaf.

---

[5] Al-Kasnazān, *Al-Anwār al-raḥmāniyya*, 1.

I am like you. I belong to the takya; I belong to the Shaikhs. I am one of your brothers—a dervish. However, the Shaikhs have assigned special obligations to me. They have placed me in Shaikh ʿAbd al-Karīm's position. This is an order from Allah, from the honourable Messenger (PBUH), then from the Shaikhs. I am one of you in Ṭarīqa, but I have more obligations, as they have placed me in the place of the honourable Messenger (PBUH).

Shaikh Muḥammad al-Muḥammad al-Kasnazān
(*Sermon*, 1 February 2018)

8

Assuming the Shaikhdom

The appointment of the Shaikh of Ṭarīqa is by the Prophet's (PBUH) choice. It is a spiritual designation that people cannot infer using reason. The present Shaikh announces who his successor will be before his departure from this world so that there would be no doubt about his identity. For example, a few years before his demise, Sultan ʿAbd al-Qādir announced that his son, Ḥusayn, would succeed him. Sultan Ḥusayn entrusted his brother, ʿAbd al-Karīm, with many responsibilities of Ṭarīqa and its dervishes when he was younger than eighteen—that is, about eight years before his death. He also told the dervishes, years before his death, that Shaikh ʿAbd al-Karīm would succeed him. Shaikh ʿAbd al-Karīm, in turn, revealed his successor seven years before he departed this world. Before leaving for hajj in 1971, he appointed Shaikh Muḥammad al-Muḥammad as his Deputy, leaving him in charge of the affairs of the takya and the dervishes. Our Shaikh followed suit by designating his eldest son, Nahro, as his General Deputy and Shaikh of Ṭarīqa after him. We will discuss this appointment in detail in Chapter nineteen.

A Shaikh may entrust his General Deputy with some of Ṭarīqa's responsibilities, such as managing the takya, but he remains the only Master of Ṭarīqa, as Ṭarīqa cannot have more than one Shaikh at a time. The General Deputy is the future Shaikh, but during the Shaikh's life, he is just another one of Ṭarīqa's disciples. When the Shaikh passes away, the General Deputy succeeds him and all of the Ṭarīqa's spiritual and worldly affairs are transferred to him.

8.1 Succeeding Shaikh ʿAbd al-Karīm

Shaikh ʿAbd al-Karīm suffered from a heart condition and for treatment, Shaikh Muḥammad al-Muḥammad had arranged to take him to London. On Wednesday morning on 1 February 1978, the Shaikh was in poor health. While sitting on a chair at home, he felt a pain in his chest and then collapsed to the ground. Someone phoned our Shaikh who hurried over to find his father sitting on the floor with the help of an assistant. He rushed him to the Republican Hospital in Kirkuk and kept him company, staying in a room opposite his Master's. One karāma of Shaikh 'Abd al-Karīm that astonished medical staff in the hospital is that a machine for treating heart conditions that had been in disuse for a while began working again when it was needed to treat the Shaikh.

Shaikh 'Abd al-Karīm stayed in the hospital for three days, during which doctors kept him sedated. As soon as he would wake up and open his eyes he would ask for a mat to pray, even though his health prevented him from doing so, before falling back into a coma. At 9:50 p.m. on Saturday 4 February 1978, the Shaikh of Ṭarīqa passed on to his Lord's presence.

After washing and shrouding the noble body and reciting the Qur'an over it, our weeping Shaikh said, "For years, not only now, I have been crying over this hour". These feelings reflect not only the tremendous grief that he felt at the loss of his Shaikh but also the Ṭarīqa's heavy burden that was now on his shoulders. Overbearing grief remained visible on our present Shaikh throughout the mourning period. He would say that his love for this world went when Shaikh 'Abd al-Karīm went.

A group of dervishes prepared a grave for Shaikh 'Abd al-Karīm in the hall of the shrines of the Shaikhs in Karbchna, which was being renovated at the time. His noble body was transferred to Karbchna on Sunday morning, with the burial ceremony completed at 1:30 p.m. Villagers stood all along the 100-kilometre-long road between Kirkuk and Karbchna to bid farewell to a Shaikh whose reputation stretched far and wide. The passing of a Shaikh of Ṭarīqa is a mere move from this world to the spirit world because the Shaikhs of Ṭarīqa are spiritually alive. The perpetual continuation of their karāmas after their departure from this life attests to this fact. With the passing of Sultan 'Abd al-Karīm, his General Deputy, Shaikh Muḥammad al-Muḥammad, succeeded him to the Shaikhdom.

Condolences were accepted at a mosque in the Iskān area and a large tent near the Shaikh's house in Kirkuk. Due to Shaikh 'Abd al-Karīm's reputation and the large number of dervishes, people who loved him, and generally all who wanted to offer their condolences, our Shaikh continued to welcome mourners for many days after the death. Many dervishes lived in remote areas where there were no quick means of communication or transportation, so it took some time for the news of the Shaikh's passing to reach them. The Iraqi president, Aḥmad Ḥasan al-Bakr, sent a representative to attend the funeral reception on his behalf. The Iraqi government also issued a decree allowing incoming mourners from Iran, where there is a large number of dervishes, to enter the country through Sulaymāniyya without needing to obtain a visa.

When a Master of Ṭarīqa passes on to the spirit world and his successor assumes the Shaikhdom, his dervishes must pledge their allegiance to the new Shaikh. This pledge may not involve taking the Ṭarīqa's entire pledge anew. Rather, it could include a brief statement in which the seeker accepts the new Shaikh as his Master. The following incidents demonstrate the fact that the designation of a Ṭarīqa's Shaikh is a spiritual affair that everyone must comply with. On the third day of mourning in our Master's guest house, Shaikh Muḥammad Ṣāliḥ, one of Shaikh ʿAbd al-Karīm's brothers, stood up and announced that he would be the first to pledge his allegiance to his nephew as the new Master. Our Master addressed Shaikh Ṭāhir, Sultan Ḥusayn's eldest son, who was about seventy years old at the time, and said something along the lines of, "You are Shaikh Ḥusayn's son. If you wish to be the Shaikh of Ṭarīqa, I am prepared to serve you as I served Shaikh ʿAbd al-Karīm". Aware that the Ṭarīqa's Shaikhs had already chosen their successor, Shaikh Ṭāhir replied that our Shaikh was the most qualified for this trust. He then gathered his brothers, children, and grandchildren and led them to kiss our Shaikh's hand and pledge their allegiance to him.

Our Shaikh officially assumed the Shaikhdom on the third day of mourning. All the caliphs and dervishes who were present pledged their allegiance to the new Shaikh by saying, "I accept you as my Master and my guide in this life and the hereafter". That pledge took about three hours to complete because of the number of disciples who were present. Still, caliphs and dervishes kept coming to pledge allegiance to the new Shaikh for more than a week afterwards.

When a new Shaikh assumes the Shaikhdom, some disciples find it difficult to accept the new Shaikh as a successor to the departed Shaikh. This difficulty arises as a result of a combination of the extreme love for the late Shaikh that grew over the years in the seeker's heart, especially if he accompanied his Shaikh for a long time, and the tremendous pain that he feels as a result of separating from that Master. The disciple may even hurt, for example, when he sees someone else sitting on his late Shaikh's chair or using any of his belongings, even if it is the new Shaikh who was appointed by the late Shaikh. This is due to the uniqueness of the love of the disciple for his Shaikh. However, by way of a karāma from the Shaikhs, the disciple's love for his departed Shaikh quickly expands to include the new Shaikh, occupying the unique place of "the present Shaikh" in his heart. It is impossible for any true lover of the departed Shaikh to not find love for the new Shaikh invading his heart so that he starts to see, love, and treat his new Master the same way he saw, loved, and treated the late Shaikh. In the previous chapter, we saw that dervishes who possess ḥāls begin to feel attracted to the future Shaikh a while before the present Shaikh's demise. They also see spiritual unveilings in dreams and wakefulness that assure their hearts and minds about the transfer of the Shaikhdom and make them accept it. They become disciples of the new Shaikh as they were disciples of the departed Shaikh. The late Shaikh continues to hold a special position in the seeker's heart, the nature and strength of which are determined by the closeness of his companionship to the departed Shaikh.

The love for the Shaikh that grows in the disciple's heart is a result of the charisma that Allah Almighty confers on the Shaikh, as He said about the Prophet Moses, "I bestowed love upon you from Me" (Ṭāhā 39). Our Shaikh used an analogy to describe how love for the new Shaikh enters the disciple's heart: the Shaikhs of Ṭarīqa make their new successor a receptacle for their honey, so anyone who loves that honey is attracted to him. Anyone who loved the Messenger (PBUH) as a Master and a guide found the same love in his heart for Imām ʿAlī after the Messenger's (PBUH) departure, as his spiritual heir. Likewise, love for the new Shaikh grows in the disciple's heart.

Some disciples would have questions or doubts about the new Shaikh's eligibility to succeed the previous Shaikh. The personal history of the new Shaikh at the time of assuming the Shaikhdom would often have been dominated by worldly preoccupations, bereft of karāmas and spiritual exploits matching those of the departed Shaikh. If the disciple does not remember that this is the case with almost every new Shaikh, he may doubt the eligibility of the new Shaikh for the Shaikhdom. Once, while visiting the Shaikh in Virginia, USA, he talked to me about how dervishes of ḥāls started to come to him about six months before the passing of Shaikh ʿAbd al-Karīm. He went on to say that even though he was his General Deputy, he was "one of the people of this world", as opposed to the people of ḥāls who are preoccupied with Ṭarīqa.[1] Being the choice of the late Shaikh, which means that he was chosen by the Prophet (PBUH) and all the Shaikhs of Ṭarīqa, ought to remove all doubt concerning a new Shaikh's qualification. Assuming the Shaikhdom starts fundamental and continuous changes in the new Shaikh that transform him into the person needed for this spiritual position.

Many karāmas occur that confirm the new Shaikh's entitlement to the Shaikhdom to help doubtful dervishes, who may have forgotten or ignored the late Shaikh's will, come back to their senses. Just as there were karāmas and spiritual unveilings regarding Shaikh Muḥammad al-Muḥammad's succession that occurred while Shaikh ʿAbd al-Karīm was alive, many miracles took place after he assumed the Shaikhdom. One of these instructive karāmas happened to a dervish named Fuʾād Jāsim from the city of Ramādī. He had a firm belief in Shaikh ʿAbd al Karīm, having witnessed many of his karāmas. About three weeks after the Shaikh's death, this dervish visited caliph Yāsīn Ṣūfī and told him that he had a question he hoped would not upset him. He went on to explain that he believed that Shaikh ʿAbd al-Karīm was the Master of Ṭarīqa and Sultan of walīs but did not know anything about Shaikh Muḥammad al-Muḥammad. It was clear that Jāsim doubted the new Shaikh's succession of his predecessor. Caliph Yāsīn reassured him that whatever applied to Shaikh ʿAbd al-Karīm was equally true of his successor. He explained that the present Shaikh does not assume the Shaikhdom because he chooses to do so. Rather, this happens according to the Prophet's (PBUH) instruction and the acceptance of all of the Ṭarīqa's Shaikhs. He warned Jāsim that questioning the present Shaikh's eligibility was no small matter.

The next day, Jāsim visited the caliph a second time and told him the

[1] Shaikh Muḥammad al-Muḥammad al-Kasnazān, *sermon*, 24 September 2016.

following:

> When I visited you yesterday, my heart was not at ease with Shaikh Muḥammad al-Muḥammad's succession of Shaikh ʿAbd al-Karīm. Your words reassured me but not completely. At night, I went to bed still thinking about this issue. I saw in a dream that I was in Medina, near the al-Salām Gate, which people enter through to visit the Prophet (PBUH). I heard the sound of the Kasnazānī dhikr drum and the voices of dervishes chanting "Ḥayy Allāh, Ḥayy Allāh". Then I heard a voice saying, "Shaikh Muḥammad al-Muḥammad al-Kasnazān has come with Kasnazānī dervishes to visit the Messenger (PBUH)". My heart rejoiced at this. I wanted to visit the Messenger (PBUH), but I thought that since our Shaikh's son and Ṭarīqa's disciples had come, I would wait to visit with them.
>
> Then I saw Shaikh Muḥammad al-Muḥammad walking in front of a large, unending crowd of dervishes who were raising the banner of Ṭarīqa Kasnazāniyya of the main takya in Ramādī. The Shaikh entered from the al-Salām Gate, and I entered after him. He walked until he faced the Messenger's (PBUH) resting place, while I was behind him. I saw the door to the noble Prophetic resting place open like a sliding door. The door to the Messenger's (PBUH) shrine also opened like a sliding door. The Messenger (PBUH) came out and embraced Shaikh Muḥammad al-Muḥammad, taking in his scent, while the Shaikh kissed the Prophet's (PBUH) hand. While the Prophet (PBUH) embraced our Shaikh, he looked at me and said, "O Dervish, I am the one who put him in Shaikh ʿAbd al-Karīm's place".

Caliph Yāsīn warned him that if he doubted the Shaikh again, faith may never settle in his heart afterwards.

Something similar happened with another caliph and cleric, Ḥājj sayyid Ṭāhā, from the Dibis province in Kirkuk. After Shaikh ʿAbd al-Karīm's departure, this dervish thought that no one could take Shaikh ʿAbd al-Karīm's place, so he did not visit Shaikh Muḥammad al-Muḥammad to pledge his allegiance to him. After a while, he had a dream where he saw several of Shaikh ʿAbd al-Karīm's caliphs whom he knew trying to open a closed door. They failed to open it no matter how hard they tried. Then, Shaikh Muḥammad al-Muḥammad came and easily opened the door for them. The dream's meaning was clear, so he visited our Shaikh and pledged his allegiance to him. When our Shaikh asked him why he had delayed the visit, he related the dream to him.

On the eighteenth day after assuming the Shaikhdom, our Shaikh was sitting in the takya's courtyard in the morning. Those who had come to offer their condolences for Shaikh ʿAbd al-Karīm's passing had already left. After a while, an elderly man walked in and greeted the caliph standing at the Shaikh's service, who returned the greeting. The man asked the caliph about "sayyid Muḥammad". The caliph asked him if he was a dervish, and he answered in the affirmative. The caliph reproached him, asking him how he could be a dervish and not know who his Shaikh was, as our Shaikh was sitting in the courtyard. The man replied:

> My father and uncles would travel on foot from our home in Hawīja[2] to visit Sultan Ḥusayn. When I was a small child, I asked to go with them to visit the Shaikh. My father tried to dissuade me from travelling with them because the trip took days to complete on foot, but I insisted on visiting the Shaikh. In Karbchna, Sultan Ḥusayn called me over to him and gave me the pledge. I haven't visited the Shaikh since then.

The caliph asked him why he came to visit the new Shaikh a short while after he had assumed the Shaikhdom even though he never visited Shaikh ʿAbd al-Karīm during his forty years of Shaikhdom. He replied that an angry-looking Sultan Ḥusayn came to him in a dream the night before and instructed him to go to Shaikh Muḥammad al-Muḥammad. At that moment, our Shaikh intervened and asked the caliph what the man wanted. He told him about the conversation they just had. Our Shaikh instructed the dervish to begin a *khatma* of "lā ilāha illallāh (there is no god but Allah)", and then "Allāh", which are the first two dhikrs of Ṭarīqa Kasnazāniyya's nineteen perennial dhikrs. A khatma of any dhikr in Ṭarīqa Kasnazāniyya means reciting that dhikr 100,000 times. The Shaikh also told him that he should continue to visit now and then. Having realised that the one who was sitting on the chair and speaking was the Shaikh, the dervish approached and greeted him.

A karāma that relates to Shaikh ʿAbd al-Karīm's death came to light on the third day after his passing. A caliph from the Gambia named Ibrāhīm ʿAbd Allāh Jāllū came to the funeral reception. He had taken the Ṭarīqa's pledge years ago when he was receiving an education in Islamic studies in Ramādī. Before his death, Shaikh ʿAbd al-Karīm

---

[2] The Hawīja district is in Kirkuk, about 160 kilometres from Karbchna.

spiritually visited the caliph and instructed him to attend the funeral reception in Kirkuk. The dervish immediately began making travel arrangements, arriving on the third day of the funeral reception.

Ibrāhīm had witnessed a karāma of Shaikh ʿAbd al-Karīm many years earlier, even before becoming a dervish. After taking the Ṭarīqa's pledge in Ramādī's main takya, he asked the caliph who gave him the pledge about a majestic man in a picture on the wall. The caliph said that it was Shaikh ʿAbd al-Karīm, the Master of Ṭarīqa. When this dervish heard this, he said "Praise be to Allah" three times and reached into his pocket and pulled out a small book that could almost fit into the palm of your hand. It was *al-Burda* (The Mantle), al-Būṣīrī's famous poem in praise of the Prophet (PBUH). He went on to tell the caliph the following:

> When I was in my third year of secondary schooling, this man (pointing to Shaikh ʿAbd al-Karīm's picture) came to me in a dream and showed me this book. He said, "My son, take this book. When you finish your secondary schooling and come to study in Iraq, come visit me in Kirkuk". At the time, I was living in my brother's house because my school was far from my family's home. The next morning, on my way to school, I visited a bookstore on my route. I found the book that the Shaikh showed me in the dream on display. When I wanted to buy it, the shopkeeper told me that I would not benefit from it because it was in Arabic, but I bought it anyway.
>
> About a month later, someone told me that my brother's house had burned down. The news shocked and disturbed me. I kept thinking about the book. When I reached the house, I found that the fire had rendered it into ashes, as it was made from wood, like all houses there. I went to the room where the bookcase was and reached into the ashes that covered the ground hoping to find the book. I found it intact—the fire had not touched it, unlike the rest of the books.

During the ceremonies on the fortieth day after Shaikh ʿAbd al-Karīm's death, our Shaikh was sitting in the outside of courtyard of the shrines in Karbchna, facing the mountain, when he advised the dervishes who were present something along the lines of:

> O Dervishes! Look after your behaviour as dervishes and your preaching. Shaikh ʿAbd al-Karīm was a piece of light from Allah. I am not Shaikh ʿAbd al-Karīm. Shaikh ʿAbd al-Karīm was the Master of Ṭarīqa for forty years, while I have only completed forty days as of today. Those present should tell

> those who aren't, and if there is anyone among you that do not see me (he rose from the chair and stood so that all the disciples could see him), know that none of you will see any blessing from me, even by this much (he pointed to his fingertip), except by way of hard work and merit.

This statement represented a change in granting spiritual gifts. Shaikh ʿAbd al-Karīm used to grant spiritual power to many caliphs and dervishes, even if they were not exceptional worshippers; the blessing was mostly gifted, rather than earned. As for the new Shaikh, he emphasised the need for the disciple to earn spiritual power from the Shaikh through the worship of Allah.

Sometime later, our Shaikh decided to perform ʿumrah. He went to Karbchna to visit the shrines. He and some dervishes who accompanied him on the visit entered the shrines. Three of them would go with him for ʿumrah. After greeting the Shaikhs and reading the Fātiḥa for their souls, he asked Shaikh ʿAbd al-Karīm for permission to perform ʿumrah. At that moment, the Shaikh's tomb began to shake, continuing to do so for more than two minutes. The vibration was visible to all who were present. It was so intense that it even tilted the covering on the shrine to one side until it fell. In addition to performing ʿumrah in the first half of 1978, our Shaikh had accompanied Shaikh ʿAbd al-Karīm on his ḥajj in 1973.

All the Kasnazānī Shaikhs wore Kurdish clothing, and so was the case with our Shaikh, although the design of his clothing differed slightly from Shaikh ʿAbd al-Karīm's style of dress. About two or three months after he assumed the Shaikhdom, he was visiting the Shaikhs in Karbchna when a caliph, who had served Shaikh ʿAbd al-Karīm, approached him, carrying an outfit similar to the clothes his predecessor used to wear. He asked him to wear what he called "the clothes of Shaikhdom" during his visit to the shrines. This request annoyed our Shaikh who answered, "Shaikhdom is not tied to clothes. Even if I wore European clothing, I would still be the Shaikh of Ṭarīqa". True Islam and nearness to Allah are not based on one's external looks, including what one wears. Rather, it is based on the love for Allah and the piety they have in their heart. Our Shaikh would often wear an Arab cloak over his Kurdish clothes when receiving guests.

8.2 Karāmas That Confirm the Muḥammadan Inheritance

Many karāmas and spiritual unveilings foretold Shaikh Muḥammad al-Muḥammad's succession of Shaikh ʿAbd al-Karīm. We have also seen several wonders that occurred after our Shaikh assumed the Shaikhdom. Here we will recount other karāmas that confirm his state of being an inheritor of the Prophet (PBUH).

On 10 October 2012, a car broke down in front of the takya's land in Saraipalya, Bangalore, India, before the takya was built. Three men got out of the car, one of whom turned out to be a businessman, another an engineer, and the third a professor of Sufism named Ḥaydar ʿAlī. Having noticed the takya's flag, when they entered through the temporary gate, they inquired about the place. Caliph ʿImād ʿAbd al-Ṣamad told them that it was a takya of Ṭarīqa ʿAlīyya Qādiriyya Kasnazāniyya whose Master was Shaikh Muḥammad al-Muḥammad al-Kasnazān al-Ḥusaynī.

The caliph offered the pledge to the professor and explained how it was necessary to take the pledge at the hand of a perfected Shaikh and explained the qualities of such a Shaikh. The words had an impact on the professor, who expressed his desire to take up Ṭarīqa. The caliph told them that their car would start after they took the pledge, as Allah would have fulfilled the good that He wanted for them in having the car break down in front of the takya. The professor said that they would see if what he promised was true, and they all took the pledge.

The professor asked whether the car would now start, and the caliph answered in the affirmative. They wanted to open the bonnet of the car to examine the engine, but the caliph dissuaded them from doing so, as he had promised them that the car would start. He asked them to get into the car, close the doors, and start the engine; the car did indeed start. Touched by the karāma, the professor got out of the car, kissed the hands and feet of the caliph, and donated a sum of money to the takya. The amazed professor said that his house was near the takya so he would stay in touch with the caliph.

The next day, he came with five or six people. He knelt at the takya's door before entering. After introducing his friends, he said that he wanted to relate something that happened to him the day before. Caliph ʿImād thought that the professor wanted to recount to his friends the karāma of the broken car starting without repair, but he was surprised with what he had to say:

> After I left yesterday, some doubts arose in my heart. I thought to myself, "I am a professor of Sufism, so how can this person teach me and give me the pledge?" I felt envious. When I arrived home, I was tired, so I slept. I had a dream in which I saw this takya, and you were sitting in this exact place in the same position. I gradually got closer to you, but I was surprised when I found that the face was not yours; it was of an older person. That man called to me, so I sat beside him. He started to tell me the same things you told me. I said, "My Master, I heard these words yesterday from someone who was sitting here. He was wearing clothes and a green shawl similar to yours, but his face was different". He replied, "Yes, that was Shaikh Muḥammad al-Muḥammad al-Kasnazān's caliph. I am the Messenger of Allah's caliph, ʿAlī Ibn Abī Ṭālib. When you put your hand in the hand of Shaikh Muḥammad al-Muḥammad's deputy, you put your hand in ours".

The professor began to cry, and those present were overcome with awe. Then he went on to say that Imām ʿAlī Ibn Abī Ṭālib added:

> We, the family of the Prophetic household, have authorised our inheritor Shaikh Muḥammad al-Muḥammad ʿAbd al-Karīm al-Kasnazān to speak on our behalf.

The very same day, caliph ʿImād phoned caliph Majīd Ḥamīd in Amman to covey to our Shaikh this karāma. He was surprised again when caliph Majīd informed him that the night before, the Shaikh had said that he has permission to speak on behalf of the Prophetic household.[3]

The following vision that caliph ʿImād saw in Bangalore, India, on 11 September 2013, confirms that our Master promotes the Messenger's (PBUH) way:

> While waiting for the time of the afternoon prayer, I fell asleep. I had a dream in which I was in Medina, peace and blessings be upon its owner. I was standing at the end of a long queue of people. We were waiting for the Prophet (PBUH) to come out from his resting place under the green dome so that we could visit him. Suddenly, everybody turned to me and said, "Come over, the Messenger (PBUH) is asking for you". I also turned around to see if these people were addressing someone behind me, but there was no

[3] Fatoohi, *The wonders of Ṭarīqa Kasnazāniyya*, 47-49.

one. The line of people split in two, allowing me to walk through the middle. I walked with extreme shyness. I saw the Messenger (PBUH) standing near the door. He looked tired and was leaning on Shaikh Muḥammad al-Muḥammad for support. Our Shaikh's right hand was stretched behind the Messenger's back to his right armpit. He (PBUH) had his left hand on Shaikh Muḥammad al-Muḥammad's shoulder. I said, "Allah is the greatest! The Messenger (PBUH) is tired? Why?" The Shaikh gestured with his noble head to come closer. Before I got closer, I could see some of the Messenger's (PBUH) features, but as I moved closer, thick clouds gathered around both of them so I could only see the Shaikh's face. When I was close, I heard the Messenger (PBUH) say, "He (meaning the Shaikh) is the only one who lifted me".[4]

A vision that our Shaikh saw on AH 17 Ramadan 1437 (22 June 2016) also reflects his deputyship of the Prophet (PBUH). He saw himself visiting the shrines of the Kasnazānī Shaikhs in Karbchna with green flags waving for his arrival. He was standing in front of Shaikh ʿAbd al-Qādir al-Kasnazān's shrine, and he and the Kasnazānī Shaikhs were all immersed in a dense, unique light. Shaikh ʿAbd al-Qādir was standing in front of the door, holding a book he was reading from. He said to our Shaikh, who was standing in front of him, "You are a caliph". Our Shaikh replied, "Yes, my beloved". Shaikh ʿAbd al-Qādir repeated more assertively, "You are a caliph". Our Shaikh replied, once more, "Yes, my beloved". Then Shaikh ʿAbd al-Qādir sharply repeated the phrase a third time, emphasizing the declaration he read from the book, "You are a caliph". This austerity seems to have been in response to the shyness and humility our Shaikh was overcome with as a result of this bestowal and because of where he was. He responded a third time, "Yes, my beloved". This vision indicates that he was Allah's caliph on earth, i.e. the Prophet's representative.[5]

The Prophet (PBUH) naming our Shaikh "Muḥammad al-Muḥammad", as we shall see in §12.3, is another indication that he was an inheritor of his Forefather (PBUH). Numerous karāmas show that Allah and the Prophet (PBUH) have elected the Shaikhs of Ṭarīqa Kasnazāniyya, including Shaikh Muḥammad al-Muḥammad, for the deputyship of the Prophet (PBUH).

---

[4] Ibid., 51.

[5] Shaikh Muḥammad al-Muḥammad al-Kasnazān, *sermon*, 1 February 2018.

Compete in preaching; compete in opening takyas; compete in having good manners; compete in doing more dhikr; compete in worshipping at night; compete in fasting often; compete in performing retreats and spiritual exercises. Do not compete in chasing after this world. This world is carrion and those who seek it are dogs. This world seeks those who run away from it and runs away from those who seek it.

Shaikh Muḥammad al-Muḥammad al-Kasnazān
(*Sermon*, 22 December 2005)

9

Retreating to Worship Allah

Following in the footsteps of the Prophet (PBUH) and the Shaikhs of Ṭarīqa, Shaikh Muḥammad al-Muḥammad went into *khalwas* (retreats) to worship Allah (exalted and high is He). His three seclusions were in the same cave that Shāh al-Kasnazān and Sultan Ḥusayn carried out their retreats at the foot of Mount Sagarma.

9.1 Three Retreats

The Shaikh's three seclusions took place in three consecutive years, all after he became the Master of Ṭarīqa. The first khalwa was less than six months after assuming the Shaikhdom in 1978 and the second and third in the following two years. Clearly, practising three khalwas in such a short period at the beginning of his Shaikhdom was meant to speed up his spiritual development.

Each khalwa began ten days before the month of Ramadan and continued throughout the month of fasting, totalling forty days. According to the Western calendar, the first khalwa began around 26 July and ended on 3 September 1978. Each of the following two seclusions began and ended eleven days before the one that preceded it, as the lunar Hijrī year is shorter than the solar Western year by eleven days. The third khalwa differed from the first two in that the Shaikh did not spend all of his time in the cave. He would remain inside it from the morning prayer until the night prayer and then return to the takya, probably because of his need to closely manage the Ṭarīqa's affairs and the impossibility of postponing everything for forty days.

Before entering his first seclusion, he visited the Karbchna shrines. When he was about to enter the cave, he read the *basmala* and the following noble verse, "Retreat to the cave. Your Lord will spread out for you of His mercy and will make easy for you your affair" (al-Kahf 18:16). This noble verse recounts Allah's order to the famed young converts to enter the cave that witnessed the miracle of their lengthy slumber and then waking up.

The cave of our Shaikh's retreat faces the Ka'ba. The walls and ceiling of this natural cave are made up of huge rocks. It is about three metres deep, and it is more than two metres high in most places, so it is possible to stand at its entrance, but it gradually narrows on some of its sides. When inside the cave, the person is completely isolated from the outside world. This makes it reminiscent of Cave Ḥirā', where the Prophet (PBUH) would seclude himself. Since our Shaikh's three seclusions were in the heat of summer, he would stay inside the cave during the day, and when the temperature would cool at night, he would go out and sit on the roof of the cave.

The Kasnazānī khalwa diet is extremely challenging to adhere to, yet our Master subjected himself to a far stricter diet, which was specific to him as the Shaikh of Ṭarīqa. He restricted his daily food intake to a very small quantity of bread, fruits, and vegetables. In the first thirteen days of his first khalwa, he limited his daily intake of bread to a quarter of a *ruqāq* bread prepared without any salt or sugar. Ruqāq bread is extremely thin; when he would break off a piece in his palm before eating it, it would not fill it. After that, he stopped eating bread completely for the rest of that khalwa and in the following two, limiting his diet to fruit, such as melons. He could only eat a few kinds of fruit because they would cause discomfort as a result of eating them without any other food. He would also eat a few pieces of boiled okra that were cooked without fat or salt because it helps in softening the stomach with its abundant fibre. A few days after this huge reduction in food intake, water and tea would start to cause acidity in the stomach.

He also put himself through additional struggles. In the first khalwa, he asked his brother-in-law, Sāmān, to accompany him without being in a state of seclusion himself, meaning without abiding by its conditions. At the time of breaking the fast, the Shaikh would ask for the best, most delicious kinds of food for his companion to eat in front of him. Shaikh Sāmān told me that as soon as the khalwa ended, it became clear to him that our Shaikh was subjecting himself to additional struggle by having his companion eat those delicious foods in front of him. He expressed his amazement about the fact that he never thought about this matter at all during the khalwa. As he put it, it was as if the Shaikh had thrown a veil over his companion that prevented him from realising that he was being used as an additional source of strife for the Shaikh so that he would not feel embarrassed. While the Shaikh would watch his companion eat as much as he liked of the tastiest of foods, the small amount of very limited foods he would eat himself throughout the entire day would not fill the palm of one hand. Commenting on the difficulty of this struggle against the self, our Shaikh said, "There are times when one wishes he could give everything he owns for a piece of bread".[1] This emphasizes the magnitude of spiritual influence that helps the person in seclusion withstand its exceptional hardships.

About thirty-five dervishes from different parts of Iraq and some from Iran joined him in the first khalwa. He delivered a sermon to them about the khalwa's rules and etiquettes. Before it began, he determined the area of seclusion for the dervishes, on the same mountain, close to his cave. Each disciple chose a small natural place suitable for seclusion or prepared one using branches and shrubs as roofs and walls. It was incumbent upon the one in seclusion to stay within the limits of the khalwa area even when leaving his place of seclusion for whatever reason. Some disciples secluded themselves on an individual basis, while others were in pairs. The Shaikh cautioned the dervishes to not busy themselves with talking instead of worship. He and the dervishes refrained from shaving their beards during the khalwa.

In every khalwa, the first dhikr that our Shaikh and the disciples would perform was the first khatma of the perennial Kasnazānī dhikrs, "lā ilāha illallāh". They would also complete a khatma of each of the other eighteen perennial wirds during the khalwa. Dervishes were instructed not to sleep at night as they had to spend it in worship. A dervish could sleep for a while after finishing his dhikrs that follow the dawn prayer.

The disciples spent most of their time alone performing their devotional duties, but they would come together at certain times of the day for congregational dhikrs. They would also recite al-Būṣīrī's al-Burda every night as a group. Also, after praying and breaking the fast, the Shaikh and the dervishes would stand in the direction of the Ka'ba to recite one hundred times each of the dhikrs "yā Khabīr (O All-Aware

---

[1] Shaikh Muḥammad al-Muḥammad al-Kasnazān, *sermon*, 25 May 2000.

One!)" and "ṣallā Allāhu subḥānahu wa-t'ālā 'alayka wa-sallam yā rasūla Allāh (may Allah (exalted and high is He) send prayers upon you, O Messenger of Allah!)".

In the morning, the dervishes taking part in the retreat would gather in front of the Shaikh's cave to hear a sermon, any instructions or remarks he had, and answers to questions related to the seclusion. When a disciple had a question or a particular issue he wanted to present to the Shaikh outside the group meeting time, for example, a private matter, he would inform the person standing at the Shaikh's service for him to arrange a meeting. Dervishes outside the khalwa were sometimes allowed to pay a short visit to the Shaikh.

9.2 Supernatural and Spiritual Experiences

Entering seclusion makes a person go through various spiritual experiences, from divine unveilings and visitations from good spirits to harassment and attacks from evil spiritual creatures trying to stop him from this practice of intense worship of Allah and to harm him. Someone who would like to enter a retreat needs a Shaikh to spiritually protect him from devils and evil spirits that try to cause him harm. He must also be ready for this most difficult experience, as our Shaikh explains:

> An ordinary person cannot complete a khalwa at all. They either cause him some harm or kill him, he may lose his mind, or he may just cut it short and run away. Anyone who claims to have completed a khalwa is a liar, unless he is a walī. A person who has not attained wilāya cannot complete a khalwa without a Shaikh. The person who has a Shaikh can do that. If one of our dervishes wishes to enter a khalwa, I would educate him and give him permission so he can do it, provided that he has a sound mind and understanding and is calm. A person who lacks reason or understanding cannot complete a khalwa.[2]

Our Shaikh said that during his three seclusions, whenever he closed his eyes, without sleeping or entering into a state of spiritual meditation, whether night or day, he would see his Master, Shaikh 'Abd al-Karīm, and his Master's Master, Shaikh Ḥusayn, standing at the

[2] Shaikh Muḥammad al-Muḥammad al-Kasnazān, *sermon*, 16 April 2016.

entrance of the cave.[3] Their spiritual presence was to protect their caliph and Deputy, the new Shaikh of Ṭarīqa, while he progressed spiritually. Our Master said that Shaikh ʿAbd al-Karīm did not leave him, that is, spiritually, for five years after he succeeded him.

Much of what happens during a retreat is kept private and is not shared with others. I will mention here some of what our Shaikh revealed of the spiritual experiences that he had during his seclusions.

For a period in one of the seclusions, devils would disseminate an extremely foul odour, like that of a rotting corpse, at the time of breaking the fast. The odour would persist until approximately the time of the night prayer. It made it difficult for the Shaikh to eat or drink.

One day, the Shaikh was lying down with his eyes closed reading dhikrs when his heart suddenly received an inspiration to order the dervish at his service, who was sitting nearby, to immediately get up and leave his post. As soon as the dervish left his place, a massive rock fell from the cave's roof onto the spot where he had been seated, which would have undoubtedly killed him had he remained in his place.

One night, a snake dangled from the roof of the cave towards our Shaikh's assistant. As soon as our Shaikh drew his sword, the snake fled. In another incident, he asked his assistant to clean his pillow, and when he lifted it, he found a very large scorpion underneath it.

The following occurrence was witnessed by all the dervishes in seclusion. At times, after the night prayer but before midnight, the part of the sky facing the opening of the Shaikh's cave would transform into something like a battlefield because of the abundance of meteors shooting across it. This indicates an abnormal level of presence and activity of, on the one hand, devils and evil jinns who try to negatively impact the divine atmosphere that the khalwa creates and, on the other, good spirits that undo their efforts. This phenomenon is a confirmation of what Allah Almighty says in the Qur'an:

> We have placed within the heaven mansions and beautified it for observers. We have protected it from every cursed devil, except one who steals a hearing and is pursued by a clear burning flame. (Al-Ḥijr 15:16–18)
>
> Indeed, We have adorned the nearest heaven with an adornment of stars and as protection against every rebellious devil. They may not listen

[3] Shaikh Muḥammad al-Muḥammad al-Kasnazān, *sermon*, 25 May 2000.

to the exalted assembly [of angels] and are pelted from every side, repelled; and for them is a constant punishment, except one who snatches [some words] by theft, but they are pursued by a burning flame, piercing [in brightness]. (Al-Ṣāffāt 37:6–10)

The following noble verse mentioned by a jinn spokesperson explicitly mentions the increase of guards in the heavens at certain times when special spiritual activities take place:

> We have sought [to reach] heaven but found it filled with powerful guards and burning flames. We used to sit therein in positions for hearing, but whoever listens now will find a burning flame lying in wait for him. (Al-Jinn 72:8–9)

This is another example of how Ṭarīqa transforms faith from being "traditional" to "authentic", as our Shaikh used to describe it. Traditional faith is the kind of faith that one inherits from his culture and holds without direct, experiential proof of its unseen foundations. Ṭarīqa causes a devoted dervish to see spiritual proofs from the unseen, which are unattainable otherwise. The dervishes in seclusion had complete faith in Allah's words, including verses that describe pelting the devils who try to infiltrate the world of good spirits. However, their witnessing of the phenomenon of the abundance of meteors with their own eyes drew them closer to the level of Iḥsān. This is the highest degree of certainty which the Prophet (PBUH) defined as follows, "[It is] to worship Allah as if you see Him; and if you cannot see Him, then verily He sees you".[4] Karāmas are the means of crossing over from "believing" in the Qur'an's truthfulness to "witnessing" it.

In another unveiling that testified to the veracity of the Qur'an, our Shaikh saw the sky in the form of an array of adjacent doors. The doors were of the usual size. When he asked about the doors, he was told that behind each was something extremely terrifying that would destroy anyone who tries to enter without permission. This is a spiritual representation of this Qur'anic verse:

> And the heavens shall be opened, becoming in the form of doors. (Al-Naba' 78:19)

After reciting, with the disciples, one hundred times each of "yā

[4] Al-Bukhārī, *Al-Jāmi' al-ṣaḥīḥ*, I, no. 50, p. 65.

Khabīr" and "ṣallā Allāhu subḥānahu wa-t'ālā 'alayka wa-sallam yā rasūla Allāh" after the sunset prayer while standing and facing the Ka'ba, the Shaikh would proceed with his personal wirds. At that time, the dervishes would begin to hear what sounded like the chirping of thousands of crickets. The sound would continue until he finished those dhikrs at the time of the night prayer, at which point it would disappear. At times, the sound would be so loud to the point where he would have to raise his voice when speaking even when addressing someone near him. One astonishing aspect of this phenomenon is the fact of it happening at night in an isolated, mountainous area, where stillness is almost ubiquitous. This phenomenon sometimes occurred even outside of the khalwa. At times, the Shaikh would go out for a walk in Amman. At the end of that walking path, there is a grove wherein there are tall pine trees. In a spot there, he would perform the sunset prayer and the Sunna prayers and read his special wirds. Sometimes, the same sounds would be heard until he finished his wirds.

In seclusion, many spiritual unveilings and visitations from Shaikhs and good spirits occur. The following is one such karāma that happened to the Shaikh in his second seclusion, which he disclosed in a speech to dervishes who were visiting him:

> A short while ago, Shaikh 'Abd al-Karīm came and called me, "Muḥammad". I answered, "Yes, my beloved". He said, "Look at my hand". There was a wire in his hand that looked like a radio antenna. He shook the wire, and a tremendous fire broke out from the city of Penjwin (in northern Iraq, on the border with Iran) to the city of Abadan (in southern Iran, on the border with Iraq). The Shaikh said, "Do you see that?" I answered in the affirmative. The Shaikh shook the wire again, and the fire spread as had happened the first time. The Shaikh said, "Tell your dervishes that we sat you in the Shaikhs' place and put the Ṭarīqa's staff in your hand. The one who sticks to you is safe, and the one who does not is responsible for that".

This unveiling happened in mid-1979. A little more than a year later, a devastating eight-year-long war between Iraq and Iran broke out.

A karāma that illustrates the spiritual benefits of retreat happened three days before the end of our Shaikh's third khalwa, i.e. on the twenty-seventh night of the month of Ramadan. This is the night that many consider *Laylat al-Qadr* (the Night of Power). The Shaikhs told our Master to inform the dervishes in seclusion that the Messenger (PBUH) was telling them to submit that night whatever requests they had. They told him that a sign of the truthfulness of this message is that when he informs the dervishes, one of them will be struck with an intense ḥāl that would cause him to take to the mountain. The next day, after breaking the fast, our Shaikh stood atop his cave, which overlooked all the dervishes' places of seclusion, and informed them of the order of the Messenger (PBUH) to present their requests to Allah (exalted and high is He) after the night prayer. An Iranian dervish named sayyid ʿAbd al-Raḥmān was struck with a ḥāl that caused him to go to the mountain. The following day, the Shaikh had to send someone to bring him back. Late in the night of the notification, a dervish and cousin of his called Mullā Muḥammad came to him having experienced a ḥāl that made him cry and laugh. The dervish asked the Shaikh for permission to speak. The latter agreed and told him that he knew what he would say. The dervish said that, while awake, he saw every disciple present his requests in the form of a scroll. He saw the honourable hand of the Messenger (PBUH) take all requests and raise them to Allah (mighty and sublime is He).[5]

Several deceased walīs who were disciples of Shaikh ʿAbd al-Karīm visited our Shaikh while he was in khalwa. This included some who passed away when he was still young. These visitors from the spirit world would ask him what he wanted from them in the way of service to Ṭarīqa, but he would dismiss them without asking for anything.

The following is another karāma that happened during one of our Shaikh's retreats. He would suffer from the intense mid-summer heat during the day inside the cave. The Shaikhs made an opening in the cave through which a cool breeze, like that of an electric air conditioner, would come to him.

Many dervishes witnessed karāmas that revealed the spiritual support of the Shaikhs to our Shaikh in his seclusion. In his second seclusion, the Shaikh's nephew, ʿAlī Ḥusayn, who was not in the khalwa, had a particular dream twice. He saw Imām ʿAlī (may Allah ennoble his face) descend from a rope from the sky to the place of seclusion.

---

[5] Shaikh Muḥammad al-Muḥammad al-Kasnazān, *sermon*, 30 June 2000; 4 December 2013.

These supernatural occurrences are just the tip of the iceberg of what happened during our Shaikh's khalwas. Most karāmas are secrets that cannot be divulged.

One day in London, our Shaikh spoke to me in detail about khalwas and supernatural events that take place in them, including some that I have mentioned earlier. He also spoke about how evil spirits target those who perform dhikrs and spiritual practices, trying to make them abandon worship and hurt them. Indeed, devils have killed many walīs and righteous people. This usually happens when the latter are in a state of inattentiveness, such as when asleep or in the toilet.

One night in Kirkuk, Shaikh Muḥammad al-Muḥammad was asleep when evil spirits attacked him and hurt him a lot. He gently addressed his Shaikh, "How can they be allowed to hurt me when I seek madad from you?" At this point, Shaikh 'Abd al-Karīm appeared spiritually. Our Shaikh shyly repeated his question. The Shaikh advised him to always have a wakeful guard near to him when he went to sleep. The presence of a wakeful guard would repeal evil spirits in most cases but a few. After this incident, our Shaikh would never sleep unless someone was awake near him.[6]

[6] Shaikh Muḥammad al-Muḥammad al-Kasnazān, *sermon*, 8 May 2000.

The takya is a spiritual school that prepares a disciple to be a worshipper, a seeker, and a good person and a reformer in society. We want a Muḥammadan (PBUH) society, a society like the society of the Companions of the Messenger (PBUH), "The forerunners, the forerunners (10)—they are the ones that are brought near [to Allah]" (al-Wāqi'a 56:10-11). We seek their moral character, "Indeed, you are of a great moral character" (al-Qalam 68:4). May Allah (exalted and high is He) send His blessings and peace upon you, O my Master, O Messenger of Allah.

Shaikh Muḥammad al-Muḥammad al-Kasnazān
(*Sermon*, 22 January 2010)

10

Moving the Central Takya to Baghdad

When Shaikh Muḥammad al-Muḥammad became the Master of Ṭarīqa in early 1978, Iraq's central takya, meaning the Shaikh's residence, was in the district of Imām Qāsim in Kirkuk in northern Iraq. This is where Shaikh ʿAbd al-Karīm al-Kasnazān settled down in 1968. Our Shaikh expanded the takya, adding an adjoining house to it and making a takya for women. He vacated his house next to the takya, where he used to live during his father's Shaikhdom, and turned it into a takya for dervishes as well.

Shortly after assuming the Shaikhdom, Shaikh Muḥammad al-Muḥammad made a very important strategic decision. He moved the central takya to Baghdad, thus moving his place of residence from Kirkuk to Baghdad. This led to the spread of Ṭarīqa like never before. When he became Master, there were only three small takyas in Baghdad: one in the al-Raḥmāniyya quarter, which was a room in a house; another in the al-Ardharūmlī quarter; and a third near the al-Gaylānī Shrine. There was only one caliph in Baghdad, named "Bāqir" (may Allah have mercy on him), who managed the al-Raḥmāniyya takya, the city's first Kasnazānī takya.

When the Shaikh visited Baghdad early in his Shaikhdom, staying in the Ibn Khaldūn hotel, near the al-Ṣarrāfiyya Bridge, he spoke to a dervish named Kāmil Shihāb (may Allah have mercy on him), who used to manage the al-Ārdharūmlī takya, about the necessity of establishing a takya in a dedicated building. He would meet with the disciples there, and they would be able to regularly practice dhikr, worship, and preach. He directed Kāmil to search for suitable land to build the central takya upon, having given him an idea of the kind of place to look for. After checking out potential sites, Hajj Kāmil proposed a plot of land in the district of Ḥayy al-Quḍāt in central Baghdad with an area of 1,365 square metres. As the land was in the suburbs of Baghdad, some Arab and Kurdish disciples thought that it was too far from the city centre and not easily accessible. When our Shaikh visited it, however, he concluded that it was the right place for the future takya.

The land was surrounded by a fence, but neighbouring houses dumped their rubbish on it. The authorities were considering more than one plan for using the state-owned land but they had not made a final decision. A karāma facilitated the Ṭarīqa's acquisition of the land. Shortly after, a large number of disciples in seven large buses visited the Shaikh in Karbchna, where he was supervising the renovation of the shrines. Hiding among the visitors was a young man named ʿAlī from the security department of the National Command of the ruling Baʿath Party in Iraq. He had been sent by security agencies to spy on Ṭarīqa. Ṭarīqa had always been a source of concern for the government, which did not understand that it was a spiritual, not a worldly, organization. Its concern was further heightened by the fact that the Ṭarīqa's Shaikh was a Kurd, as were many of its dervishes. The central government was in conflict with Kurdish political and armed wings. Our Shaikh was sitting with guests in his house, which is located on a hill about 250 metres away from the Shaikhs' tombs. He suddenly summoned caliph Muḥammad Maḥmūd (may Allah have mercy on him), who served as his administrative deputy among caliphs and dervishes, described the spy to him, and told him to deliver a message to him.

Caliph Muḥammad found the visitor among disciples near the shrines. He took him aside and delivered our Shaikh's message to him: Karbchna was a safe zone, so there was no need for the pistol he was hiding. Also, there were Kurdish fighters in surrounding areas that could cause trouble for him if they knew that he was armed. Muḥammad asked the visitor to leave the pistol with him. He would accompany him on the way back after the visit had ended and return it to him in Sangāw after he and the rest of the dervishes had crossed the danger zone and entered the total safety zone, where there were no Kurdish fighters. The man looked shocked and denied that he was carrying a weapon. When he found that Muḥammad was absolutely confident in the Shaikh's assertion, the astonished man acknowledged that this was the case and gave him his pistol. He asked the dervish to take him to see the Shaikh. When our Shaikh received him, he repeated what he had said before, that Karbchna was safe, and that it was best not to carry a weapon in this area since Kurdish fighters might misunderstand the situation and hurt him if they came to know that he was armed. He reassured him once again that the caliph would return his weapon to him in Sangāw. He told him that Ṭarīqa had nothing to hide to be spied on and that the main concern of the Shaikh and dervishes was to remember and worship Allah. He urged the visitor to write an accurate and detailed report to whoever sent him of what he saw. He also asked him to come and see him again afterwards.

ʿAlī became a sincere disciple. He used his connections to secure the approvals needed for building the takya on the land in Ḥayy al-Quḍāt. A karāma turned this man from a spy on Ṭarīqa into one of its good disciples. He came at the perfect time to provide an important service for Ṭarīqa, helping to expedite the building of the new central takya in Baghdad.

The takya's land was registered in 1979, about a year after our Master assumed the Shaikhdom, and its construction began in 1980. The Shaikh regularly visited Baghdad to oversee the construction work. In the beginning, he would stay in a hotel, but when his visits became longer, he rented a house. The takya opened in 1982, so he visited it more frequently until he moved with his family that year to permanently reside in his home in the takya. Baghdad became the Ṭarīqa's preaching hub.

The takya was designed and built under our Master's direct supervision. He appointed Shaikh Sāmān Maʿrūf as the lead engineer. He asked him to make a mosque that could accommodate those who prayed and performed dhikr, a hall for dervishes, some of whom would stay in the takya, and a house for the Shaikh, which would also never be without guests. When he said that he wanted the dhikr yard to be large, Shaikh Sāmān said that it was difficult to do that. Influenced by the size of the small dhikr yard in the Kirkuk takya, he said that he believed that the area the Shaikh wanted for the yard would be too large for the expected number of dervishes. The Shaikh replied that the Shaikhs bring as many disciples as a takya can accommodate: the bigger the takya is, the greater the number of disciples. He asked him to make the dhikr yard as large as possible. Thanks to continuous preaching, dervishes started to fill the takya's yard on Monday and Thursday nights, when dhikr circles were held. About a decade later, the Shaikh reiterated the same words when commenting on the building of the takya in his farm in Dora, which Ṭarīqa started to use for some religious celebrations when the central takya could not accommodate attendees.

The Master asked for a special hall for women to be built, where female preachers could educate female dervishes and those who wanted to learn about Ṭarīqa. Therein, his mother would also receive those who wanted to visit her to seek her prayers or advice. When the dhikr circles were established on Monday and Thursday nights, the sleeping room, which overlooks the takya's courtyard where the dhikr was held, was also reserved for women, so that they may participate in the dhikr at a distance from men.

The Shaikh made the door of the takya's mosque a replica of the new door that was designed for the shrines in Karbchna. He did not want to use pillars inside the hall of the mosque, which was twenty-two metres long and seventeen metres sixty-five centimetres wide. Shaikh Sāmān said that the mosque's huge dome, whose peak was seventeen metres above the mosque's floor, needed to be supported by pillars. The Shaikh repeated his request to not have any pillars inside the mosque. Sāmān said that even though he, as the engineer, thought that supporting pillars were necessary, he would make the dome without them, relying on our Shaikh's spiritual influence. Two days after casting the dome and putting up temporary wooden pillars to allow the building materials to harden, the caliph who was supervising the construction noticed that one of the wooden pillars had tilted. Shaikh Sāmān reiterated that the dome was supposed to be supported by pillars but expressed no concern for it since it did not collapse during the casting process. After the mosque's completion, a huge, very heavy chandelier was also hung from the dome's roof.

After the dome was covered from the outside and a crescent moon was placed on its peak, Shaikh Sāmān saw in a dream Shaikh Ismāʿīl al-Wilyānī's hand supporting the dome. One day, when a group of engineers asked our Shaikh how the dome of the takya's mosque stood without supportive pillars, he replied, "Shaikh ʿAbd al-Karīm's hand is supporting it until the Day of Resurrection". Shaikhs Ismāʿīl al-Wilyānī and ʿAbd al-Karīm here represent the Shaikhs of Ṭarīqa in general and their spiritual protection of the takya. Even large explosions near the takya as a result of aerial bombardments during the Gulf War did not affect the mosque's dome—further proof of its being under the protection of Ṭarīqa's Shaikhs.

Dervishes usually take part in the building of takyas because it is a blessed effort, as takyas are Allah's houses wherein preaching and dhikr take place. When establishing the main takya in any given city, it is not only disciples from that city that participate in building it, but dervishes from other cities also come to help. This is how, for instance, the central takya in Baghdad was built.

The following is one of the karāmas that accompanied the building of the central takya in Baghdad. Our Shaikh, who was in Kirkuk at the time, sent caliph Aḥmad Ḥusayn and another caliph named Muḥammad to a factory in the city of Erbil to buy marble for the takya. He specified the type of marble to them, its colour and dimensions, and the required amount. The factory's manager apologised and said that what they wanted was unavailable. The Shaikh asked them to once again go to the same factory and ask for the marble. Hesitantly, Aḥmad reiterated that the factory's manager told them that the marble was unavailable but that he would go again as this was the Shaikh's wish. Our Shaikh patted him on the back encouragingly and said, "Go Kasnazānī, Kasnazānī". When they reached the factory, Muḥammad felt too embarrassed to ask for the marble again, so Aḥmad alone went to the manager's office. He told those present in the office that he knew that they had already told him that they did not have this kind of marble, but that he had returned to check once again to be sure, in deference to the Shaikh's wish. The manager restated that they did not have that kind of marble. An employee there who was writing something put his pen aside and asked the caliph to follow him to the storehouse because he was reminded of the possible availability of this kind of marble. He removed a cover that revealed the marble that the Shaikh wanted. The available amount matched the desired quantity. Stunned, the employee said, "Your Shaikh knows our factory better than us!" This karāma reminds us of a muʿjiza of Jesus (peace be upon him), which was his ability to know what people had stored in their homes, "I inform you of what you eat and what you store in your houses" (Āl ʿImrān 49).

The most important thing that you can spend your time and effort working on is preaching. For us, preaching is the greatest worship. Preaching is the greatest deed in Ṭarīqa. Enjoining good and forbidding evil is the most important thing because you teach people to worship, direct them towards Allah (exalted and high is He), implement the Muḥammadan Sharia (PBUH). You are educators: learn and teach people. You take your knowledge from the Shaikhs and the Muḥammadan Sharia and convey it to people and teach them.

Shaikh Muḥammad al-Muḥammad al-Kasnazān
(*Sermon*, undated)

11

Calling People to Allah and His Prophet (PBUH)

Following in the footsteps of their great forefather, the Messenger of Allah (PBUH), the Kasnazānī Shaikhs dedicated their lives to calling people to the way of Allah and, sacrificing what was precious and dear for this purpose. Just like all of the Masters of Ṭarīqa before him, Shaikh Muḥammad al-Muḥammad never stopped this effort, even for a day. He would remind disciples of the necessity of preaching and supported them with everything they needed to convey Allah's words, His remembrance, and the Prophet Muḥammad's (PBUH) message to people all over the world. Preaching is not limited to inviting non-Muslims to Islam and urging negligent Muslims to strongly hold on to religion. Rather, every action in the way of enjoining good and forbidding evil is an act of preaching, even when preaching to those who are committed, practising Muslims. Our Shaikh said:

> It is impermissible to stop preaching. One must preach daily, even to his family, extended family and relatives. Preaching is of utmost importance.[1]

He went on to say, "My every concern is Ṭarīqa and preaching". Another one of his sayings about preaching that he used to reiterate is, "Through preaching, obligations are enjoined".[2] Preaching leads non-Muslims to Islam and teaches them its obligations of praying, fasting, almsgiving, and performing hajj, and it also reminds heedless Muslims of them. Preaching leads people to Islam and reminds them of it. Embracing Islam means upholding its obligations. Hence, "Through preaching, obligations are enjoined".

In extolling the virtues of preaching and giving the pledge, our Shaikh related that upon returning home, Shaikh ʿAbd al-Karīm would

---

[1] Shaikh Muḥammad al-Muḥammad al-Kasnazān, *sermon*, 22 December 2005.

[2] Shaikh Muḥammad al-Muḥammad al-Kasnazān, *sermon*, 2 March 2013.

sometimes be asked about his apparent joy. He would say that he was happy because he had just given the pledge to someone.[3] This situation reminds us of a piece of advice that the Messenger (PBUH) gave to his spiritual caliph, Imām ʿAlī Ibn Abī Ṭālib, the day he sent him to conquer Khaybar, "If one person is guided through you, it would be better for you than getting red camels".[4]

After Shaikh Muḥammad al-Muḥammad assumed the Shaikhdom, the preaching of Ṭarīqa Kasnazāniyya expanded like never before. He intensified the various activities of calling people to Allah, including:

- Founding takyas
- Increasing the number of preaching caliphs, training them, and sending them to preach all over the world
- Continuously giving sermons
- Authoring and publishing books and encouraging caliphs to write about Ṭarīqa
- Facilitating the study of darbāsha karāmas by scientists

We have talked earlier about karāmas but we have discussed them in considerable detail in other books.[5] In this chapter, we will focus on the other four areas of preaching: founding takyas, developing caliphs and preachers, giving sermons, and authoring and publishing Sufi books and promoting Sufi culture.

11.1 Scaling Up the Building of Takyas

One example of the unprecedented spreading of Ṭarīqa Kasnazāniyya during Shaikh Muḥammad al-Muḥammad's Shaikhdom is that what began as 3 small takyas in Baghdad had grown to over 130 by the time he migrated from Baghdad at the end of 2000. This growth took place despite the severe constraints by the government and its security services to limit the spreading of Ṭarīqa, which included ordering the closure of the majority of takyas in Baghdad, as we will see in detail in

---

[3] Shaikh Muḥammad al-Muḥammad al-Kasnazān, *sermon*, 22 December 2005.

[4] Al-Bukhārī, *Al-Jāmiʿ al-ṣaḥīḥ*, II, no. 2846, p. 173. Arabs considered red camels as the most precious property that a person can have.

[5] Fatoohi, *Shaikh Muhammad al-Muhammad*, 91-130; Fatoohi, *Al-Taṣawwuf*, 55-90; Fatoohi, *The wonders of Ṭarīqa Kasnazāniyya*.

Chapter seventeen. Every day, the central takya in Baghdad was bursting with disciples and others taking the pledge. On Monday and Thursday nights, which were when major dhikrs would take place, the attendees at the takya would number in the hundreds.

On days of religious celebrations, the takya could not accommodate all of the disciples. On days of Eid, there would be a long queue of disciples, each waiting for half an hour or more before it was their turn to greet the Shaikh. In 1998, our Shaikh hosted the annual celebration of the Prophetic birth in his orchard in Dora, as the main takya could no longer accommodate the thousands of people who attended. He had intended for the orchard to host future celebrations of this noble anniversary, but restrictions imposed by the government meant that the next two had to be held in the central takya with relatively limited attendance.

Our Master visited many of the new takyas that were opened in Baghdad, where a celebration of the Messenger's (PBUH) birth would be hosted followed by the Kasnazānī dhikr to bless the new takya. He instructed and supervised the construction of the main takya in Basra, southern Iraq, which was completed in 1992. Hundreds of large and small takyas were built throughout Iraq. This led to numerous Arabs taking the Kasnazānī pledge and the fulfilment of Shaikh ʿAbd al-Qādir al-Kasnazān's revelation in 1912 when he looked at his swaddled newborn son, ʿAbd al-Karīm, "What Allah wills, what Allah wills. Allah (exalted and high is He) will guide many Arabs at the hands of the son of this man to the true path".

From time to time, our Shaikh would visit the main takyas in various cities and would be involved in supervising them because the main takya in each city is the preaching hub and means for the instructions of the Shaikh to be disseminated to secondary takyas, and consequently to all disciples, in that city. He stopped these visits after he migrated to Sulaymāniyya and then Amman after that, and also because of his health and the unstable political and security situation in Iraq.

After migrating to Sulaymāniyya, he lived in the area of Mamūstyān and started building a massive takya in Bākhī Bikhtiyārī to be the new central takya. He asked Shaikh Sāmān to be the engineer in charge but he also personally supervised the construction work. When his house in the takya was completed towards the end of 2002, he moved to live there.

Kasnazānī takyas also spread during the era of our Shaikh to different countries around the world. Takyas are places of Allah's dhikr and a place that the spirits of the Shaikhs and angels attend, so it is not surprising that building a takya is often accompanied by karāmas. We will recount here how the first dedicated takyas in India and Sudan were built and some amazing wonders that happened in the process.

In 1994, our Shaikh started regularly sending caliph Yūsuf Ḥusayn (may Allah have mercy on him) on long preaching visits in India. Over the next fifteen years or so, Ṭarīqa Kasnazāniyya developed a following mainly in Banglore, but in some other cities as well. About thirty small takyas were built. But the absence of a dedicated building as a takya restricted the spreading of Ṭarīqa. In 2011, our Shaikh launched a new preaching campaign in India, sending caliph ʿImād ʿAbd al-Ṣamad on regular visits. Before he first sent him out, he advised him as follows, "We have been wanting to establish a takya in Bangalore for about twenty years. Your goal is to preach and establish a takya". The first specialised takya was established in India, in the city of Bangalore, through an amazing karāma whose events began in June 2012. This is the story, as told by caliph ʿImād:

> Carrying out my Shaikh's order, during my preaching tours I searched for a suitable plot of land to establish a takya. Whenever I found a potential place, I would tell the honourable Shaikh about it, but he did not want any of these places because they were far from where caliphs and dervishes lived.
>
> I then had a dream where I saw the honourable Shaikh driving his old red Landcruiser and I was sitting beside him. He said to me, "My son, do you see that yellow-lighted lamp?" I said, "Yes". He said, "I want you to get land in this area". I said, "With the spiritual influence of the Shaikhs, I will do so". Then he said, "My land is there. There are documents that show that it is in my name. Try to find these documents". I promised him that I would, then we left the place with him driving the car. While we were going back, I saw a train pass near the place. Then I woke up. I began to ask if there was a railroad nearby whenever I was shown a plot of land.
>
> A while later, I had a second dream. The honourable Shaikh was sitting in a car and I was standing next to it. He asked me from the car window, "My son, have you found the place?" I told him that I was still searching, then I woke up. When I told the honourable Shaikh about the two dreams, he commented, "Allah willing, the Shaikhs will give you what you have

seen".

About a week later, I was in Shadab Nagar in the centre of Bangalore, close to where all the caliphs lived, when a Muslim real estate agent came to me with documents for a plot of land that was on sale in Saraipalya. I told him that it was very small, as I needed a tract of land that had an area of no less than one thousand metres squared because it would be a takya. He had other small portions of land neighbouring that land, so I told him that I needed between eighteen to twenty of those small adjoining plots. The agent said that they would be costly. At the time, I didn't have any money, but I put my trust in Allah.

I asked him what his name was and he said, "Muḥammad Irshād". When I heard his name, I felt a fluttering in my chest. I saw in the name the first sign from my Master that this was the land for the takya. His first name, "Muḥammad", was the honourable Shaikh's name, and his last name, "Irshād" (preaching), was what the takya would do. Caliphs Zakariyyā Ibrāhīm Shaikh, Fayrūz Khān 'Azīz, and Ja'far Muḥammad Ḥanīf, who live in Bangalore, witnessed this and the wonders that followed.

It was afternoon when we went to inspect the land. An indescribable feeling came over me. It was as if I had entered Paradise because we had passed by a railway. Then I saw the streetlight that I saw in my dream. I told my companions that this was the yellow-lighted lamp, and I told them about the two dreams. I told them that the two signs in the dream that we saw on the land and the fact that the agent's name was Muḥammad Irshād constituted a definitive indication that this was indeed the takya's land.

The area had a Hindu majority. There were two or three Muslim households and they had a small mosque made of mud. After we performed Wird al-'Aṣr, I told the caliphs that we would stay until darkness fell so that they could see the yellow light with their own eyes. The area was filled with mosquitoes, so my companions tried to dissuade me from staying, but I insisted on waiting for darkness to descend.

After we performed the sunset prayer, we kept waiting for streetlights to light up so that we could check the colour of that streetlamp. About half an hour passed and the streetlights were still off. I asked Fayrūz and Ja'far to ask the owner of a small shop under the streetlamp why the streetlights did not light up and what colour that streetlamp was. He told them that the power was out until nine o'clock and that the colour of the light was white. When they told me what he said, I swore that it was yellow. They were taken aback by my insistence, as the shopkeeper must know better the colour of the streetlight that lit his shop every night!

I asked my companions to stay there until power was restored so that we could determine the light's colour. We were there at the mercy of the mosquitoes for another hour and a half. A while after we performed the night prayer and its dhikr, the power came. Zakariyyā noted that the light was white. I swore a second time that it was yellow. He started to laugh hysterically when he saw the resoluteness of my belief despite it being contradicted by what the shopkeeper had said and what the eye saw. While Zakariyyā was laughing, he was soon baffled when the white light began to turn yellow. It became apparent that the bulb was a halogen bulb. I asked the caliphs to go back to the shopkeeper and ask him why he had said that the light was white. The man came out of his shop to look at the light. When he saw that it was yellow, he also seemed astonished. He said that he would swear that the light was white and that he was absolutely sure of this since he had owned this shop for many years.

Another wondrous thing in what happened, which was the secret behind the honourable Shaikh in the dream mentioning that the colour of that streetlight was yellow, was that all the other streetlights were white; this was the only streetlamp that was yellow! The caliphs wept because of the karāma they had seen. I restated what I said earlier, that this land definitely belonged to Ṭarīqa. We started the process of purchasing the land.

Two days later, Muḥammad Irshād came to me with a man he introduced as a mediator between us and the landowners. I asked him what his name was, and he said Aḥmad Irshād! The signs kept coming. After we paid the down payment, we went to an office where we met a person named ʿAbbās, who represented the landowners. When I greeted ʿAbbās, he began kissing my hands and feet and delighted me by surprising me with the fact that, for more than fifteen years, his late mother had been a disciple of the honourable Shaikh ʿAbd al-Karīm al-Kasnazān. She had taken the pledge at the hand of ʿAbd al-Razzāq Sharīf, a caliph of the honourable Shaikh ʿAbd al-Karīm. Expressing his desire to serve Ṭarīqa, ʿAbbās said that he would try to secure a reduction of the land's square foot price.

He took us to meet a Muslim individual who was the senior person responsible for a large amount of land, including the one that we wanted to buy. This man said that he also wished to serve the takya project since it belonged to the honourable Shaikh ʿAbd al-Qādir al-Gaylānī's Ṭarīqa. He offered to bear the cost of the takya's opening ceremony. I thanked him and asked him what his name was. He stunned me by replying that his name was "Irshād".

When I informed the honourable Shaikh that the name of the first individual was Muḥammad Irshād, the second, Aḥmad Irshād, and the third, Irshād, he commented, "Your Shaikh is the Quṭb al-Irshād,[6] Allah be praised,

---

[6] The term "Quṭb", which literally means "pole", is a high Sufi spiritual rank. The title

and Ṭarīqa is a Ṭarīqa of irshād (preaching). This takya is for you, Allah willing, by the spiritual influence of our Master al-Gaylānī, may Allah sanctify his secret, and by the spiritual influence of Shāh al-Kasnazān, may Allah sanctify his secret".

Indeed, we purchased the land and built a takya on it, just as the honourable Shaikh said and as the chain of astounding karāmas indicated.[7]

Construction of the takya began and was completed in 2013. Development work continued in the following years until the takya became one of the most beautiful takyas and mosques in the city.

Shaikh Muḥammad al-Muḥammad also introduced Ṭarīqa Kasnazāniyya to Sudan, where there are now many takyas and numerous seekers. After the Iraqi reciter of the Qur'an Hajj 'Alā' al-Dīn al-Qaysī (may Allah have mercy on him) returned from an official trip to Sudan in 1994, he informed our Shaikh that he had given the Ṭarīqa's pledge to Professor Ḥasan Aḥmad Ḥāmid, one of the most prominent scholars there. The latter had recently seen Shaikh 'Abd al-Qādir al-Gaylānī in a vision instructing him to spread Ṭarīqa Qādiriyya in Sudan. This vision came true when he took the pledge of Ṭarīqa Kasnazāniyya.[8] Our Shaikh sent caliph Ṭāhā 'Ubayd al-Ṭā'ī to Sudan and told him that he would find that the Shaikhs had paved the way for him to preach.

Accompanied by two other caliphs, Ṭāhā arrived in Khartoum on Tuesday 11 January 1994. They headed straight for Professor Ḥāmid's house. They told him about what our Shaikh had entrusted them with and gave him a letter from our Shaikh to be delivered to Sudan's president, Omar al-Bashir, asking for permission to build a Kasnazānī takya in Sudan. The letter was meant to introduce Ṭarīqa to the president and to prevent any misunderstanding about what Ṭarīqa wanted in establishing itself in Sudan, especially since the Ṭarīqa's Shaikhs were from another country.

The unexpected visit stunned Professor Ḥāmid. That morning,

"Quṭb al-Irshād" means "pole of preaching".

[7] Fatoohi, *The wonders of Ṭarīqa Kasnazāniyya*, 79-83.

[8] For more details, see Fatoohi, *Shaikh Muhammad al-Muhammad*, 46-48; Fatoohi, *Al-Taṣawwuf*, 50-51.

before the three dervishes arrived, his sister-in-law, who was living with his family, had told him that she had had a dream that night. She saw that a messenger had left Baghdad three days earlier and was headed towards him. Professor Ḥāmid sent for his sister-in-law and told her that her dream had come true. The messenger she had seen in her dream was the caliph who was sent by Shaikh Muḥammad al-Muḥammad al-Kasnazān. He noted, though, that the messenger had arrived on the same day he left Baghdad, not three days after, as she had seen in the dream. The caliph interjected here, giving another detail about his trip that confirmed the vision's accuracy. He left Baghdad for Amman on Sunday 30 October, but he had to stay in Amman for two days, waiting for the only weekly flight from Amman to Khartoum on Tuesday. Indeed, his trip took three days, not one day as Professor Ḥāmid thought!

The next morning, Professor Ḥāmid took the three dervishes on a tour of the al-Ṣāfiya neighbourhood where he lived, searching for a building that could be rented as a place for a takya. They would then send our Shaikh's letter to the president to obtain the state's approval. After several hours during which they visited many places, they did not find a suitable building. When they returned to the house at around three in the afternoon for lunch, Ṭāhā remembered a dream he had seen the night before about the takya's location. He saw a big mosque wherein there was a tall minaret. Next to it, there were simple, old, terraced houses. On the other side of the street, there was a yard in front of the mosque the size of a football pitch. In the middle of it, there was a very large house, so it was isolated from any other structure. In that house, there was one very tall tree that had many branches. When the caliph recounted his dream, Professor Ḥāmid was surprised, and said, "It seems like you know the area better than me!" He went on to say that the big house belonged to someone called Muḥammad al-Ṭayyib, and that the mosque was well known, named "Ummat al-Ijāba". They were located in Shambāt al-Ḥilla, which was about a kilometre away from al-Ṣāfiya.

On their way to visit the site, Professor Ḥāmid explained that al-Ṭayyib had registered a mosque with the office of religious endowment that he wanted to build on that large expanse of land. However, he built a big house that was about a thousand square metres that no one lived in. It was used from time to time as a retreat to memorize the Qur'an. The tree was a doum palm that had grown over the years where water that students used for ablution ran. Another distinguishing feature of the tree was that it was the only one in the area, as the small houses in that residential neighbourhood had no gardens. After arriving at the house, they all noted the dream's accurate description of it. Professor Ḥāmid agreed that it would make for a suitable takya. They met al-Ṭayyib who agreed to rent out the house as a takya. This was how the first Kasnazānī takya in Sudan was established. Our Shaikh appointed Professor Ḥāmid, who became a member of the Islamic jurisprudence council in Sudan, as his deputy in the country. Many takyas were later opened in various cities in Sudan.

The karāmas of building the takyas in Bangalore and Khartoum belong to that intricately detailed type of karāma that includes various people, places, and times. These demonstrate the tremendous divine force that is behind every muʿjiza and karāma.

11.2 Developing Caliphs and Sending Them to Preach

In Ṭarīqa Kasnazāniyya, every dervish must preach because calling people to Allah has always been one of the most important duties of Muslims since the time of our Master Muḥammad (PBUH). This is an even greater duty for caliphs, i.e. dervishes who have been given formal permission to preach. In addition to their responsibility to invite people to Ṭarīqa, caliphs are authorised to give the pledge of Ṭarīqa Kasnazāniyya on behalf of the Shaikh. Our Shaikh's focus on preaching made him greatly increase the number of caliphs. He began to give formal permission to preach to all who could call people to Allah and had the desire to do so. He would reiterate that the best caliphs and dervishes are those that preach the most.

He organised intensive educational courses for some active caliphs to raise their level of knowledge of Ṭarīqa and Sharia so that they could preach to people in the best way possible. Obviously, a preacher who speaks about Islam and Ṭarīqa with knowledge and expertise can answer people's questions and respond to ill-informed claims and arguments. Kasnazānī dervishes, in general, became more knowledgeable and developed a greater understanding of Sufism. Islamic scholars lectured in these courses and the participants received official certifications. The study covered several subjects, such as Sharia, Sufism, creed, and jurisprudence. The first course was held in 1994, at the Institute of Imāms and Preachers in Baghdad, the second in the summer of 1996, at the central takya in Baghdad, and the third in 2005, at the central takya, which was now in Sulaymāniyya.

The Shaikh was keen that every caliph and dervish be a true representative of Ṭarīqa. He would always mention the importance of following the example of the Prophet (PBUH), "There has certainly been for you in the Messenger of Allah an excellent example for anyone whose hope is in Allah and the Last Day and [who] remembers Allah often" (al-Āḥzāb 33:21), who had the highest moral character, "Indeed, you are of a great moral character" (al-Qalam 68:4). Dervishes should be examples for people to follow:

> We, Kasnazānī dervishes, must be the cleanest of people in society, so that they may follow our example, so that they may follow the simplest Kasnazānī dervish.[9]

Our Shaikh would continuously advise disciples and caliphs, and he would also intervene to solve problems that arose among them and advise those who have erred. He would try to mend relations between dervishes when there was a disagreement or conflict. He wanted them to be brothers who were affectionate to each other for Allah's sake, who were prepared to move past the mistakes they made with one another. In his preaching assembly, he would reiterate that were it not for envy, aversion, and other ill feelings between caliphs, "Ṭarīqa would span from east to west". He often reminded disciples of the Prophetic ḥadīth, "Believers are like a building whose parts support one another".[10] The Prophet (PBUH) laced his noble fingers together to demonstrate closeness and support when he said this. Our Shaikh would also mention this ḥadīth, "In their mutual love, compassion, and sympathy, the believers are like a body. When a part of it suffers, the whole body responds to it with wakefulness and fever".[11]

---

[9] Shaikh Muḥammad al-Muḥammad al-Kasnazān, *sermon*, 22 January 2010.

[10] Al-Bukhārī, *Al-Jāmiʿ al-ṣaḥīḥ*, I, no. 471, p. 171.

[11] Muslim, *Ṣaḥīḥ*, IV, no. 2586, p. 1999-2000.

Our Master was a teacher with a big heart that tolerated anyone who erred, confessed their mistake, and rectified their behaviour. At the same time, he was firm with anyone who insisted on distorting the image of Ṭarīqa with damaging words or actions. Individuals were dismissed from Ṭarīqa because they became a source of harm for it and for people in general.

He sent caliphs to preach and give people the Ṭarīqa's pledge in Islamic and non-Islamic countries—from the largest, most modern, and wealthiest cities of the developed world to the smallest, oldest, and poorest villages in the third world. He sent preachers to India, Malaysia, Sudan, Kenya, Benin, Togo, Comoro Islands, Britain, Germany, the former Soviet Union, the United States of America, and other countries. He also permitted giving the pledge over the phone and the internet to those who could not find a caliph near their place of residence or for whom travelling for that purpose was difficult.

Reflecting the fact that Allah made religion for women as much as for men, and recognising their significant role in developing individuals and society as a whole, the Shaikh increased the number of female caliphs as well. A large number of female preachers in Ṭarīqa now teach women about Islam and its spiritual side. These relevant words are from one of our Shaikh's sermons:

> O Kasnazānī dervishes! Convey your message to everyone, to every individual in society, men and women, young and old. Convey the Muḥammadan message because Ṭarīqa belongs to everyone. Ṭarīqa enjoins good and forbids evil.[12]

11.3 Delivering Sermons

From his ascension to the Shaikhdom, and in keeping with the conduct of the Shaikhs of Ṭarīqa before him, our Shaikh was always keen to speak to disciples about religious affairs and remind them of their obligations to Allah, their families, and society. Before his health forced him to attend circles of dhikr less frequently, he would lead Wird al-ʿAṣr every day, missing it only when preoccupied with other Ṭarīqa affairs.

He would also always attend the dhikr circles held on Monday and

[12] Shaikh Muḥammad al-Muḥammad al-Kasnazān, *sermon*, 22 January 2010.

Thursday nights, in addition to the celebrations of Eid and other religious occasions. When leading Wird al-ʿAṣr, he would sometimes deliver a sermon before or after the dhikr. As for Monday and Thursday nights, he usually gave a sermon after the dhikr ended and before the singing of odes of praise began. After moving from Sulaymāniyya to Amman, due to the nature of the building of the takya and his health, he no longer attended dhikr circles and assemblies of odes. He only attended the latter when they were hosted in his assembly. He did not stop preaching and delivering sermons to dervishes and others who visit his private assembly to his last days.

He was in a constant state of preaching, whether his assembly was attended by disciples who came to visit him and listen to his words that reminded them of Allah and His Messenger (PBUH) or people who came for any particular reason; whether the attendees were in the hundreds, a few, or even one individual. On many occasions, I found myself alone in his assembly yet he spoke to me exactly as he would preach to a group of visitors of any size. The journey to Allah, religious issues, and the state of Muslims were always topics for sermons, conversations, and dialogues, even in his private assembly. They were closest to his heart. For example, when he went to Moorfield Hospital in London on 11 May 2000 for a procedure on his eyes, Shaikh Nahro, Hajj Laṭīf, who was the Shaikh's personal assistant, and I accompanied him. When he was sitting on the bed waiting to be taken to the operating theatre, he did not talk about the surgery or anything related to it, nor did he show any signs of anxiety, as an average person would. Instead, he spoke to us about various topics, including pious restraint (waraʿ) in Sufism; the need for the Sufi seeker to not take the concessions of Sharia, but rather, to demand the greatest degree of commitment from himself; the need to avoid backbiting; being vigilant in observing the heart's thoughts and repelling bad whispers; the immortality of the spirit in Ṭarīqa; and the types of dhikr drums and using them along with tambourines in performing dhikr.

This was also the case when he was in The Johns Hopkins Hospital in Baltimore, Maryland, USA, for a kidney transplant. During his stay in the hospital, he would always preach to medical staff. Such instances illustrate his unique disposition and the dedication of his entire life to preaching and serving Islam, Muslims, and people in general.

The Shaikh's preaching, just like the rest of his affairs, was directed by the Shaikhs. One day in 1981, our Shaikh left his home in the Baghdad takya and headed towards the takya's mosque, accompanied by Shaikh Sāmān, the engineer in charge of building the takya. While they were crossing the takya's courtyard leading to the mosque, Sāmān asked him to give a sermon to dervishes urging them to work, noting that some had not been helping enough with the building work. Our Shaikh smiled and replied that the matter was not in his hands; when the Shaikhs wanted him to speak, he spoke with ease and fluency, but when they did not want him to speak, he was unable to speak. This reminds us of Shaikh ʿAbd al-Qādir al-Gaylānī's words that explain the difference between the speech of a self-appointed preacher and of one who is an instrument in Allah's hand, having drawn him near and made him well acquainted with Him:

> The Prophet (Allah's prayer and peace be on him) said, "When someone comes to know Allah, his tongue becomes exhausted",[13] meaning that he becomes mute. The tongue of His lower self, passion, natural inclination, habit, telling of lies, slander, and falsehood will become dumb, whereas the tongue of his inward will speak, and the tongue of his heart, innermost being, essences, truthfulness, and purity will speak. The tongue of his falsehood will become dumb, but the tongue of his truth will speak. The tongue of his talking about things that are of no concern to him will become incapable of speech, whereas the tongue of his heart will speak about things that concern him. The tongue of his quest for his lower self will become dumb, whereas the tongue of his quest for the True One will speak. In the early stage of acquiring knowingness, speech will stop and the person's whole existence will melt away. He will become extinct to himself and everyone else. Then, if the True One (mighty and glorified is He) wills, He will resurrect him. If He wants him to speak, He will create for him a tongue with which He enables him to speak. He will cause him to speak what He wants of words of wisdom and secrets. His speech will be a remedy within a remedy, a light within a light, a truth within a truth, a rightness within a rightness, and a purity within a purity, for he will speak only at the command of Allah (mighty and glorified is He) using his heart. If he speaks without being commanded to do so, he will perish. He will not speak unless he is given a command, or as a result of an irresistible thing that overcomes

---

[13] Al-Rāzī, *Al-Tafsīr al-kabīr*, 15, p. 113.

him.[14]

Most of our Shaikh's sermons were in Arabic because the majority of attendees were usually Arabs. Sometimes, he would deliver sermons in Kurdish when most attendees were Kurds. When he preached to those who did not speak Arabic or Kurdish, such as English speakers, a disciple would translate. He used simple language that made his profound words easy to understand by even the simplest of people. Hence, he often spoke in the vernacular, using Standard Arabic only when necessary.

There is a striking resemblance between our Shaikh's words and the sermons of al-Ghawth al-Āʿẓam, Shaikh ʿAbd al-Qādir al-Gaylānī, who delivered them in his school in Baghdad. The words of a Muḥammadan inheritor not only address the intellect but also touch the inner depths of the heart. The words of a Shaikh well acquainted with Allah stem from a heart brimming with divine love, hence they contain light and spiritual energy. They penetrate the barriers of the seeker's self and the obstacles of his worldly interests to impact his heart.

The Shaikhs of Ṭarīqa do not use sermonising as a means to flaunt their religious or spiritual knowledge because their speech is directed by Allah and is in His cause. They focus their words on what increases the seeker's determination to worship Allah and obey Him. Our Shaikh limited his preaching to particular topics that reminded seekers of the requisites of travelling on the path to Allah, citing noble verses; honourable ḥadīths; the Messenger's (PBUH) deeds, states, and manners; and the conduct, words, and karāmas of Ṭarīqa's Shaikhs. When he cited Allah's words or the Prophet's ḥadīths, the listener would find a special delight in them and an effect on the heart every time they were mentioned, which was not lessened by them being repeated. This was something that anyone who listened to his words experienced directly. Shaikh Muḥammad al-Muḥammad said:

> We always reiterate verses, ḥadīths, and sayings of the Shaikhs, "So remind, if the reminder should benefit" (al-Aʿlā 87:9). This is so that you may benefit, O seeker! So that you may reflect once again on the Shaikh's sayings, the sayings of the Shaikhs, because the words of the Shaikh and the

---

[14] Al-Gaylānī, *Purification of the Mind*, 184-185.

Shaikhs are consistent with the Sunna and the Book.[15]

Our Shaikh said the following in regard to what he focused on in his exhortation:

> Some say, "the Shaikh repeats himself". Of course, I repeat words to the disciple, so that I may teach him and help him understand. I tell him the same thing every time, I even repeat it a thousand times. If you do not follow what I say, what am I to do? Of course, the Shaikh repeats himself because he speaks from what he has. He is like a shopkeeper who sells what he has in his shop, nothing else! My shop sells worship, my shop sells good conduct, my shop sells my dhikrs and my wirds. I speak about my dhikrs and my wirds. I speak about my Ṭarīqa. I speak about my conduct. I talk about what I have, about what I can talk about. I don't have anything else. These are my goods.[16]

These words speak of the Shaikh's utmost humility and show that the only objective of his sermons was to educate the seeker spiritually.

There are many videos and audio recordings of his sermons on the internet.

11.4 Authoring and Publishing

Shaikh Muḥammad al-Muḥammad published four books in Arabic, including a unique Sufi encyclopaedia. They educate the reader about the fundamentals of the Sufi way in general and Ṭarīqa Kasnazāniyya in particular. They teach the seeker about the requisites of Ṭarīqa, namely, refined manners, conduct, and various forms of worship. Some of these books have been translated into other languages. These publications are all available for free download on the internet.

The following is a summary of the Shaikh's published books in order of their date of publication:

1) **Title:** *Al-Anwār al-Raḥmāniyya fīl-Ṭarīqa al-ʿAliyya al-Qādiriyya al-Kasnazāniyya* (Lights of the Merciful One in Ṭarīqa ʿAliyya Qādiriyya Kasnazāniyya).

Place and Date of Publication: This book was first published in Baghdad in 1988. It was published again in Cairo in 1990 by Madbouly Bookshop.

---

15 Shaikh Muḥammad al-Muḥammad al-Kasnazān, *sermon*, 11 January 2014.

16 Shaikh Muḥammad al-Muḥammad al-Kasnazān, *sermon*, 18 September 2013.

Summary: The Shaikh made his first book a detailed introduction to the historical and creedal fundamentals of Sufism and the seeker's code of conduct on the Sufi path. In addition to noble Qur'anic verses, the Messenger's (PBUH) ḥadīths, and the author's views, the book cites the views of a large number of Sufi Shaikhs and scholars to illustrate that Ṭarīqa is not only an indivisible part of Islam but it is also its spirit, and to emphasize that practising it is at the core of Islam. The book presents much information about Ṭarīqa Kasnazāniyya, including its Shaikhs, dhikrs, and devotional practices.

Contents: The book contains an introduction to Sufism and what it means to be a Sufi. It presents the various stations, states, and practices of Sufism, including repentance, companionship, love, spiritual bonding, listening to devotional odes, dhikr, internal strife, silence, vigil, isolation, seclusion, inner thoughts, fear, hope, truthfulness, sincerity, patience, satisfaction, gratitude, asceticism, pious restraint, and reliance.

The book also covers the proper etiquettes of disciples in the Shaikh's assembly, in the takya, and with their fellow dervishes, as well as when eating, sleeping, dressing, sitting with others, travelling, and visiting their Shaikh. It also addresses important Sharia issues, such as purity, ablution, and prayer.

The book explains the karāmas of walīs and how they are a continuation of the miracles of the Prophet Muḥammad (PBUH). It discusses Sufi practices that are often objected to by those who are ignorant of their reality and origins in Sharia, such as asking for the intercession of walīs, asking for spiritual support, and kissing the hands of righteous people and paying homage to them. Additionally, the book touches on some of the fundamental mistakes that some people who practise Sufism make, such as following a deceased Shaikh instead of a living one or taking more than one Shaikh. It looks at the lives of the Shaikhs of Ṭarīqa Kasnazāniyya and provides a commentary on its dhikrs, method of giving the pledge, seclusion, and spiritual exercises.

2) **Title**: *Jilā' al-khāṭir min kalām al-Shaikh 'Abd al-Qādir* (Purification of the Mind: From Shaikh 'Abd al-Qādir's Words).

Place and Date of Publication: Baghdad, 1989.

Summary: This is a manuscript containing forty-five sermons that Shaikh 'Abd al-Qādir delivered at his school in Baghdad. Our Shaikh edited the manuscript using three different copies of it from the Qādiriyya Shrine Library, the Iraqi Museum Library, and the al-Awqāf Library in Baghdad. This was the first time this manuscript had been edited and published.

He did not publish the forty-five sermons as separate chapters in the book, as they occur in the manuscript and as is the tradition of editing manuscripts, including those of Shaikh ʿAbd al-Qādir's sermons. He employed a creative technique to help the general reader and the practising Sufi to benefit more from the words of al-Ghawth al-Āʿẓam. He divided the contents of the sermons into forty chapters, each covering a particular Sufi subject, such as patience, forgiveness, and extinction. The compiled passages from the different sermons on each subject were put in their respective chapters. This thematic organization makes it easier for the reader to study Shaikh ʿAbd al-Qādir's sayings about each of these important themes.

Contents: Our Master prefaced the book with an introduction to the exceptionally devout life of Shaikh ʿAbd al-Qādir. The chapters of the book are as follows: good behaviour in the company of Shaikhs, repentance, the mediator, love, trust, renunciation, fear, patience, sincerity, truthfulness, sorrow, satisfaction, piety, striving against the lower self, the blessings of remembrance [of Allah], the works of the heart, the knowledge of walīs, putting knowledge into practice, spending on the poor, seclusion, solitude, the definition of the Sufi, extinction, pardoning, the light of the believer, denouncing this world, the fruit of knowledge, denouncing hypocrisy, the benefits of the month of Ramadan, the benefit of mercy, the prohibition of injustice, neglecting what is of no concern, humility, denouncing dissimulation, envy, the curtailment of hopes, death, thinking well of others, having a sense of shame, and enduring affliction.

3) **Title:** *Al-Ṭarīqa al-ʿAliyya al-Qādiriyya al-Kasnazāniyya* (Ṭarīqa ʿAliyya Qādiriyya Kasnazāniyya).

Place and Date of Publication: Baghdad, 1998.

Summary: There are common themes between this book and *al-Anwār al-Raḥmāniyya*, but this book addresses them differently, expands on their coverage, and covers many new topics. It does not replace al-Anwār al-Raḥmāniyya but completes it. It clarifies issues that cause controversy and disagreement between scholars. The book is primarily based on Qur'anic verses, Prophetic ḥadīths, and the perspectives and sayings of Shaikhs and scholars.

Contents: Like *al-Anwār al-Raḥmāniyya*, this book also discusses the stations of Ṭarīqa: repentance, reliance, fear, hope, truthfulness, sincerity, patience, pious restraint, asceticism, satisfaction, and gratitude. It covers the history of the Shaikhs, dhikrs, and etiquettes of Ṭarīqa Kasnazāniyya. It discusses in detail the greatness of the Messenger (PBUH) and the noble Qur'an, the unique status of the Prophetic household, and the symbol that Imām Ḥusayn embodies. The book also discusses the status of Imām 'Alī as the bearer of Ṭarīqa's knowledge after the Messenger (PBUH). It looks into the meaning of the Shaikh being a Muḥammadan inheritor. It discusses the subject of karāmas, including the proof of their validity in the Qur'an and Sunna, as well as the karāmas of the household of the Prophet (PBUH), the Companions, and the Kasnazānī Shaikhs.

The book devotes an entire chapter to the subject of intercession and seeking a means to draw near to Allah, due to its significance and because it is the biggest objection some people raise against Sufism. Citing the noble Qur'an and the honourable Prophetic Sunna, the book demonstrates the validity of seeking Allah's help through the Prophet (PBUH) and the people of his household, visiting the shrines of walīs, and seeking blessings through relics of the Messenger (PBUH) and righteous people. The book also touches on the permissibility of listening to devotional odes.

4) **Title:** *Mawsū'at al-Kasnazān fīmā aṣṭalaḥa 'alayhi ahlu al-taṣṣawuf wal-'irfān* (Al-Kasnazān Encyclopaedia of Terms Coined by the People of Sufism and Gnosticism).

Place and Date of Publication: Damascus, 2005, Dār al-Maḥabba.

Summary: This twenty-four-volume encyclopaedia is the first of its kind. There are numerous encyclopaedias on various subjects, but this work is the only encyclopaedia specialising in Sufism. In preparing it, Shaikh Muḥammad al-Muḥammad consulted hundreds of sources, including 150 manuscripts that had not been edited before, such as *Jawāhir al-asrār wa-laṭā'if al-anwār* by Shaikh 'Īsā, son of Shaikh 'Abd al-Qādir al-Gaylānī, and *Marātib al-qurra fī 'uyūn al-qudra* by Shaikh Ibn 'Arabī.

The massive task of compiling an encyclopaedia of such breadth requires a team of experts in various sub-sciences. Our Shaikh conducted this enormous research project and compiled this monumental encyclopaedia with the help of a handful of dervishes who assisted him in finding manuscripts and printed sources that he would look over and select material from for the encyclopaedia. They would also make photocopies of sources he wanted and would sometimes look through sources for whatever he asked them to search for.

Working on this monumental project took more than a quarter of a century. In the beginning, our Shaikh did not declare that the goal was to produce an encyclopaedia of Sufism. He would speak about collecting the opinions of Shaikhs on various Sufi terms, but later, he began referring to the idea of compiling an encyclopaedia.

In its preface, the author mentions the objectives behind developing this quantitatively and qualitatively enormous work:

- Shedding light on the history of Sufism since its inception to the present era, especially in a time when the world is spiritually famished
- Filling the need in the Islamic literature for this kind of lexical Sufi work, in a time when encyclopaedias and dictionaries for various other religious sciences abound
- Shedding light on the origins, principles, phases, and criteria of Sufi terminology within a modern framework of lexical mapping
- Uncovering meanings of sciences, primary sources, and doctrinal foundations of Sufis; also, unveiling Sufis' spiritual stations, ranks, states, inner experiences, and stations of nearness to Allah Almighty that they have been granted
- Revealing the interdependence between the past and the present of Sufi terms and their shared objectives, despite the multiplicity and diversity of their Ṭarīqas
- Making Sufi terminology easier to understand
- Providing a comprehensive Sufi reference for researchers and students of this field

- Facilitating tracing the development of each term by listing the opinions about it in chronological order[17]

Contents: This encyclopaedia contains thousands of terms that Sufis have exclusively used in their books and sayings, in addition to general terms that they ascribed Sufi meanings to, such as Allah's beautiful names and the names of the Messenger (PBUH). It also includes common words, such as "house" and "tree", that Sufis have used as symbols and metaphors, giving them technical meanings. It mentions the various meanings of each term according to several Sufis.

For any given term, the encyclopaedia first introduces its linguistic meaning in the dictionary, followed by the places where it appears in the Qur'an, then its instances in the Sunna, if at all, before covering its meanings according to Sufi Shaikhs. One creative aspect of the encyclopaedia is that it organises the perspectives of Shaikhs in chronological order, making it easier to track the development of each term and its transformation over time. For further benefit, the encyclopaedia refers to the opinions of some researchers that have reported the views of Sufi Shaikhs and have commented on them. It also mentions the meaning of any given term according to Ṭarīqa Kasnazāniyya Shaikhs.

The first term in the encyclopaedia is the letter "ʾalif" and the last is "the Grand Days". The number of terms and words exceeds ten thousand. The terms fill twenty-two volumes, and the twenty-third volume is dedicated to biographies of influential Shaikhs, scholars, and researchers whose views are covered in the encyclopaedia. The twenty-fourth and final volume contains several indexes, including an index of terms and an index of words and the encyclopaedia sources.

Scholars and academics have praised the uniqueness, importance, and comprehensiveness of the encyclopaedia and have noted that it is a precious addition to Sufi literature in particular and Islamic literature in general.

Our Shaikh also compiled two books of supplications for the followers of Ṭarīqa Kasnazāniyya:

1) **Title:** *Al-Ṣalawāt al-Kasnazāniyya* (Kasnazānī Prayers (on the Prophet (PBUH))).

---

[17]Al-Kasnazān, *Mawsūʿat al-kasnazān*, I, pp. 12-13.

Place and Date of Publication: Baghdad, 1990.

Contents: This is a compilation of some of the most beautiful and powerful prayers upon the Prophet (PBUH). Prayers upon the Messenger (PBUH) have a special status in Ṭarīqa Kasnazāniyya, and Sufism in general, as we will see in detail in §12.3. Our Shaikh compiled and printed this book in the 1990s, but collecting prayers upon the Prophet (PBUH) was an ongoing project under his supervision. By the time of his passing, the compiled prayers would fill more than ten volumes when published.

2) **Title:** *Ḥizb al-Wāw* (Ḥizb of the Letter Wāw).

Place and Date of Publication: Amman, 2003.

Contents: This unique dhikr was spiritually communicated to our Shaikh in 2013. It consists of every Qur'anic verse that starts with the letter "wāw", listed in their order in the muṣḥaf. He said that this wird came about "by Allah's command to the honourable Messenger (PBUH), to the Shaikhs, and the Shaikhs communicated it to me".[18]

He used to oversee the production of Ṭarīqa's educational literature in the form of brochures and booklets, such as the booklets *The Concept of Ṭarīqa in Islamic Sharia* and *The Dhikrs of Ṭarīqa 'Aliyya Qādiriyya Kasnazāniyya*. At the time of his passing, he had several other books in preparation.

---

[18] Shaikh Muḥammad al-Muḥammad al-Kasnazān, *sermon*, 12 September 2013.

If you abandon dervishhood, if you abandon dhikr, if you abandon your wirds, the Shaikhs abandon you. Wirds and dhikrs are the disciples' shields. Our weapons, our tanks, our fighter jets, are Allah's dhikr (exalted and high is He). We die on Allah's dhikr. We live on Allah's dhikr. We die for the sake of Allah's dhikr (exalted and high is He). We live for the sake of Allah's dhikr (exalted and high is He). Our food, the soul's food, is Allah's dhikr (exalted and high is He). Do not forget your dhikrs and your wirds.

Shaikh Muḥammad al-Muḥammad al-Kasnazān
(*Sermon*, 7 January 2010)

12

Developing the Dhikrs of Ṭarīqa

Allah conferred on our Master many unveilings that made him change some of the dhikrs that he inherited from his Shaikhs and introduce new ones. These changes included the daily, perennial, and circle dhikrs. He also introduced temporary dhikrs. Allah also honoured our Shaikh with a great dhikr called "Ḥizb al-Wāw".

12.1 Perennial Dhikrs

In the era of Shaikh ʿAbd al-Karīm al-Kasnazān, there were nineteen perennial dhikrs, each of which was read 82,000 times, except "yā wadūd", which was read 65,000 times. Shaikh Muḥammad al-Muḥammad made two changes to these dhikrs. After coming out of his first seclusion, about six months after assuming the Shaikhdom, he made it so every one of the nineteen dhikrs is read 100,000 times. As already mentioned, in the terminology of Ṭarīqa Kasnazāniyya, this specific number is known as "khatma". It is derived from the Arabic root *kh-t-m*, which means "complete" or "conclude".

The second modification happened in the middle of 1996. He replaced the dhikr of "Allāhumma ṣallī ʿalā sayyidinā Muḥammadi wa-ʿalā ʾālihi wa-ṣaḥbihi wa-sallim taslīmā (O Allah! Send prayer on our Master and on his lineage and companions and salute him with a perfect salutation)" with another formula that the Shaikhs of Ṭarīqa conveyed to him, known as al-Ṣalāt al-Waṣfiyya, "Allāhumma ṣallī ʿalā sayyidinā Muḥammadi ʾl-waṣfi wal-waḥyi war-risālati wal-ḥikmati waʿalā ʾālihi wa-ṣaḥbihi wa-sallim taslīmā (O Allah! Send prayer on our Master whose quality, revelation, message, and wisdom are most praised (Muḥammad), and on his lineage and companions, and salute him with a perfect salutation)".

12.2 Daily Dhikrs

The Shaikh added new daily dhikrs and changed the numbers of some that he inherited. We will mention here some of these changes.

In the 1980s, our Master added the recitation of the Qur'anic chapter *al-Īkhlāṣ*, along with the *basmala*, two hundred times. Consisting of four verses, reciting this chapter with the *basmala* two hundred times a day reaps a reward equivalent to reading one thousand verses. This brings to mind this ḥadīth of the Messenger (PBUH), "Anyone who reads one thousand verses for Allah's sake, Allah writes his name alongside the prophets, the truthful, martyrs, and the righteous".[1]

In the early 1990s, our Shaikh introduced the recitation of the following dhikr three times after each of the five obligatory prayers, "Allahu ḥādirī (Allah is present with me), Allahu nāẓirī (Allah sees me), Allahu shāhidun ʿalay (Allah is a witness on me). Allahu maʿī (Allah is with me), Allahu muʿīnī (Allah is my helper), wa-huwa bi-kulli shayʾin muḥīṭ (and He encompasses everything)". This is a wird of Shaikh ʿAbd al-Qādir al-Gaylānī that he received from Shaikh Maʿrūf al-Karkhī. Our Master said that this dhikr embodies Iḥsān,[2] religion's third pillar, which is, in the words of the Prophet (PBUH), "To worship Allah as if you see Him; and if you cannot see Him, then verily He sees you".[3] One can only reach this level of awareness of Allah by way of divine unveilings that draw him closer to the spirit world while he is in this world.

In March 2016, the Shaikh added one recitation of the following dhikr after every prayer, "Astaghfiru Allah (I seek forgiveness from Allah), al-ladhī lā ilāha illā Huwa (whom there is no god besides), ar-Raḥmān ar-Raḥīm (the Gracious, the Merciful), al-Ḥayyu al-Qayyūm al-ladhī lā yamūt (the Ever-living, the Sustainer of Existence who never dies), wa-atūbu ʾilayhi (and I repent to Him). Rabbī ighfir lī (My Lord, forgive me!)".

He introduced three alterations to Wird al-ʿAṣr, which is performed an hour before the sunset prayer. This dhikr was a gift from Shaikh ʿAbd al-Qādir al-Gaylānī to the Shaikhs of Ṭarīqa Kasnazāniyya. It was

---

[1] Al-Bayhaqī, *Al-Sunan al-kubrā*, IX, no. 18575, p. 291.

[2] Shaikh Muḥammad al-Muḥammad al-Kasnazān, *sermon*, 22 January 2010; 4 August 2013.

[3] Al-Bukhārī, *Al-Jāmiʿ al-ṣaḥīḥ*, I, no. 50, p. 65.

communicated to Shaikh ʿAbd al-Qādir al-Kasnazān shortly before his passing, but he instructed that it should become part of the dhikrs of Ṭarīqa in the Masterdom of his successor, Shaikh Ḥusayn. Wird al-ʿAṣr was made up of nine dhikrs, each of which was read thirty-three times, and it did not change during the time of Shaikh ʿAbd al-Karīm. Sometime after assuming the Shaikhdom of Ṭarīqa, Shaikh Muḥammad al-Muḥammad increased it to fifty. In 2005 or 2006, he increased the number a second time to sixty-six. In early October 2010, he added "yā arḥama ar-Rāḥimīn (O Most Merciful of the merciful)" to the end of Wird al-ʿAṣr, which he described as a "supplication", distinguishing it from the nine dhikrs.

On the evening of Sunday 28 January 2018, after a celebration of the Prophet's (PBUH) birth, our Shaikh marked the return of Shaikh Nahro from the USA by leading a recitation of Wird al-ʿAṣr. Performing this dhikr at night is a rare occurrence, if not unprecedented. After the worshippers completed the final dhikr of "yā Raḥīm", he began the dhikr of "lā ilāha illā Allāh" one hundred times. He named this addition to Wird al-ʿAṣr the "Victory Dhikr". The supplication of "yā arḥama ar-rāḥimīn" may be read as many times as desired after "lā ilāha illā Allāh", should the seeker like to do so.

Like Shaikhs Ḥusayn and ʿAbd al-Karīm, Shaikh Muḥammad al-Muḥammad often led Wird al-ʿAṣr. Even when he was away from the takya—for example, in a car—he would perform Wird al-ʿAṣr alone.

12.3 Prayers upon the Prophet (PBUH)

One dhikr that our Shaikh introduced, in the 1980s, was a formula of reading prayers upon the Prophet (PBUH). In 2013, in Amman, he referred to this prayer in his following talk about reading prayers upon the Prophet (PBUH) in general:

> In ours, Ṭarīqa ʿAliyya Qādiriyya Kasnazāniyya, we have the greatest khatma, which is "lā ilāha illā Allah (there is no god save Allah) Muḥammadun rasūlu Allah (Muḥammad is the Messenger of Allah) ṣallā Allah taʿālā ʿalayhi wa-sallam (prayer and peace of Allah (high is He) be upon him)". Look at the greatness that Allah conferred on the honourable Messenger (PBUH). After the declaration of oneness comes honouring the Messenger (PBUH), reading prayers upon the honourable Messenger (PBUH). He has ordered us to do this, "Indeed, Allah and His angels read

prayers upon the Prophet. O you who have believed, read prayers upon him and send greetings of peace" (al-Āḥzāb 33:56). He has given us a gift. Reading prayers is a gift, reading prayers is mercy, reading prayers is a blessing, reading prayers is a treasure, reading prayers is earning sustenance, reading prayers is winning this life and the Day of Resurrection, reading prayers is Paradise, reading prayers is light, reading prayers draws one closer to Allah and to the honourable Messenger, "If he [My servant] comes one span nearer to Me, I go one cubit nearer to him. If he comes one cubit nearer to Me, I go a distance of two outstretched arms nearer to him".[4] When you read prayers upon the honourable Messenger (PBUH), you draw nearer to Allah. We have this khatma, the greatest khatma in Islamic Sufism, the greatest khatma in Islam, the greatest khatma in our Ṭarīqa. Whoever wants to test it out may try. This khatma is not found in other Ṭarīqas; you may search if you want to! I have perhaps thousands of Sufi books. No Shaikh has this khatma besides your Kasnazānī Shaikhs. This happened by an order. By Allah, by Allah, by Allah, the dhikr of "lā ilāha illā Allah Muḥammadun rasūlu Allah" came by an order. This order came to me when I was in Baghdad. This dhikr was conveyed to me by an order. Undoubtedly, all Sufi matters are from Allah (exalted and high is He) through the honourable Messenger and the Shaikhs.[5]

Our Shaikh included the recitation of this formula one hundred times in the daily dhikrs after the dawn and night prayers. In January 2006, he added the phrase "fī-kulli lamḥatin wa-nafas (with every look and breath), ʿadada mā wasiʿahu ʿilmu Allah (as many times as Allah's knowledge encompasses)" to this dhikr. The formula of the prayer thus became "lā ilāha illā Allah (There is no god save Allah) Muḥammadun rasūlu Allah (Muḥammad is the Messenger of Allah) ṣallā Allah taʿālā ʿalayhi wa-sallam (prayer and peace of Allah (high is He) be upon him), fī-kulli lamḥatin wa-nafas (with every look and breath), ʿadada mā wasiʿahu ʿilmu Allah (as many times as Allah's knowledge encompasses)".

---

[4] This is the full text of the Qudī ḥadīth that the Messenger (PBUH) conveyed from Allah, "I am just as My slave thinks I am, and I am with him if he remembers Me. If he remembers Me in himself, I too remember him in Myself; and if he remembers Me in a group of people, I remember him in a group that is better than them. If he comes one span nearer to Me, I go one cubit nearer to him. If he comes one cubit nearer to Me, I go a distance of two outstretched arms nearer to him. If he comes to Me walking, I go to him running" (ibid., III, no. 7129, p. 693).

[5] Shaikh Muḥammad al-Muḥammad al-Kasnazān, *sermon*, 12 September 2013.

One afternoon in July 1996, after coming out of his private room, he told dervishes that he had been honoured with a new formula of prayers upon the Messenger (PBUH) that had not been granted to anyone before, "Allāhumma ṣallī ʿalā sayyidinā Muḥammadi ʾl-waṣfi wal-waḥyi war-risālati wal-ḥikmati waʿalā ʾālihi wa-ṣaḥbihi wa-sallim taslīmā (O Allah! Send prayer on our Master whose quality, revelation, message, and wisdom are most praised (Muḥammad), and on his lineage and companions, and salute him with a perfect salutation)". At the time, he called al-Ṣalāt al-Waṣfiyya "the seal of all Kasnazānī prayers on the Prophet (PBUH)". He also described it as being "authored" by the Messenger (PBUH):

> This formula of prayers (on the Prophet) is not from me. Rather, it was communicated to me. Look at how blessed al-Ṣalāt al-Waṣfiyya is. It is from him, from the light, from the honourable Messenger (PBUH). In the past, we did not have this formula of prayers (on the Prophet (PBUH)). It is very blessed, as it is from him. It is he who has informed us of it. This is why we read it continuously. This formula of reading prayers (on the Prophet) did not exist in any book. It is from him, from the honourable Messenger. He communicated it, so we communicated it…how beautiful and how blessed it is! He himself granted this formula of reading prayers (on the Prophet), it was authored by him. How beautiful it is! Try as you may, your mind would never comprehend the blessing of al-Ṣalāt al-Waṣfiyya because it came about by his wish, by his order, and by the command of Allah (exalted and high is He).[6]

Our Shaikh added the recitation of al-Ṣalāt al-Waṣfiyya one hundred times to the daily dhikr after the night prayer. Al-Ṣalāt al-Waṣfiyya also replaced the following formula of reading prayers upon the Prophet (PBUH), which is read at least one thousand times every day at any time of the day, "Allāhumma ṣallī ʿalā sayyidinā Muḥammadi waʿalā ʾālihi wa-ṣaḥbihi wa-sallim taslīmā (O Allah! Send prayer on our Master Muḥammad and on his lineage and companions, and salute him with a perfect salutation)". It also took its place in the daily and perennial dhikrs.

As a result of the special spiritual power of al-Ṣalāt al-Waṣfiyya, Shaikh Muḥammad al-Muḥammad would sometimes instruct dervishes

[6] Shaikh Muḥammad al-Muḥammad al-Kasnazān, *sermon*, 1 May 2018.

who were facing various difficulties to perform a khatma of it. Before receiving al-Ṣalāt al-Waṣfiyya, our Shaikh would direct disciples in such circumstances to read the renowned formula of reading prayers upon the Messenger (PBUH) known as al-Ṣalāt al-Nāriyya (The Fiery Prayer):

> Allahumma ṣalli ṣalātan kāmila, wa-sallim salāman tāmman ʿalā sayyidina Muḥammad al-laththī tanḥallu bihi al-ʿuqad, wa-tanfariju bihi al-kurab, wa-tuqḍā bihi al-ḥawāʾij, wa-tunālu bihi al-raghāʾib, wa-ḥusnu al-khawātim, wa-yustasqā al-ghamāmu biwajhihi al-karīm, waʿalā ʾālihi wa-ṣaḥbihi, fī kulli lamḥatin wanafa, biʿadadi kulli maʿlumin laka (O Allah, read complete prayers and salute with a perfect salutation our Master Muḥammad, by whom all difficulties are solved, all calamities go away, all needs fulfilled, all cherished desires obtained, and good ends to life achieved; and rain-showering clouds are requested by means of his noble countenance; and on his family and companions in every moment and every breath, as many times as is in Your knowledge.[7]

Al-Ṣalāt al-Waṣfiyya replaced al-Ṣalāt al-Nāriyya.

Shaikh Muḥammad al-Muḥammad would frequently mention noble Ḥadīths about the merits of prayers upon the Messenger (PBUH), such as, "Whoever reads one prayer upon me, Allah reads prayer upon him ten times".[8] In regard to the greatness of prayers upon the Prophet (PBUH), he said, "No one knows the secrets of this prayer besides Allah, the Messenger (PBUH), and those firmly rooted in the knowledge of the spirit".

He confirmed that reading prayers upon the Prophet (PBUH) realises one's wishes and solves various problems. He would often advise dervishes who would consult him about difficulties and problems they had to read prayers upon the Messenger (PBUH) in abundance. He would also stress that any supplication must be preceded by, infused with, and ended with prayers so that it may be accepted. The supplication must be "wrapped" with reading prayers upon the Prophet (PBUH).[9] He used to speak often about the specialness of reading prayers upon the Prophet (PBUH), as in these words:

---

[7] Al-Nabhānī, *Daʿwat tashrīfāt*, 61; Al-Nazilī, *Khazīnat al-asrār*, 183.

[8] Muslim, *Ṣaḥīḥ*, I, no. 408, p. 306.

[9] Shaikh Muḥammad al-Muḥammad al-Kasnazān, *sermon*, 3 October 2013.

> Read much prayers upon the Messenger (PBUH) because these prayers will be a light for the seeker on the Day of Resurrection. This is an attribute of Allah (exalted and high is He). Allah (exalted and high is He) says to you—see how much Allah loves His servants as He gives you the best thing, the dearest thing for the seeker—He says, "Indeed, Allah and His angels read prayers upon the Prophet. O you who have believed, read prayers upon him and send greetings of peace". Prayers and peace be upon you, O Messenger of Allah! Read much prayers upon the Messenger (PBUH). With reading prayers upon the Messenger, you earn his love. The start of any supplication is reading prayers upon the Messenger. No request for any servant is answered unless he reads prayers on the Messenger at its beginning and its end. Between the two prayers, Allah willing, your request would be answered. Keep up your wirds, your practice of your Ṭarīqa, your dhikrs, in particular the prayers upon the Messenger.[10]

As we have mentioned, the Shaikh also compiled different formulas of reading prayers upon the Messenger of Allah (PBUH) in a book entitled *al-Ṣalawāt al-Kasnazāniyya* that was published in 1990. Collecting various such formulas remained an ongoing project of his until his passing.

The love of our Shaikh for the Messenger (PBUH) was unique. It showed in his words, face, movements, and actions. The signs of that infatuation would show on him whenever the name of our Master Muḥammad (PBUH) or any of his titles was mentioned. This love often materialised as tears and weeping. This was witnessed by anyone who attended our Shaikh's preaching sessions or saw him listen to odes of praise. Indeed, this endless love for the Prophet (PBUH) would show on him even when he (PBUH) was mentioned casually, at any time, and in any situation. I would like to mention one example from a private assembly of our Shaikh in Amman. His office manager, Muḥammad al-Kātib, was reading out the titles of manuscripts in a library catalogue so that the Shaikh could indicate those that he wanted photocopies of to read. Each time al-Kātib read out a manuscript title that contained the name or a title of the Prophet (PBUH), our Shaikh raised his right hand from where it was resting on the chair as a sign of greetings and respect, as if he were greeting someone present and visible.

Another example from personal experience comes from my last visit

[10] Shaikh Muḥammad al-Muḥammad al-Kasnazān, *sermon*, 28 September 2012.

to him at the end of October 2019, when he was in Virginia, USA. He liked to engage his table guests with various discussions. One night, we were having dinner when I mentioned the status of the person who sings odes of praise of the Prophet (PBUH) and the fact that our Shaikhs enjoyed listening to them. One of those present at the dinner was caliph Majīd Ḥamīd, the most senior singer of odes of praise in our Ṭarīqa. Our Master wanted to second what I had just said and started to commend the singers of odes of praise. He went on to say, "The person who praises the beloved…", but he broke down and could not continue his words. His body shook with the intensity of his weeping. When he calmed down, he tried to continue his words, but love overtook him again, stopping him for a second time, before he finally managed to finish his words. I never saw our Shaikh love anyone or anything more than the Prophet (PBUH). Indeed, I have not seen any lover love his beloved the way our Shaikh loved the beloved of Allah (PBUH). The title of this book is an expression of this fact.

Our Shaikh would often call the Prophet (PBUH) "the beloved". He would stress that love for the Messenger (PBUH) is the door to obtaining nearness to Allah:

> Everything that we have spoken about is linked to one thing, which is loving the beloved (PBUH), "The religion in the sight of Allah is Islam" (Āl ʿImrān 3:19). "Islam" means "Muhammad", "Muhammad" means the gifted mercy, "We have not sent you [O Muḥammad!] except as a mercy to the worlds" (al-Anbiyāʾ 21:107). For anyone who seeks mercy, it is Muhammad; for anyone who seeks religion, it is Muhammad; for anyone who seeks the hereafter, it is Muhammad; for anyone who seeks resurrection, it is Muhammad. He is the intercessor of the sinful, the master of messengers, the master of prophets and messengers, the master of walīs and prophets.
>
> Loving of the beloved is to love Allah (exalted and high is He): 'Say [O Muhammad!], "If you should love Allah, then follow me, and Allah will love you and forgive you your sins"' (Āl ʿImrān 3:31). You should understand that these matters are all linked to the love of the beloved. Without love for the beloved, your deeds would not succeed. You can make your action succeed by wrapping it with love for the beloved, with reading prayers upon the beloved (PBUH). Prayers upon the beloved wrap your worship, clean your worship, and refer it to Allah (exalted and high is He), "We have not sent you [O Muhammad!] except as a mercy to the worlds". With the gifted mercy of Islam, you wrap your worship. Reading prayers upon the beloved (PBUH) is

> a light that takes the human being to Allah (exalted and high is He). If the love of the Messenger is written on the board of the heart, everything you do, Allah willing, reaches Him. If there is no love of the beloved in your heart, there is no worship in it. Religious matters in Islam are linked to the belief in the beloved.[11]

Our Shaikh became wholly consumed by his love for the Prophet (PBUH). One indicator of this extinction of the self and the lofty spiritual status that it took him to is that the noble Prophet (PBUH) distinguished him with a special gift. He appended one of his glorious titles to our Shaikh's name to honour and single him out, changing his name from "Muḥammad" to "Muḥammad al-Muḥammad". Our Master announced this favour on 18 May 2016. "Muḥammad al-Muḥammad" expresses the Prophet's (PBUH) endorsement of our Shaikh, roughly meaning "Muḥammad who belongs to me" or "Muḥammad whom I have chosen for myself".

On 11 August 2017, following his daily routine, the Shaikh left his public assembly for his private room at around 1 a.m. to sleep until around 2:30 a.m., after which he would start his worship. When he woke up, he contacted his personal assistant, ʿĪsā al-Mazrūʿī, and asked him to come up. He asked who was in the takya, to which ʿĪsā said that there were some dervishes. The Shaikh then told him to convey a message to them. He had just been given the glad tidings that as soon as a person intends to read prayers upon the Messenger (PBUH) and prepares himself and his prayer beads for it, Allah Almighty forgives him his sins by the Messenger's (PBUH) blessings.

In my last visits to him in Amman in 2018-2019, I noticed that when dervishes would inform him about difficulties they were having, the Shaikh would now only prescribe dhikr of prayers upon the Prophet (PBUH). He would go on to talk about its blessings and you could see the joy on his face.

One example of daily behaviour that articulates the way he was consumed by love for the Prophet (PBUH) was demonstrated when he would leave his private room for his public assembly where he would meet dervishes and visitors. On his way to his chair, there was, on the wall, a very beautiful tapestry rug of the Green Dome and the Prophetic

---

[11] Shaikh Muḥammad al-Muḥammad al-Kasnazān, *sermon*, 27 February 2013.

Mosque. He would stand in humbleness in front of the rug and read al-Fātiḥa and prayers. This was the first thing he would do in his public assembly.

During his last months in Amman before his last visit to the USA, the Shaikh used to read this supplication, which is Kurdish poetry:

> Yā ṣāḥibay mādīnay munawwara,
> Bafarmū toy minī 'aowarā.

This may be translated as follows:

> O, the inhabitant of the Illuminated City,
> Please say "you are from me, so come".

This is another indication of how our Shaikh was consumed by love for the Prophet (PBUH). It describes his spiritual extinction (*fanā'*) in his Master (PBUH) and he used it to ask his Master (PBUH) to call him to be with him.

12.4 Dhikr Circle

The Shaikh introduced many alterations to the dhikr circle. It now begins with the following supplication:

> Yā dā'ima l-faḍli 'alā al-bariyya, yā bāsiṭa l-yadayni bil-'aṭiya, yā ṣāḥib al-mawāhib as-saniyya, ṣalli 'alā Muḥammadin khayri l-bariyya, waghfir lanā yā Rabbanā fi-hādhihi al-'ashiyya (O You of permanent favour on the creation! O You whose hands are outstretched with gifts, O You of brilliant attributes, read prayers on Muḥammad, the best of creation, and forgive us, our Lord, on this night).

A slightly different version of this prayer is attributed to the Companion Ibn 'Abbās.[12]

He also changed the formulas of *istimdād*, that is seeking spiritual support, from the Prophet (PBUH) and Imām 'Alī Ibn Abī Ṭālib (may Allah ennoble his face), by adding to them words of Shaikh Muḥyiddīn Ibn 'Arabī.[13] Below is the formula of seeking support from the Messenger (PBUH), with the addition beginning from the phrase

---

[12] Al-Nabhānī, *Sa'ādat al-dārayn*, 246-247; Al-Nabhānī, *Da'wat tashrīfāt*, 107.

[13] These words of Shaikh Ibn 'Arabī are quoted by Al-Mar'ashī, *Mulḥaqāt Al-'Ihqāq*, 33, 107. The latter, in turn, quoted them from Al-Iṣbahānī, *Sharḥ ṣalawāt chharda ma'ṣūm*, 293.

"al-ḥamdu lillāhi rabbi l-ʿālamīn" (Praise be to Allah, Lord of the worlds) and extending to the end of the phrase "wal-mubarqaʿi bi l-ʿamāʾ (the one veiled by heavy clouds)". The addition consists of a supplication in praise of Allah followed by a formula for reading prayers upon the Prophet (PBUH) that includes many of his spiritual attributes and titles:

> Madad yā sayyidanā wa-nabiyyanā wa-shafīʿa dhunūbinā. Yā ṣāḥiba l-āyāt wal-muʿjizāt, wa-yā ṣāḥiba dalāʾili l-khayrāt wa-khawāriqi l-ʿādāt, wa-yā sayyida s-sādāt, ḥabība rabbi l-ʿālamīn, wa-khātima n-nabiyyīn wa-sayyida l-mursalīn. Al-ḥamdu lillāhi rabbi l-ʿālamīn, ḥamdān azaliyyan bi abadiyyatihi wa-abadiyyan bi azaliyyatihi, sarmadan bi iṭlāqih, mutajalliyan fī-marāyā āfāqih, ḥamda l-ḥāmidīn wa-dahra d-dāhirīn. Ṣalawātu Allahi wa-malāʾikatihi wa-ḥamalati ʿarshihi wa-jamīʿi khalqihi min arḍihi wa-samāʾihi ʿalā sayyidinā wa-nabiyyinā, aṣli l-wujūdi wa-ʿayni sh-shāhidi wal-mashhūd, wa-awwali al-awāʾil, wa-adalli ad-dalāʾil, wa-mabdaʾi l-anwāri al-azalī wa-muntahā al-ʿurūji l-kamālī. Ghāyati l-ghāyāt, al-mutaʿayyin bi n-nashaʾāt. Abi l-akwān bi fāʿiliyyatihi, wa-ummi l-imkān bi qābiliyyatihi. Al-mathali l-aʿlā l-ilāhī, hayūlī l-ʿawālimi ghayri l-mutanāhī. Rūḥi l-arwāḥ wa-nūri l-ashbāḥ, fāliqi iṣbāḥi l-ghaybi wa-rāfiʿi ẓulmati r-rayb. Muḥtadi t-tisʿati wat-tisʿīn. Raḥamatin lil-ʿālamīn. Sayyidina fīl-wujūd, ṣāḥib liwāʾi l-ḥamdi wal-maqāmi l-maḥmūd, wal-mubarqaʿi bi l-ʿamāʾ, ḥabīb Allah Muḥammad al-Muṣṭafā ṣallā Allah taʿāla ʿalayhi wa-sallim (Grant us support, O our Master, our Prophet, and intercessor of our sins! O possessor of signs and miracles. O possessor of waymarks of goodness and paranormal occurrences. O Master of Masters, Beloved of the Lord of the worlds, Seal of Prophets and Master of Messengers. Praise be to Allah, Lord of the worlds, everlasting praise with His eternality and eternal praise with His everlastingness, perpetual praise with His absoluteness, manifest praise in the mirrors of His horizons, praise of those who praise, lasting throughout all time. Prayers of Allah, His angels, the bearers of His throne, and all of His creation from His earth and His sky, be upon our Master and Prophet, the source of existence, the essence of the witness and what is witnessed, foremost of the foremost, the greatest of proofs, the beginning of pre-eternal lights and end of perfected ascension, the destination of all destinations, the establisher of what is established, the father of the universes by his action, the mother of all ability by his capability, the highest divine example, the endless fabric of the universe, the soul of souls and light of spirits, the cleaver of the dawn of the unseen and lifter of the darkness of doubt, the origin of the ninety-nine, mercy to all the worlds, our Master in existence, the bearer of the standard of

praise and the station of praiseworthiness, and the one veiled by heavy clouds, Allah's Beloved, Muḥammad, the Chosen One, Allah Almighty's prayers and peace be upon him).

The following is the formula of seeking spiritual support from Imām ʿAlī. Our Master's addition begins from the phrase "wa-ʿalā sirri l-asrāri (and on the secret of secrets)" and ends at the phrase "Imāmi l-aʾimmati (Imām of imāms)", and it contains spiritual titles and attributes of the Imām:

> Madad yā sayyidī wa-sanadī wa-murshidī wa-tāja raʾsī wa-nūra ʿaynī. Fārisa l-mashāriqi wal-maghārib, ṣāḥib muẓhiri l-ʿajāʾib wal-gharāʾib, asad Allahi l-ghālib. Wa-ʿalā sirri l-asrāri wa-mashriqi l-anwār, al-muhandisi fīl-ghuyūbi l-lāhūtiyya. Unmūdhaji l-wāqiʿi wa-shakhṣi l-iṭlāqi, al-munṭabiʿi fī-marāyā l-anfusi wal-āfāq. Sirri l-anbiyā'i wal-mursalīn, sayyidi l-awṣiyāʾi waṣ-ṣiddīqīn. Ṣūrati l-ilāhiyya, māddati l-ʿulūmi l-ghayri l-mutanāhiyya, aẓ-ẓāhiri l-burhān, al-bāṭini bi l-qadri wal-shaʾn, basmalati kitābi l-wujūd, ḥaqīqati n-nuqṭati l-bāʾiyya, al-mutaḥaqqiqi bi l-marātibi l-insāniyya. Ḥaydari ājāmi l-ibdāʿ, al-karrāri fī-maʿāriki l-ikhtirāʿ, as-sirri l-jalī wan-najmi th-thāqib, Imāmi l-aʾimmati ʿAlī Ibn Abī Ṭālib ʿalayhi ṣ-ṣalāti was-salām. (Grant us support, O my Master, my supporter, my guide, the crown of my head and light of my eye, the knight of the east and the west, the companion of the manifester of wonders and marvels, the victorious lion of Allah! And on the secret of secrets and source of lights, the architect of divine unseen. The paradigm of reality and absolute man, he who is printed on the mirrors of selves and horizons, the secret of the prophets and messengers, the master of guardians and the truthful. The Divine picture, the unending essence of knowledge, the one whose proof is apparent, the one whose rank and stature are hidden, the basmalah of the scripture of existence, the reality of the dot of the letter bāʾ, the one who realized the levels of humanity, the brave lion of the forts of ingenuity, the ferocious fighter in battles of contrivance, the manifest secret and the penetrating star, the Imām of all Imams, ʿAlī Ibn Abī Ṭālib, prayers and blessings be upon him).

The dhikr circle came to an end with the recitation of this ṣalāt, "Allahumma ṣalli was sallim wa-bārik ʿalā an-nabī Muḥammad wa-ʾāli Muḥammad, sayyidi ar-rijāli al-mufaḍḍal, yā baḥra al-kamāl yā Muḥammad (O Allah, send prayers, peace, and blessings upon the Prophet Muḥammad and the family of Muḥammad, the preferred one, Master of men, O sea of perfection, O Muḥammad!)", followed by al-

Ṣalāt al-Waṣfiyya. The sessions of odes of praise and sermons were also concluded by these two formulas of prayers on the Prophet (PBUH).

Shaikh ʿAbd al-Karīm al-Kasnazān used to attend the final portion of the dhikr circle, which is accompanied by drums and tambourines. He would stand for a short while outside the circle without entering it, before going to sit on his chair in front of the circle while the dervishes completed the dhikr. Our Shaikh also used to attend the same part of the dhikr circle, but he would enter the circle's centre. One day he commented on this, saying that "Shaikh ʿAbd al-Karīm knew why he did not enter the circle and I know why I enter it".

While standing in the circle, he would sometimes correct the way some dervishes would stand or do the dhikr movements. Nearing the end of the dhikr, when the dervishes sat on the ground, he would leave the circle and go to sit on his chair in front of the circle, where dervishes would visit him after the dhikr ended. He would sometimes deliver a sermon, then a session of odes of praise would be held.

At times, he would raise his foot during the dhikr and move it slightly so that he would stay leaning on his other foot and his cane. This was a gesture of humility and subservience to grand Shaikhs when their spirits attended the dhikr circle. As we have mentioned before, the Shaikh's poor health stopped him from attending the dhikr circle in the later stages of his life, except on some special occasions.

12.5 Temporary Dhikrs

In addition to the Ṭarīqa's permanent dhikrs—that is, the daily and perennial dhikrs and the dhikr circle—our Shaikh would sometimes instruct dervishes to perform certain dhikrs temporarily. The reasons behind these wirds were not always disclosed. Often, the dhikr was limited to a certain number, although some wirds would end after a certain time or with the conclusion of a situation or event. The instruction was often to read these dhikrs instead of the perennial ones. The disciples would return to complete the perennial wirds from where they left off after completing the temporary wirds. As an example of a temporary dhikr, on 10 February 2017, the Shaikh instructed the disciples to read the dhikr "lā ilāha illallāh" 100,000 times and the dhikr "lā ilāha illallāh, Muḥammad rasūl Allāh, ṣallallāhu taʿālā ʿalayhi wa-sallam (there is no god but Allah, Muḥammad is the Messenger of Allah, Allah's peace and blessings be upon Him)" 135,000 times. The reward for reciting the dhikrs was to be gifted to the Ṭarīqa's Shaikhs. The dhikrs were to be read with the intention of the fulfilment of whatever purpose our Shaikh had then in his heart.

12.6 Individual Dhikrs

Our Shaikh would at times prescribe a special dhikr for a dervish or a group of dervishes for an undisclosed Ṭarīqa matter. He would also often instruct a disciple to perform a certain dhikr a specific number of times or for a fixed period. This was usually for a need that the disciple sought his help in fulfilling, such as increasing sustenance, curing an illness, or removing some harm.

Here is an example from personal experience. In June 2016, I started to have a strange, uncomfortable feeling in my heart after walking for around ten minutes. I would also at times feel a palpitation, in particular when eating. The palpitation would become so fast at times that it made me feel as if my heart would burst out of my chest. In September of that year, I went to visit our Shaikh in Virginia. At the end of the twelve-day visit, before saying goodbye to him to fly back home, I informed him of my condition. He asked about the details, and I told him that I had an appointment with a heart specialist three days later. He told me not to worry and to do a khatma of "lā ilāha illallāh" and, Allah willing, the condition would go away. He went on to quote two Prophetic ḥadīths, "the best dhikr is 'lā ilāha illallāh'"[14] and "whoever says 'lā ilāha illallāh' shall enter Paradise",[15] and the Qudsī ḥadīth "'lā ilāha illallāh' is My fortress; whoever enters My fortress is saved from My torment".[16] Upon my return, I was diagnosed with an arrhythmia and the specialist asked me to monitor myself and see him again if my condition developed further. Before I finished the khatma that our Master prescribed for me, the condition completely disappeared and I did not need to see the doctor again.

---

[14] Al-Tirmidhī, *Al-Jāmiʿ al-kabīr*, V, no. 3383, p. 393.

[15] Al-Ṭabarānī, *Al-Muʿjam al-kabīr*, VII, no. 6348, p. 55.

[16] Al-Muttaqī Al-Hindī, *Kanz al-ʿummāl*, I, no. 158, p. 52.

12.7 Ḥizb al-Wāw

While the term "wird" refers to a dhikr that a person recites regularly, a "ḥizb" is a dhikr that a person reads when he likes, such as when he has a specific need. Our Shaikh said that the thought came to him that many Shaikhs had their own ḥizbs but he did not have one. In 2013, he was granted a special ḥizb called Ḥizb al-Wāw. He described this ḥizb as an "order from Allah to the honourable Messenger (PBUH), to the Shaikhs, and the Shaikhs conveyed it to me".[17]

This ḥizb consists of every Qur'anic verse that begins with the letter "wāw", totalling 2,128 verses, sequentially ordered as they appear in the muṣḥaf. The first verse is "Those who believe in what has been revealed to you [O Muḥammad] and what was revealed before you and of the Hereafter, they are certain [in faith]" (al-Baqara 2:4), and the last verse is "From the evil of an envier when he envies" (al-Falaq 113:5). The Shaikh described this unique ḥizb as "a tremendous thing", which could only be read with his permission when it was first announced and printed. The best time to read it is during the last third of the night, and a person may complete its recitation over more than one night.

[17] Shaikh Muḥammad al-Muḥammad al-Kasnazān, *sermon*, 12 September 2013.

Let's say that there are only five hours between the time you go to bed and the dawn prayer. Give yourself three or four hours and give one hour to Allah, to your grave, to your Ṭarīqa. Wake up, perform ablution, and perform a few prostrations. Focus on Allah and start your worship, dhikrs, and wirds until the muezzin calls for the prayer. Perform the Sunna two prostrations before the dawn prayer. In the eyes of Allah, these two prostrations, as the Messenger said, are "better than this world and all it contains".[1] These two prostrations are Sunna of the Messenger before the dawn prayer. Then, perform the prayer of dawn and complete your wirds. Then sleep a little before waking up to go to work. Do your work until the afternoon prayer is called for, so you perform the prayer, and so on. Night worship is a necessary duty for the seeker. The seeker who does not perform night worship does attain those results, "Arise [to pray] the night, except for a little" (al-Muzzammil 79:2), "And in a part of the night, pray with it (the Qur'an) as additional worship for you that your Lord may raise you to a praised station" (al-ʾIsrāʾ 17:79).

Shaikh Muḥammad al-Muḥammad al-Kasnazān
(*Sermon*, 9 September 2013)

[1] Muslim, *Ṣaḥīḥ*, IV, no. 2449, p. 1903.

13

Worshipping and Qiyām al-layl

Shaikh Muḥammad al-Muḥammad loved performing dhikr and prayers and worshipping in general. He would urge dervishes to worship and would try to bring worshipping closer to their hearts. He gave students the permission to prioritise their studies over dhikrs during exam times and compensate for what they missed later. Yet he insisted that the obligatory prayers must be upheld all the time. He would reiterate Prophetic ḥadīths about the importance of prayers and them being the cornerstone of religion.[1]

He never stopped praying, not even for a single day. When he was bedridden by illness, he would perform whatever was possible of the prayer movements. When body movements were not possible—for instance, because his body was wired up to medical devices—he would emulate the prayer movements with his head.

Our Shaikh used to be amazed by how little Shaikh 'Abd al-Karīm used to sleep, but after succeeding him to the Shaikhdom, the Shaikhs instructed him not to sleep before reading the dawn prayers and his dhikrs and the sun had risen. He recounted that in the early days, he once felt sleepy while sitting on his chair waiting for the sun to rise. His neck started to gradually dangle until his chin touched his chest. At this point, he saw Shaikhs Ḥusayn and 'Abd al-Karīm on his right and left, respectively, each strongly shaking one of his arms and saying, "What are you doing?" It felt as if he had committed a serious fault, so he woke up in a panic. He said that he was not asleep when this happened but was only feeling sleepy.

The Shaikh used to urge dervishes to compete in performing *qiyām al-layl* (night worships)[2] and would describe for them its beauty:

> There is something that is critical for the seeker who would like to reach

---

[1] Al-Tirmidhī, *Al-Jāmi' al-kabīr*, VI, no. 3788, p. 125.

[2] Shaikh Muḥammad al-Muḥammad al-Kasnazān, *sermon*, 22 December 2005.

high ranks in spiritual matters, which is qiyām al-layl, "And in a part of the night, pray with it as additional worship for you that you Lord may raise you to a praised station" (al-Isrā' 17:79). Look how you should sacrifice, O seeker! How beautiful it is when you worship in the night and there is no one between you and your Lord. You repent and ask for forgiveness. You perform ablution and prostrate. To whom? For al-Raḥmān! You prostrate to your creator. You prostrate to the one in whose hand are all matters of this world and the hereafter. You prostrate to this creator who created you. He created everything and counted it. You prostrate to Him, "So prostrate and draw near" (al-'Alaq 96:19). How beautiful it is when you prostrate, draw near to Allah. Ask in your heart, in your prostration, "seek Me and you will find Me".[3]

As for the Shaikh himself, he performed qiyām al-layl every day, even when he was over eighty. He would demand of himself the kind of worship that people are rarely capable of. After leaving his public assembly, usually between midnight and 1 a.m., he would go to his private room to get some sleep. He would wake up around 2:30 a.m. and start preparing for qiyām al-layl. After performing ablution, he would get changed, comb his hair, and wear perfume, as if he were expecting a very important guest. He would explain this by saying that a person must be in the most beautiful condition when preparing to meet Allah. His personal assistant would then provide him with a few bottles of water and then leave him alone on the prayer mat, facing the qibla, to start his worship and dhikrs. After having a kidney transplant in 2010, he could not sit on the prayer mat so he would worship while sitting on a chair.

Our Shaikh would continue with his dhikrs until the call of the dawn prayer. After performing this prayer, he would go back to his dhikrs and continue worship until seven-thirty or eight o'clock, that is, after sunrise. During this daily seclusion, he would not speak to anyone nor would anyone speak to him at all. He used to read his dhikrs in a low voice. 'Īsā al-Mazrū'ī, who was the Shaikh's personal assistant from 2004 until his death, said that during his qiyām al-layl and performing dhikr, an augustness would show on the Shaikh such that even he would feel a sense of awe when looking at our Shaikh's face.

When going to bed for some sleep after finishing his worship, the

---

[3] Shaikh Muḥammad al-Muḥammad al-Kasnazān, *sermon*, 3 October 2013.

Shaikh would look exhausted, as if he had been doing hard physical work for long hours. ʿĪsā said that even when our Shaikh was asleep, his sleep was not deep, as he used to hear him asking for madad from the Shaikhs and remembering Allah every now and then. After sleeping for two to three hours, he would wake up to start his worship and daily duties in managing the affairs of Ṭarīqa. In the later stages of his life, his health condition and the medications he had to take limited what he could do.

Our Shaikh would let go of his beads only to sleep or perform ablution. Whether sitting alone to worship, speaking to people about Islam, receiving visitors, or doing anything else, his beads would always be in his hand, moving with the movement of his tongue and heart in remembering Allah. When he ate, he would put the beads around his neck, which he would also do at times when going to the markets. If his hands were kept busy by something that forced him to put the beads aside, he would pick them up as soon as possible. When talking about dhikr, he would at times mention a story involving Shaikh Junayd al-Baghdādī. Shaikh Junayd was once asked, "Why do you still carry the beads even though you have arrived at this honourable position?" He replied, "This is the way through which I arrived at my Lord, so I would not depart it".[4]

Following in the steps of all Kasnazānī Shaikhs, Shaikh Muḥammad al-Muḥammad would join dervishes in performing Wird al-ʿAṣr and the dhikr circle. However, since Shaikhhood is a unique and special spiritual rank, a Shaikh has dhikrs that are particular to him that would differ from those of the disciples.

He had special wirds that he would read after the dawn prayer until sunrise, walking while reading them, sometimes from his bedroom to an adjacent yard if available, or simply to the bedroom's entrance, even if it was a short distance. It seems that walking while reciting these particular dhikrs was one of their requirements. The Qur'an tells us that dhikr may be performed in any posture and position, as in this description of worshippers, "Who remember Allah while standing, sitting, and lying on their sides and give thought to the creation of the heavens and the earth" (Āl ʿImrān 191).

[4] Al-Qushayrī, *Al-Risāla al-qushayriyya*, 80-81.

Another special worship the Shaikh carried out early in his Shaikhdom, when he was living in Kirkuk, was to pray four prostrations one hour before the call to the noon prayer. The timing was so precise that he would stand on the prayer rug a minute or two before the time for this prayer, looking at his watch until it was exactly one hour before the noon prayer, at which point he would begin praying. Whenever there was someone in his assembly that did not know of this daily practice, he would inform them before the prayer that the time for the noon prayer had not yet arrived, so that they would not be confused.

He had wirds where he would not speak to anyone except by gesture when reading them. At times, he performed such dhikrs after the sunset prayer until the time of the night prayer. When a person did not understand his gesturing, he waited until he finished that dhikr, and then spoke to them about what he wanted. Shaikh ʿAbd al-Karīm would also devote himself to worship after the sunset prayer. His personal assistant would leave him alone and return only when he neared the end of his wirds.

Shaikh Sāmān, who is married to the Shaikh's sister and whose sister was married to the Shaikh, sometimes had to sleep in the Shaikh's bedroom in his house in Karbchna because there was no space in other rooms. He relates that our Master would often read the Qur'anic chapter of Yāsīn when he went to bed. One astonishing thing he noticed was that sometimes our Shaikh would doze off while reading Yāsīn, but when woke up, he would go back to completing the chapter from the verse he had been reading before he fell asleep!

The following special spiritual experience demonstrates how remembering Allah was fused with our Master inwardly and outwardly. Before having a kidney transplant in 2010 in the USA, the Ṭarīqa's Shaikhs told him that they had already performed the surgery in their spiritual hospital, so the operation in the hospital of this world would be successful. After waking up from the anaesthesia, the Shaikh found himself *outwardly* reading the last two verses of the chapter of al-Tawba, "There has certainly come to you a Messenger from among yourselves. Grievous to him is what you suffer; [he is] concerned over you and to the believers is kind and merciful. If they turn away [O Muḥammad], say: 'Sufficient for me is Allah; there is no deity except Him. On Him I have relied, and He is the Lord of the Great Throne'" (al-Tawba 9:128-129), while he found himself *inwardly* reading the two verses of the Prophet Jonah's supplication and Allah's answer, "'There is no deity except You; exalted are You. Indeed, I have been of the wrongdoers.' We responded to him and saved him from distress. And thus do We save the believers" (al-Ānbiyā' 21:87-88). The Prophet Jonah called out this supplication when he was in the whale's belly, while our Shaikh was inwardly reading these two verses while he was under the effects of anaesthesia. There seemed to be an element of similarity in the Prophet Jonah's being in the whale's depths, temporarily isolating him and his senses from his natural surroundings, and our Shaikh's being anaesthetised, temporarily isolating his external existence from the world.

You have won in this great and blessed occasion [of the birthday of the Prophet (PBUH)]. Allah willing, it is the anniversary of the descent of the light from Allah (exalted and high is He) to our planet, to the earth. He gave us this gift so that we can be blessed by this scent, blessing, and grace from Allah (exalted and high is He) to this nation. This blessing and grace is not something anybody can get; it calls for thanking and praising. Allah has given us this blessed occasion, "Allah would not punish them while you [O Muḥammad!] are among them; and Allah would not punish them while they seek forgiveness" (al-Anfāl 8:33).

Shaikh Muḥammad al-Muḥammad al-Kasnazān
(*Sermon*, 1 May 2018)

14

Introducing the Muḥammadī Calendars

For Sufi Shaikhs, the birth of Muḥammad (PBUH) has a unique sacred status among Islamic events because he is the Prophet of Islam, the one to whom the Qur'an was revealed, and the means of guiding people. His birth represents the descent of Allah's light among people, "There has come to you from Allah a light and a clear Book" (al-Mā'ida 4:15). It also marks Allah's sending of special mercy to people, "We have not sent you except as a mercy to the worlds" (al-Ānbiyā' 2:107). Shaikh Muḥammad al-Muḥammad described the noble birthday as "the birth of the light on planet Earth, the birth of the light, the birth of the spirit, the birth of existence. Everything was created for his sake. Everything followed him. [He is] the beloved, the elect (PBUH)".[1] He refers here to the fact that the light of the Prophet (PBUH) was the first thing that Allah created and that the rest of the creation was because of him. Many miracles accompanied this unique universal event, including the shaking of the mansion of the Persian emperor and the fall of fourteen of its terraces, the extinguishing of the temple fire that was worshipped in Persia, and the subsiding of the waters of the lake of Sāwa.[2]

Celebrating the Prophetic birth is one of the greatest religious practices in Ṭarīqa. The Prophet (PBUH) is the door to Allah; remembering and reading prayers on him are forms of remembering Allah, and loving him grows the love of Allah in the heart and makes Allah love the servant. Allah says that a Muslim must give precedence to the Messenger (PBUH) over everyone else and anything:

> Say [O Muḥammad], "If your fathers, your sons, your brothers, your

---

[1] Shaikh Muḥammad al-Muḥammad al-Kasnazān, *sermon*, 19 November 2018.

[2] Al-Āṣbahānī, *Dalā'il al-nubuwwa*, 139.

wives, your relatives, wealth which you have obtained, commerce wherein you fear decline, and dwellings with which you are pleased are more beloved to you than Allah and His Messenger and jihad in His cause, then wait until Allah executes His command. Allah does not guide the defiantly disobedient people". (Al-Tawba 9:24)

A Muslim who does not celebrate the birth of the Messenger (PBUH) should not celebrate anyone or anything else. This celebration is an acknowledgement of Allah's favour of sending His noble Prophet (PBUH) and is in obedience to His order. Shaikhs of Ṭarīqa and scholars have said much about the virtue of celebrating the noble Prophetic birth, such as Shaikh Ḥasan al-Baṣrī's words, "I wish I had as much gold as Mount Uḥud so that I can spend it on reading [in praise of] the birth of the Messenger (PBUH)".[3]

14.1 The Muḥammadī Calendar

On the night of AH 12 Rabīʿ al-Awwal 1412, which corresponds to 19 September 1991 CE, our Shaikh put forward an initiative that represents a permanent celebration of the Prophetic birth and reveres and venerates the noble Messenger (PBUH). He proposed a new lunar calendar that dates events relative to the birth of the Prophet (PBUH). He led a research team of seekers of Ṭarīqa, of which I was honoured to be a member, to carry out this project.

This calendar dates Islamic history relative to its real beginning. It presents a practical solution to a specific difficulty in the study of early Islamic history. Historians usually indirectly divide Islamic history into three periods that are dated using three different reference years. The first period is from the birth of the Messenger (PBUH) to the beginning of the revelation of the glorious Qur'an. For instance, biographical works of the Messenger (PBUH) state that he married sayyida Khadīja when he was "twenty-five years old"[4] and that he was "thirty-five years old"[5] when he wisely advised the tribes of the Quraysh about how to place the Black Stone in the Kaʿba, sparing them a potential war among themselves. The reference year for this period is his birth year.

---

[3] Al-Bakrī, *Iʿānat al-ṭālibīn*, III, p. 364.

[4] Ibn Hishām, *Sīrat al-nabī*, I, p. 242.

[5] Ibid., I, p. 248.

The second period extends from the first revelation of the Qur'an to the Prophetic migration, which is dated relative to the revelation year. For example, the first migration of a group of Muslims from Mecca, which was to Abyssinia, is said to have happened in "the month of Rajab of the fifth year after prophethood was conferred on the Messenger of Allah (PBUH)"[6] and that the Prophet travelled to Ṭā'if "in the last few nights of the month Shawwāl of the eleventh year after prophethood was conferred on the Messenger of Allah (PBUH)".[7]

The third period is the one that followed the migration of the Prophet (PBUH) from Mecca to Medina. Its reference year is the year of migration, which is the first year of the Hijrī calendar. Accordingly, early Islamic history has been dated using three different reference years, which is almost the equivalent of using three different calendars.

The "Mīlādī Muḥammadī", or "Muḥammadī" for short, calendar is not a replacement for the Hijrī calendar. In addition to its religious significance, it can have practical benefits because of its use of the year of noble Prophetic birth as a common reference year for all periods of Islamic history.

The Muḥammadī year consists of twelve months, each of which starts when its respective lunar crescent becomes visible, as is the case in the Hijrī calendar. As this calendar celebrates the birth of the Prophet (PBUH), its first month and year are the birth's month and year, respectively. Therefore, the date of the noble birth according to the Muḥammadī calendar is 12/1/1, as he was born on day 12. The Muḥammadī year begins two months after the beginning of the Hijrī year because the Hijrī month of the noble birth, Rabī' al-Awwal, is the third month of the Hijrī year. The Hijrī year retains the order of months of the Arabic pre-Islamic calendar. Our Shaikh called the first year of the Muḥammadī calendar the "year of light", instead of its common name in historical sources as the "year of the elephant". The new name derives from Allah's description of the Prophet Muḥammad (PBUH) as "light" in this verse, "There has come to you from Allah a light and a clear Book" (al-Mā'ida 4:15).

Intended to commemorate Islam's main symbol, the Messenger

---

[6] Ibn Sa'ad, *Kitāb al-ṭabaqāt al-kabīr*, I, p. 173.

[7] Ibid., I, p. 180.

Muḥammad (PBUH), and Islam in general, the Muḥammadī calendar's months have been named after great Islamic characters, symbols, and events. For the month names to have historical significance, they were chosen to celebrate events that happened in their respective months. These are the names of the Muḥammadī months and why they have been chosen:

1) **Al-Nūr** (the light): This is the birth month of the Messenger (PBUH). In the same way that our Shaikh called the year of the noble birth the "year of light", this month derived its name from the Qur'anic description of the Prophet (PBUH).

2) **Al-Quds** (Jerusalem): This is one of Islam's most sacred cities, embracing the Aqṣā Mosque to which the Messenger (PBUH) was first transported at night before being taken to the heavens. In this month, Saladin liberated Jerusalem in the famous Battle of Ḥiṭṭīn (M 637 / AH 583).

3) **Al-Karrār** (the attacker): In this month, the conquest of Khaybar took place (M 71 / AH 7). After a fifteen-day siege, the Muslim army attacked this fortified city for two days but without success. When the army came back on the second unsuccessful day, the Messenger made his well-known declaration, "By Allah, I will give the standard tomorrow to a man who loves Allah and who Allah and His Messenger love, who is an attacker (karrār), not one who flees, and who will conquer it by force".[8] The next day, he called for Imam ʿAlī Ibn Abī Ṭālib and tasked him with conquering the fort, which he did.

4) **Al-Zahrā**ʾ (the brilliant one): This is the title of sayyida Fāṭima, daughter of the Messenger (PBUH). She was born on day 20 of this month (M 38 / AH 17). The Prophet said about her virtues, "Fāṭīma is a part of me; anything that hurts her hurts me too".[9]

5) **Al-Isrā**ʾ (the night journey): This is the month in which Allah (exalted and high is He) took the Messenger at night from the Ḥarām Mosque in Mecca to the Aqṣā Mosque in Jerusalem (M 52 / 3 BH), "Exalted is He who took His Servant by night from the Ḥarām Mosque to the Aqṣā Mosque, whose surroundings We have blessed, to show him of Our signs. Indeed, He is the Hearing, the Seeing" (al-Isrāʾ 17:1).

---

[8] Abū al-Fidāʾ, *Al-Mukhtaṣar*, I, p. 140.

[9] Muslim, *Ṣaḥīḥ*, IV, no. 2449, p. 1903.

6) **Al-Qādisiyya:** This month witnessed the Battle of Qādisiyya (M 69 / AH 15) in which the Muslims defeated the army of the Persian Sasanian empire and that led to the conquest of Iraq.

7) **Ramadan:** This is the name of this month in the glorious Qur'an, "The month of Ramadan [is that] in which was revealed the Qur'an, a guidance for the people and clear proofs of guidance and criterion" (al-Baqara 2:185).

8) **Al-Naṣr** (the victory): In this month, the Muslims defeated an alliance involving the tribe of Quraysh in the Battle of the Trench (M 59 / AH 5).

9) **Al-Bayʿa** (the pledge): This is the month of the pledge of Riḍwān (M 60 / AH 6), which the Qur'an mentions, "Certainly Allah was pleased with the believers when they pledged allegiance to you [O Muḥammad] under the tree, and He knew what was in their hearts, so He sent down tranquillity upon them and rewarded them with an imminent conquest" (al-Fatḥ 48:18).

10) **Al-Ḥajj** (the pilgrimage): This is the month in which Muslims perform pilgrimage to the Ḥarām Mosque in Mecca.

11) **Al-Hijra** (the migration): The first month of the Hijrī year. The actual migration of the Prophet (PBUH) from Mecca is reported to have begun at the end of the second month and his arrival in Medina was in the following month.

12) **Al-Futūḥ** (the conquests): In this month, the conquest of Nahāwand (M 74 / AH 21) took place. This is also known as the "conquest of conquests" because it was a decisive battle in the eventual Muslim conquest of the Persian empire. There were also other important battles in this month, such as the raid of Abwāʾ or Waddān (M 55 / AH 2), the first Muslim raid, and the conquest of Ctesiphon (M 69 / AH 16), the capital of the Sassanid empire.

Table 14.1: The Muḥammadī Months and Their Hijrī Equivalents

Muḥammadī		**Hijrī**	
No.	**Month**	**No.**	**Month**
1	Al-Nūr	3	Rabīʿ al-Awwal
2	Al-Quds	4	Rabīʿ al-Thānī
3	Al-Karrār	5	Jamādā al-Uwlā

4	Al-Zahrā'	6	Jamādā al-Ākhira
5	Al-Isrā'	7	Rajab
6	Al-Qādisiyya	8	Sha'bān
7	Ramadan	9	Ramadan
8	Al-Naṣr	10	Shawwāl
9	Al-Bay'a	11	Dhū al-Qi'da
10	Al-Ḥajj	12	Dhū al-Ḥijja
11	Al-Hijra	1	Muḥarram
12	Al-Futūḥ	2	Ṣafar

The Muḥammadī calendar is fifty-three years and ten months ahead of the Hijrī calendar. This is the period between the start of the first Muḥammadī year, that is, the "year of the light", and the start of the first Hijrī year. The days of the months in both calendars are the same because both follow the lunar month, which starts with the first visibility of the lunar crescent. But the months and years differ. We will now discuss the conversion between Hijrī and Muḥammadī dates.

14.1.1 Converting Hijrī into Muḥammadī Dates

The general formula for converting a Hirjī date into its Muḥammadī equivalent is as follows:

Muḥammadī date = Hijrī date + 53 years + 10 months (1)

14.1.1.1 Calculating the Month

A Hijrī month is converted into its Muḥammadi equivalent as follows:

For Hijrī months 1-2:

Muḥammadī month = Hijrī month + 10 (1.1)

For Hijrī months 3-12:

Muḥammadī month = Hijrī month - 2 (1.2)

One of these two formulas is used regardless of the year.

14.1.1.2 Calculating the Year

Calendars do not use year zero. The first Hijrī year, that is, AH 1, is preceded by year 1 before Hijra (BH), which may be numerically represented as -1. Similarly, the first Muḥammadī calendar is preceded by year M -1. Accordingly, there are two different pairs of formulas for converting Hijrī years into Muḥammadī years, depending on the Hijrī date.

These two formulas are used for calculating the year for any date except for the period BH 2/54 - BH 12/1:

For Hijrī months 1-2:

Muḥammadī year = Hijrī year + 53 (1.3)

For Hijrī months 3-12:

Muḥammadī year = Hijrī year + 54 (1.4)

Example: Muslims conquered Mecca peacefully on 20 Ramadan in the eighth Hirjī year, i.e. AH 20/9/8. The equivalent Muḥammadī date is calculated as follows:

- The day is the same in the two calendars, so the Muḥammadī day is 20.

Given that the Hijrī month is number 9, formulas 1.2 and 1.4 are used:

- Muḥammadī month = 9 - 2 = 7
- Muḥammadī year = 8 + 54 = 62

The date of the conquest of Mecca according to the Muḥammadi calendar is 20/7/62, that is, 20 Ramadan 62.

If the Hijrī date is between month 2 of year BH 54 and month 12 of year BH 1, then formulas 1.3 and 1.4 are replaced with the following two formulas for calculating the Muḥammadī year:

For Hijrī months 1-2:

Muḥammadī year = Hijrī year + 54 (1.5) instead of (1.3)

For Hijrī months 3-12:

Muḥammadī year = Hijrī year + 55 (1.6) instead of (1.4)

Example: The night journey of the Prophet (PBUH) from the Ḥarām Mosque to the Aqṣā Mosque happened on 27 Rajab of year three before Hijra. This is how to convert it to the corresponding Muḥammadī date:

- The day is the same in the two calendars, so the Muḥammadī day is 27.

Given that the Hijrī month is number 7 and the date is in the period BH 2/54 – BH 12/1, formulas 1.2 and 1.6 are used:

- Muḥammadī month = 7 - 2 = 5
- Muḥammadī year = -3 + 55 = 52

The Muḥammadī date of the night journey is 27/5/52, that is, 27 al-Isrā' 52.

14.1.2 Converting Muḥammadī into Hijrī Dates

The general formula for converting Muḥammadī dates into Hirjī dates is as follows:

$$\text{Hijrī date} = \text{Muḥammadī date} - 53 \text{ years} - 10 \text{ months} \qquad (2)$$

14.1.2.1 Calculating the Month

A Muḥammadi month is converted into the corresponding Hijrī date as follows:

For Muḥammadi months 11-12:

$$\text{Hijrī month} = \text{Muḥammadi month} + 10 \qquad (2.1)$$

For Muḥammadi months 1-10:

$$\text{Hijrī month} = \text{Muḥammadi month} + 2 \qquad (2.2)$$

14.1.2.2 Calculating the Year

The following two formulas are used for calculating the year for any date except the period M 1/1 - M 10/5:

For Muḥammadi months 11-12:

$$\text{Hijrī year} = \text{Muḥammadī year} - 53 \qquad (2.3)$$

For Muḥammadi months 1-10:

$$\text{Hijrī year} = \text{Muḥammadī year} - 54 \qquad (2.4)$$

Example: The Muslims conquered Mecca on M 20 Ramadan 62. This date can be converted into its Hijrī equivalent as follows:

- The day is the same in the two calendars, so the Hijrī day is 20.

Given that the Muḥammadī month is 7, formulas 2.2 and 2.4 are used:

- Hijrī month = 7 + 2 = 9

- Hijrī year = 62 - 54 = 8

The date of the conquest of Mecca according to the Hijrī calendar is 20 Ramadan 8.

If the Muḥammadī date is between month 1 of year 1 and month 10 of year 54, which is before the first Hijrī year, then formulas 2.3 and 2.4 are replaced with the following formulas to calculate the Hijrī year:

For Muḥammadī months 11-12:

Hijrī year = Muḥammadī year - 54 (2.5) instead of (2.3)

For Muḥammadī months 3-12:

Muḥammadī year = Hijrī year - 55 (2.6) instead of (2.4)

Example: The Prophet (PBUH) was born on 12 of the first month, al-Nūr, of the first Muḥammadī year, i.e. M 12/1/1. The equivalent Hijrī date is calculated as follows:

- The day is the same in the two calendars, so the Hijrī day is 12.

Given that the Muḥammadī month is 1, formula 2.2 is used to calculate the Hijrī month:

- Hijrī month = 1 + 2 = 3

As the Muḥammadī month is 1 and the date is in the period 1/1-10/54, formula 2.6 is used to find the Hijrī year:

- Hijrī year = 1 - 55 = -54

The date of the noble Prophetic birth according to the Hijrī calendar is BH 12/3/-54, i.e. BH 12 Rabīʿ al-Awwal 54.[10]

14.2 The Solar Date of the Birth of the Prophet (PBUH)

The Shaikh's introduction of the Muḥammadī calendar was accompanied by another initiative to calculate the date of the birth of the Messenger (PBUH) according to the Gregorian calendar, the ubiquitous Western calendar.

There is a consensus that the Hijrī day and month of the Prophetic

[10] Al-Kasnazān et al., "Nahjun jadīdun".

birth are known to be 12 Rabīʿ al-Awwal, which corresponds to 12 al-Nūr in the Muḥammadī calendar, and the year of birth is the "year of the elephant", which corresponds to 570 CE. This makes it possible to calculate the Gregorian date of the birth of the Prophet (PBUH). This date was found to be Friday 2 May 570. Our Master used to celebrate this date every year in the same way he commemorated its Hijrī equivalent.

14.3 The Muḥammadī Shamsī Calendar

The solar calendar is no less important than the lunar one in the Islamic world. The official calendar in many Islamic countries is the Gregorian one, which is a solar calendar that reckons time from the hypothetical date of the birth of Jesus (PBUH). The Qur'an points out the benefits of using the sun and the moon in the reckoning of time:

> [He is] the cleaver of daybreak and has made the night for rest and the sun and moon for calculation. That is the determination of the Impregnable, the Knowing. (Al-Ānʿām 6:96)
>
> It is He who made the sun a shining light and the moon a derived light and determined for it phases that you may know the number of years and account [of time]. Allah has not created this except in truth. He details the signs for a people who know. (Yūnus 10:5)

Less than three years after introducing the Muḥammadī calendar, Shaikh Muḥammad al-Muḥammad initiated another project to celebrate the birth of the Prophet (PBUH). On the anniversary of the noble birth according to the Gregorian calendar, on 2 May 1994, he proposed a new solar calendar that reckons time from the month of the noble birth. To distinguish it from the lunar "Muḥammadī" calendar, this calendar was called "Muḥammadī Shamsī", where "Shamsī" means "solar". The first Muḥammadī Shamsī month, which is the birth month, corresponds to the fifth month in the Gregorian calendar. Accordingly, the Muḥammadī Shamsī calendar starts four months after the start of the Gregorian year. In other words, the Gregorian date of the noble birth on 2/5/570 CE converts to 2/1/1 in the Muḥammadī Shamsī calendar.

Most of the months of this calendar have been named after weather and seasonal changes that happen in those months in the Arabian peninsula where Prophet Muḥammad (PBUH) was born and from where Islam spread. These are the names of the months:

1) **Al-Raḥma** (the mercy): This is the month of the birth of the Messenger whom the Qur'an described with this word, "We have not sent you [O Muḥammad] except as a mercy to the worlds" (al-Ānbiyā' 21:107).

2) **Al-Firdaws** (paradise): Fields are full of fruits, vegetables, and seeds in this month, which evokes the concept of Paradise.

3) **Al-Shams** (the sun): This is the first month of the hot summer.

4) **Al-Ruṭab** (dates): In this month, dates ripen. The date palm is considered to be a blessed tree in Islam.

5) **Al-Riḥla** (the journey): The migration of the Messenger (PBUH) took place in this month. He left Mecca on day 8 and arrived in Medina two weeks later, on day 22.

6) **Al-Ghayth** (rain): Rain starts falling in this month.

7) **Al-Bard** (cold): This is the first month of winter.

8) **Al-Thalj** (snow): Snow starts falling in this month.

9) **Al-Rīḥ** (wind): This month usually has strong winds.

10) **Al-Zar'** (planting): The first month of planting the summer plants.

11) **Al-Burāq** (the Burāq): The Messenger's (PBUH) ascension to the heavens was in this month. Burāq is the name of the means that he used in his journey.

12) **Al-Rabī'** (spring): The first month after the vernal equinox.

Table 14.2: The Muḥammadī Shamsī Months and Their Gregorian Equivalents

Muḥammadī Shamsī		**Gregorian**	
No.	**Month**	**No.**	**Month**
1	Al-Raḥma	5	May
2	Al-Firdaws	6	June
3	Al-Shams	7	July
4	Al-Ruṭab	8	August
5	Al-Riḥla	9	September
6	Al-Ghayth	10	October
7	Al-Bard	11	November
8	Al-Thalj	12	December

9	Al-Rīḥ	1	January
10	Al-Zarʿ	2	February
11	Al-Burāq	3	March
12	Al-Rabīʿ	4	April

The Muḥammadī Shamsī calendar lags 569 years and 4 months behind the Gregorian calendar. This is the time between the beginning of the first Gregorian year, which is the hypothetical year of the birth of Jesus (PBUH), and the beginning of the first Muḥammadī Shamsī year, which is the year of the birth of the Prophet Muḥammad (PBUH). The days in both calendars are the same, as they both follow the solar month, but the months and years differ. We will see now how to convert dates between the Muḥammadī Shamsī and Gregorian calendars.

14.3.1 Converting Gregorian into Muḥammadī Shamsī Dates

The general formula for converting Gregorian dates into Muḥammadī Shamsī dates is as follows:

Muḥammadī Shamsī date = Gregorian date - 569 years - 4 months (3)

14.3.1.1 Calculating the Month

A Gregorian month is converted into its Muḥammadi Shamsī equivalent as follows:

For Gregorian months 5-12:

Muḥammadī Shamsī month = Gregorian month - 4 (3.1)

For Gregorian months 1-4:

Muḥammadī Shamsī month = Gregorian month + 8 (3.2)

14.3.1.2 Calculating the Year

The following formulas are used for converting Gregorian years into Muḥammadī Shamsī years, except for dates in the period 1/1-4/570 CE:

For Gregorian months 5-12:

Muḥammadī Shamsī year = Gregorian year - 569 (3.3)

For Gregorian months 1-4:

Muḥammadī Shamsī year = Gregorian year - 570 (3.4)

Example: The night journey of the Messenger (PBUH) was on 6 March 620 CE. The corresponding Muḥammadī Shamsī date is as follows:

- The day is the same in the two calendars, so the Muḥammadī Shamsī day is 6.

Given that the Gregorian month is number 3, formulas 3.2 and 3.4 are used:

- Muḥammadī Shamsī month = 3 + 8 = 11
- Muḥammadī Shamsī year = 620 - 570 = 50

The Muḥammadī Shamsī date of the night journey is 6/11/50, which is 6 al-Burāq 50.

If the Gregorian date is between month 1 of year 1 CE and month 4 of year 570 CE, then formulas 3.3 and 3.4 are replaced with the following two formulas to calculate the Muḥammadī Shamsī year:

For Gregorian months 5-12:

Muḥammadī Shamsī year = Gregorian year - 570 (3.5) instead of (3.3)

For Gregorian months 1-4:

Muḥammadī Shamsī year = Gregorian year – 571 (3.6) instead of (3.4)

14.3.2 Converting Muḥammadī Shamsī into Gregorian Dates

The general formula for converting Muḥammadī Shamsī dates into Gregorian dates is as follows:

Gregorian date = Muḥammadī Shamsī date + 569 years + 4 months (4)

14.3.2.1 Calculating the Month

A Muḥammadī Shamsī month is converted into its Gregorian equivalent as follows:

For Muḥammadī Shamsī months 1-8:

Gregorian month = Muḥammadī Shamsī month + 4 (4.1)

For Gregorian months 9-12:

Gregorian month = Muḥammadī Shamsī month - 8 (4.2)

14.3.2.2 Calculating the Year

The following formulas are used for converting Muḥammadī Shamsī years into Gregorian years, except for dates in the period 9/570-1/12 before Muḥammadī Shamsī (BMS):

For Muḥammadī Shamsī months 1-8:

Gregorian year = Muḥammadī Shamsī year + 569 (4.3)

For Muḥammadī Shamsī months 9-12:

Gregorian year = Muḥammadī Shamsī year + 570 (4.4)

Example: The Prophet (PBUH) arrived in Medina having migrated from Mecca on 22 May 53 MS. The Gregorian date is calculated as follows:

- The day is the same in the two calendars, so the Gregorian day is 22.

Given that the Gregorian month is number 5, formulas 4.1 and 4.3 are used to calculate the Gregorian year:

- Gregorian month = 4 + 5 = 9
- Gregorian year = 569 + 53 = 622

The Gregorian date of the arrival of the Messenger (PBUH) to Medina is 22 September 622.

If the Muḥammadī Shamsī date is between month 9 of year 570 BMS and month 12 of year 1 BMS, then formulas 4.3 and 4.4 are replaced with the following formulas for calculating the Gregorian year:

For Muḥammadī Shamsī months 1-8:

Gregorian year = Muḥammadī Shamsī year + 570 (4.5) instead of (4.3)

For Gregorian months 9-12:

Gregorian year = Muḥammadī Shamsī year + 571 (4.6) instead of (4.4)

Both Muḥammadī calendars, lunar and solar, are products of the love of our Shaikh for the Prophet (PBUH). They are one form of his creativity in honouring and venerating the Prophet Muḥammad (PBUH) and celebrating his noble birth.

O Kasnazānī dervishes! What is incumbent upon you is incumbent upon me; obedience is incumbent upon us, "Obey Allah and obey the Messenger and those in authority among you" (al-Nisā' 5:59). The seeker must obey the Shaikh because the Shaikh obeys Allah (exalted and high is He), obeys the honourable Messenger, and obeys the Shaikhs. From a spiritual standpoint, I and you are connected from Shaikh to Shaikh, to the honourable Messenger, to Allah (exalted and high is He). Dervishhood is not merely taking the pledge then you go away and that's all. No! Dervishhood is being spiritually connected through Ṭarīqa. You are spiritually connected to your Shaikh's soul, from Shaikh to Shaikh, to the honourable Messenger, to Allah (exalted and high is He).

Shaikh Muḥammad al-Muḥammad al-Kasnazān
(*Sermon*, 27 September 2012)

15

Caring for Holy Sites

The shrines of Imams and Shaikhs are especially sacred to Sufis because they are blessed places visited and inhabited by righteous souls and angels. There are innumerable karāmas, a few of which are mentioned in this book, that confirm the sanctity of these places. Our Shaikh looked after the renovation of holy sites and visited them regularly.

15.1 Renovation of Holy Sites

The efforts of our Master in this field started before he assumed the Shaikhdom. In 1977, Shaikh ʿAbd al-Karīm obtained the Ministry of Endowments' agreement to help financially with the renovation of the shrines in Karbchna, supervised by the Ministry's regional office in Kirkuk. He put his Deputy, Shaikh Muḥammad al-Muḥammad, in charge of the project.

Our Shaikh wanted to use stone from Karbchna to build the exterior of the mosque, takya, and shrines. The Ministry engineer argued that this would increase the project's cost, but the Shaikh assured him that he would be responsible for obtaining the approval for the additional cost. Stone had not been used before in construction in Karbchna. It was brought from a quarry behind Shāh al-Kasnazān's reservoir. Our Shaikh used the same stone to build his house in Kirkuk. He brought marble from Mount Sagarma and used it to build the flooring of both his house in Kirkuk and, later, the central takya in Baghdad. The use of stone and marble from Karbchna was intended to seek the blessings of the village. One of the Shaikh's sayings about the virtues of this blessed village states, "The light of the Messenger (PBUH) has shone a thousand times on Karbchna's shrines, its mountain, and the village in its entirety. Everything in Karbchna is blessed".

Skilled engravers and carvers from Kirkuk carved the exterior of the building. A few months after starting the renovation of the mosque and the shrines, Shaikh ʿAbd al-Karīm passed away. Our Shaikh completed the reconstruction before the late Shaikh's forty-day death anniversary. The tombs of Shāh al-Kasnazān and Sultan ʿAbd al-Qādir were originally in one room and the tombs of Sultan Ḥusayn and Sultan ʿAbd al-Karīm were in another, but the four tombs are now housed in one hall topped by a large dome.

Our Shaikh also decided to place a golden crown, two meters high, on each tomb and build a large new door for the entrance of the hall. He sent for caliphs from Sanandaj, Iran, who were skilled in designing with gold, and caliphs from Isfahan, Iran, who were deft engravers. He met them in Karbchna on Shaikh ʿAbd al-Karīm's forty-day death anniversary. He discussed his design ideas with them, which they would sketch out and present to him, and he would approve or ask for changes to be made to them. The inscriptions and ornamentations he settled on were of the kind known locally as Karbalāʾiyya, which is the style of patterns found in Karbala. After the designs were completed, the craftsmen went back to Iran and began work.

After obtaining land for the central takya in Baghdad, the Shaikh asked for the door of the takya's mosque to be of the same design as the door to the hall of the shrines in Karbchna. The symbolic meaning of his decision was that the door of the takya's mosque in Baghdad would be the door to the hall of the shrines of the Shaikhs in Karbchna, as he was their successor as the Master of Ṭarīqa.

It took four years and three months to manufacture the tombs' crowns and the two doors because it was precise manual work. The work was completed in mid-1982. Amazingly, as the pieces could not be transported by car because of the closed borders between Iraq and Iran due to the ongoing war between the two countries, dervishes carried and transported them on foot from Isfahan in Iran to Karbchna! The hall's door was particularly heavy, with each side needing to be carried by several men. The area through which the cargo had to be transported was rugged and mountainous. It was sometimes difficult to walk through even without a load, let alone carrying such a heavy and large load. The transporting required crossing snow-covered mountains. The crossing road of Mount Sūrīn, in particular, was very narrow, in places even for a person walking alone without carrying anything. Also, crossing the border in secret and without approval forced the dervishes to avoid well-known paths. Instead, they took secret, rugged roads to cross over the ten-kilometre-long no man's land between the two warring countries. They would only travel at night to avoid army troops seeing them. The transporting process took eleven days. Despite these measures, army troops discovered them more than once and opened fire on them. It was through karāmas that the bullets would sometimes hit them but would not harm them. Transporting the tombs' crowns and the hall's door, each section of which required several dervishes to carry, was extremely difficult and dangerous.

Our Shaikh refurbished the interior of Karbchna's hall of shrines. Its flooring was made of precious marble, its ceiling was ornamented with beautiful patterns, dazzling chandeliers were installed, and the walls were decorated with pieces of ceramic with fine inscriptions and a blue stripe with the noble lineage inscribed on it. The hall dome was plated from inside with reflective mirrors that gave the hall a brilliant lustre. It has a door leading to the front yard and another leading to the adjacent mosque.

On the forty-day death anniversary of Shaikh ʿAbd al-Karīm, a walī called Kāka ʿAzīz was sitting with caliph Yāsīn Ṣūfī in the corner of the wall that separates the mosque from the shrines, and behind them was Shāh al-Kasnazān's tomb. Kāka ʿAzīz suddenly said that he saw Shaikh ʿAbd al-Qādir al-Kasnazān demolish the wall of the mosque that was in front of them, which was facing the valley, which had just been constructed. Thinking that the demolition would be instructed by our Shaikh, Yāsīn remarked that the construction had taken a long time and great effort to complete, so it was inconceivable that it would be torn down. Kāka ʿAzīz replied that he only said what had been revealed to him, which was that Shaikh ʿAbd al-Qādir al-Kasnazān would demolish that wall but not the others. When Yāsīn asked just exactly what would happen to the wall, Kāka ʿAzīz answered that it and its roof would suffer damage. During the Iraq-Iran war, which began about two and a half years after this incident, the Iraqi army targeted Karbchna in a campaign that destroyed many villages, including mosques and shrines, in Kurdistan that the government suspected were inhabited by collaborators with anti-government Kurdish fighters. The buildings of the hall of the shrines and the mosque were damaged but the walls and roofs were not affected, except for the wall that Kāka ʿAzīz saw Shaikh ʿAbd al-Qādir's hand demolish, which collapsed. The army also blew up the living halls of the dervishes. Later, our Shaikh renovated them completely and installed a dome at the centre of the mosque standing on four concrete columns and used Islamic arabesque to beautify the mosque, inside and out, in addition to refurbishing its furniture.

At the time of deciding the design of the takya's mosque in Baghdad, the Shaikh thought of replacing the crown on Shaikh ʿAbd al-Qādir al-Gaylānī's tomb. He obtained the approval of the authorities. When the crown was completed in 1983, dervishes sent it to Kirkuk, where he was at the time. He asked for it to be transported to the central takya in Baghdad and kept it there for one night to seek its blessings. The following day, it was moved to Shaikh ʿAbd al-Qādir's shrine in Baghdad. Surprised that the crown was from Iran, one of the people in charge of the shrine asked our Shaikh how this was possible. The borders between the two countries were closed and monitored on both sides by armies prepared to open fire on anyone who crossed them. He answered, "How did our Master al-Gaylānī throw his wooden shoe from Baghdad to India?", citing a karāma of al-Ghawth al-Āʿẓam. A disciple from today's Pakistan was visiting the Shaikh in Baghdad when someone tried to assault his daughter in Pakistan. The Shaikh knew what was about to happen so he threw his wooden shoe from Baghdad, hitting the assaulter and saving the young woman from harm.

One karāma that happened during the transportation of the crown from Iran is that the dervishes who were carrying it did not feel the cold when they had to sleep in rugged snow-covered areas. Instead, they would feel hot to the point of sweating!

The old crown was removed and placed atop Shaikh Junayd al-Baghdādī's tomb. The following karāma happened at the replacing of the crown. Caliph Yāsīn Ṣūfī, who was one of the dervishes charged with replacing the crown, took a palm-sized piece of silver from the old crown. He wanted to have six or seven ornamental rings made out of it for blessings, keeping one for himself and gifting the others to certain dervishes who possessed ḥāls. After the work was completed, he went back to his family in Erbil and asked his cousin, who was a jeweller, to turn the piece of blessed silver into rings. The cousin did not have a mould for ornamental rings and offered, instead, to make it into plain rings. Yāsīn agreed and emphasized to his relative the importance of using up the entire silver piece and not allowing any to go to waste because of where it came from. The caliph kept the matter a secret and told no one about it.

After he returned to Ramādī, where he lived to preach about Ṭarīqa, a walī named Aḥmad Sūr (may Allah have mercy on him) visited him in the takya. He surprised the caliph by saying:

> Last night, Shaikh ʿAbd al-Qādir informed me of the following, "Yāsīn has taken fifteen rings from my tomb. Tell him to give you one".

The caliph answered:

> O Hajj Aḥmad! I took a piece of silver to make rings from it. It could produce six or seven, but it could not produce as many as fifteen. I intended to give you one of them even before this message had come.

Hajj Aḥmad replied:

> O dervish! I am only telling you what Shaikh ʿAbd al-Qādir al-Gaylānī has told me. Otherwise, was I with you that I should know about this matter? He is the one who said that you had taken fifteen rings from his tomb and instructed me to tell you to give me one.

About a week later, Yāsīn's nephew visited his uncle and gave him an enclosed package that his mother asked him to deliver to him. When he opened it, he found that it contained the rings. There were fourteen of them, so he told his nephew that one ring was missing. The latter laughed in surprise and said that when his mother found out that the rings were made from a piece of Shaikh ʿAbd al-Qādir's tomb, she kept one for herself for the blessing. The total number of rings was indeed fifteen, just as Shaikh ʿAbd al-Qādir had informed Hajj Aḥmad Sūr.

Later on, those in charge of the shrine replaced the crown that our Shaikh had made with another made out of silver, produced in India. When our Shaikh came to know of this, he commented that he had done his duty in service to the shrine and refurbished its crown. The crown he made was transferred from Baghdad and placed on the tomb of Shaikh ʿAbd al-ʿAzīz, son of Shaikh ʿAbd al-Qādir al-Gaylānī, in the city of ʿAqra in Nineveh in northern Iraq. The Shaikh also renovated the patio that surrounds Shaikh ʿAbd al-Qādir's shrine, inlaying it with high-quality marble.

He rebuilt Shaikh Ismāʿīl al-Wilyānī's shrine in ʿAqra and clothed it in a gold shroud. This project took more than five months to complete, during which time the finest calligrapher of Baghdad penned Qur'anic verses, prayers on the Prophet (PBUH), dhikrs, and poetry in the place. Craftsmen from Isfahan created the golden shroud. The noble shrine was erected on the birthday of Shaikh ʿAbd al-Qādir al-Gaylānī on AH 11 Rabiʿ al-Thānī 1427, 9 May 2006 CE.

Our Shaikh also funded and implemented the project of delivering water and electricity to Prophet Jonah's mosque in Mosul.

15.2 Visiting Holy Sites

Naturally, our Shaikh loved to visit holy sites and shrines. When he was in Baghdad, he would regularly visit Shaikh ʿAbd al-Qādir's shrine, as well as other shrines of Shaikhs of Ṭarīqa, such as Maʿrūf al-Karkhī, Sarī al-Saqaṭī, and Junayd al-Baghdādī. In 1995, after a visit to the holy shrines in Karbala and Najaf, the government told him not to visit them again. It feared the development of closer relationships between Ṭarīqa and Shia religious leaders. He would also visit the shrines of Imām Mūsa al-Kāẓim and his grandson, Imām Muḥammad al-Jawād, in Baghdad once a year. At other times, he would frequent the area near the shrines without entering, avoiding problems with the authorities.

There were periods when he could not visit Karbchna due to the military conflict between the government and Kurdish forces in northern Iraq and, later, as a result of the Iran-Iraq war. He would send dervishes who lived in nearby areas to visit the shrines on his behalf. He would also sometimes send someone to visit other holy places in his place.

The Shaikh would have his reasons for visiting certain holy sites at specific times. At times he would disclose those reasons while at other times, he would not. For example, one morning in 1993, before going out for his daily visit to a manuscript library in Baghdad, he informed caliphs in the takya that a dark-skinned man would come. He said that this man was his guest and instructed them to ask the visitor to wait for him until he returned. He also asked caliph Majīd Ḥamīd, who would accompany him on his daily visit to manuscript libraries, to stay in the takya to wait for the man's arrival.

Later, a Sudanese man with a limp came and sat in the room where dervishes rested and slept. Caliph Majīd saw him when he entered the takya but he did not think that he was the man that our Shaikh referred to. Given his simple and plain clothing and undistinguished condition in general, he did not see anything in him that could interest the Shaikh and make him a special guest among the many visitors to the takya every day. When our Master returned to the takya, before going to his house, he asked about the man. Majīd told him about the arrival of a dark-skinned man but that he wasn't sure whether he was the man he was waiting for. Instead of our Shaikh sending for him, as was the custom when he wanted to speak with a dervish, he went to see him in the dervishes' resting room. He started by telling the guest that Shaikh Junayd al-Baghdādī had visited him the night before and told him that he would send him a man who had an affliction and asked him to help him. The Shaikh asked the guest whether he had visited Shaikh Junayd al-Baghdādī's shrine. Amazed, the man answered that he had indeed visited him the day before. He added that in the morning, he felt a strong desire to visit the Kasnazānī takya. Then our Shaikh asked him about his affliction. He answered that while working, hot tar fell on his foot and severely burned it. Hot tar can penetrate deep into the body and may even cause permanent disability. Our Shaikh reassured the man that he would remain under his care until he was cured. He asked some dervishes to take the guest to a doctor to receive treatment. The visitor stayed in the takya until he was completely cured. When he returned to Sudan, he founded a Kasnazānī takya there. Our Master was delighted with the visit of the man, describing him as "a gift from our Master Junayd al-Baghdādī". As a result, he went to visit his shrine. His visits to the shrine of Shaikh ʿAbd al-Qādir were often due to visions that he saw or in response to a call from the Shaikh to visit him.

Our Shaikh would show the utmost veneration in his visits to holy sites. When he visited Shaikh ʿAbd al-Qādir, he would always kiss the gate's threshold. He would never turn his back to the noble tomb during the visit. The following incident illustrates the level of reverence and the immense humility that he demonstrated when he visited Shaikh ʿAbd al-Qādir al-Gaylānī. One morning at the end of the 1990s, he decided to visit the shrine and some dervishes who were in the takya at the time accompanied him. On the way to the shrine, he told Shaikh Sāmān, who was with him, that Shaikh ʿAbd al-Qādir had summoned him and honoured him that night. He did not elaborate further. When the car arrived on the shrine's street, he disembarked before it reached the shrine to walk to it—one of his etiquettes in visiting the blessed shrine. The caliphs and dervishes followed him. Instead of crossing the outside patio that separates the street from the building hosting the shrine to enter the courtyard, he headed towards a dog sitting in the shade on the patio. He addressed him gently, asking him to allow him to stand in his place to greet Shaikh ʿAbd al-Qādir from there! Dervishes who were with him were deeply touched by this scene of tremendous humility. The dog left its place, so our Shaikh stood on that spot. He faced the noble shrine and addressed its owner. The dervishes who were near to him heard him speak to Shaikh ʿAbd al-Qādir but they did not understand anything he said.

The way our Master treated the dog on this occasion was not unprecedented. In another visit to the shrine of Shaikh ʿAbd al-Qādir, he was only accompanied by Shaikh Sāmān and his chauffeur. When they arrived at the patio in front of the shrine building, he turned towards his companion and told him that he would stand a little with a friend of his. Shaikh Sāmān did not understand what he meant given that the place was empty, as it was about two o'clock in the afternoon on a very hot summer day. The Shaikh walked towards a reddish dog that was taking shade near a wall. He stood next to it and lifted one of his feet a little above the ground and started to move it, balancing himself on his other foot and his staff. He would make this symbolic gesture to humble himself in the presence of great Shaikhs, including when Shaikhs' souls attended the dhikr circle. He remained standing there for a short while then headed to visit the honourable shrine. This dog was the friend our Master had referred to!

That night at the takya, our Shaikh told Shaikh Sāmān to ask some dervishes to wash the takya's yard and the front patio all the way to the street, the next morning, before he left his house for the takya. In the morning, after the dervishes finished cleaning, he left for the takya. Not long after, the dog that was outside the shrine of Shaikh ʿAbd al-Qādir the day before came from the street and headed towards the takya's door, crying with visible tears and an audible voice. When the Shaikh saw the dog, he asked a caliph to tell the dervishes in the takya that this dog was not impure, so that they would not stop him from entering. The dog went to the kitchen and sat under a table where he could still be heard weeping. After a while, a dervish gently picked him up and left him outside the takya. Evidently, this was not normal behaviour for a dog. Allah knows the reality of that creature.

Our Master's behaviour on his visit to the shrine was meant to stress his humility and avoid any sense of pride because of the blessings he received from Shaikh 'Abd al-Qādir and the Ṭarīqa's Shaikhs. This action is reminiscent of words that he often reiterated that a true dervish is in his loyalty and obedience to his Master like a dog to his owner.

The following is an instructive lesson of our Master's to dervishes regarding imitating a dog in its loyalty. He saw a child outside the main takya in Basra throwing stones at a dog that was following him. The dog would dodge the stones and continue to accompany the child. He asked those in attendance to call the child to him. When he came, the Shaikh asked him why he was throwing stones at the dog. The child said that he wanted to stop it from walking behind him, but to no avail. Our Master then asked him why the dog was following after him, and the child replied that the dog loved him. The Shaikh nodded his head in agreement and said to the present dervishes something along the lines of, "This is how a seeker must be with his Shaikh. He must not get angry with his Shaikh and must come to him as soon as he beckons to him". Shaikh 'Abd al-Qādir al-Gaylānī had the following to say:

> O young man, when the servant knows the True One (mighty and glorified is He), He draws his heart completely near, rewards him with everything, confers on him the ultimate intimacy, and bestows on him the ultimate honour. Once he gets used to these, He takes them away from him, leaves him empty-handed, sends him back to his lower self, and establishes a veil between Himself and him in order to test him and see how he will respond. Will he escape? Will he deviate or remain steadfast? If he stands firm, He removes the veil from him and returns him to his previous situation. Have you not seen how the father puts his son to the test? He sends him out of his house, locks the door in his face, and waits to see what he does. If he finds that his son remains on the doorstep, does not go to his neighbour, does not complain about him, and does not abandon polite behaviour, he reopens the door, allows him in, embraces him, and honours him more than before.[1]

[1] Al-Gaylānī, *Purification of the Mind*, 86.

The seeker is like a car that always needs fuel. The seeker needs to perform dhikr, to ask for spiritual help, to see the Shaikh, to come close to the Shaikh, to listen to odes of praise, and stories. Why did Allah say, "We narrate to you [O Muḥammad!] the best of narratives" (Yūsuf 3)? So that the seeker may feel reassured and become stronger spiritually, so that Muslims may feel stronger, "Indeed, We will support Our messengers and those who believe in the life of this world and on the Day when the witnesses will stand" (Ghāfir 51).

Shaikh Muḥammad al-Muḥammad al-Kasnazān
(*Sermon*, 25 May 2000)

16

Listening to Odes of Praise

The impact of any statement on a listener is not made solely by its words. Other factors, such as the identity of the speaker, his style of speech, and his voice, also affect the listener. When a speaker wants to threaten listeners, he speaks in an intimidating manner, and when he wants to earn their affection, he addresses them in a gentle, calm tone, and so on. These factors are important even when reading Allah's Book. Reciting the Qur'an in a beautiful voice and with melodies that touch the innermost corners of the heart increases the impact of Allah's words on the listener. The Messenger of Allah (PBUH) said, "Beautify the Qur'an with your voices, for a beautiful voice increases the Qur'an's beauty".[1] It is human nature to be influenced by beautiful sounds and melodies. This natural phenomenon can be seen even in small children. Indeed, it is scientifically proven that even animals and plants respond to music, as it has been shown to aid in their growth and accelerate their recovery from injuries.

Sufis have always attached importance to composing and singing odes in praise of the Messenger (PBUH) and the Shaikhs of Ṭarīqa. Mentioning them and remembering their qualities affix love for them in the heart. This, in turn, plants Allah's love in the heart because they are His callers and special servants. Songs of praise have a special role in reminding the traveller on the path to Allah of the First Guide (PBUH) and those who followed his noble way, increasing the love for them in the heart and the impact of this love by remembering them. A song of praise emanates from love and inspires love. When a beautiful voice sings it to a beautiful rhythm, its effect multiplies. This is why Muslims of Medina improvised the first ode of praise in Islam, *Ṭala'a al-badru 'alaynā* (The Full Moon Rose Upon Us), when they welcomed the Light of Islam (PBUH) when he arrived as a migrant from Mecca.

---

[1] Al-Dārimī, *Musnad Al-Dārimī*, IV, no. 3544, p. 2194.

Among the Shaikhs of Ṭarīqa Kasnazāniyya whose religious poetry has been compiled and published are Imām ʿAlī Ibn Abī Ṭālib[2] and Shaikh ʿAbd al-Qādir al-Gaylānī.[3] Shaikh Ismāʿī al-Wilyānī wrote poems in the Bāhdīnī dialect of the Kurdish language while Shaikh ʿAbd al-Karīm Shāh al-Kasnazān composed a long poem. It is also said that Shaikhs ʿAbd al-Qādir and Ḥusayn wrote poetry but these manuscripts were burned when the British army occupied Karbchna in the middle of 1919, in retaliation to the two Shaikhs and the dervishes who fought the occupation forces.

Ṭarīqa Kasnazāniyya has a large heritage of brilliant odes, in Arabic, Kurdish, and Persian. In Shaikh ʿAbd al-Karīm al-Kasnazān's time, most odes were in Kurdish because Ṭarīqa was mainly present in Kurdish areas. In Shaikh Muḥammad al-Muḥammad's time, the Ṭarīqa's base changed to Baghdad and the number of Arabic-speaking dervishes surpassed its Kurdish followers, so Arabic became the language of most new odes. Encouraged by our Shaikh, who was fond of praising, remembering, and reminding people of the Prophet (PBUH), Ṭarīqa's writers excelled in authoring dozens of poems, in both classical Arabic and the Iraqi dialect, in praise of the Messenger (PBUH) and the Shaikhs of Ṭarīqa. Ṭarīqa Kasnazāniyya has a huge treasure of odes of praise that one can never feel to have listened to enough. One poet who has many poems that are still being sung is caliph Bāsim Jawād Kāẓim (may Allah show mercy to him).

Excluding some famous songs of praise of the Prophet (PBUH), such as al-Būṣīrī's al-Burda, the odes that our Shaikh and the dervishes of our Ṭarīqa would listen to were authored by Kasnazānī dervishes and exclusively focused on the feats and karāmas of Ṭarīqa Kasnazāniyya Shaikhs. The benefits of odes for a seeker are growing love for the Prophet (PBUH) and the Shaikhs of his Ṭarīqa in his heart and increasing his belief that they are his means to draw closer to Allah.

One poet whose poetry our Master particularly loved was caliph ʿAlī Fāyiz (may Allah show mercy to him), who was martyred by sectarian

---

[2] ʿAlī Ibn Abī Ṭālib, *Dīwān al-imām ʿAlī*. There is near consensus that some or much of the poetry that is attributed to Imām ʿAlī is inauthentic (Khafājī, "Introduction", 20.) It is unlikely, however, that all attributed poetry is inauthentic.

[3] Al-Gaylānī, *Dīwān ʿAbd al-Qādir al-Jīlānī*.

terrorists in 2007. Speaking about Sufi poetry of praise during his visit to London in 2000, our Master lauded ʿAlī Fāyiz and said that, in his opinion, his Sufi poetry was better than that of Aḥmad Shawqī (1870-1932), who is traditionally called "the Prince of Poets". Our Shaikh also commended the poetry of caliph Dr ʿAbd al-Salām al-Ḥadīthī who continues to add beautiful poems to the treasure of Kasnazānī songs of praise. I have quoted in this book poetry from both poets.

Ṭarīqa Kasnazāniyya has talented singers that our Shaikh used to invite to sing in his assembly. He particularly enjoyed listening to Majīd Ḥamīd who sang for him odes of praise for almost three and a half decades. Caliph Majīd has a very beautiful and capable voice to which his perfection of the musical maqams has added even more beauty and creativity. Our Shaikh used to ask him to sing odes of praise even when commuting in the car. He also used to ask for a short piece of singing before he left his assembly for his private room. After caliph Majīd moved to live in the USA, caliph Ḥasan ʿAbd al-Karīm, who has a beautiful voice, became the singer in our Shaikh's assemblies.

Usually, two or three odes would be sung after the dhikr circles on Monday and Thursday nights. Songs of praise would also be performed at religious celebrations, such as the celebration of the Prophetic birth and the birth of Shaikh ʿAbd al-Qādir al-Gaylānī. Dervishes also like to sometimes sing odes in takyas at other times.

When our Shaikh's health allowed him to attend dhikr circles, he would stay for the session of songs of praise that followed the dhikr. After his health deteriorated, he stopped attending the dhikr circles but the singing of odes in his assembly continued. It would be attended by the dervishes who were present in the takya. He continued to attend the religious celebrations that the central takya hosted.

He was greatly moved by odes, with his tears and body movements often expressing what his heart harboured. He was particularly affected when the Prophet (PBUH) was mentioned. Mention of Imām Ḥusayn and the suffering he went through also particularly affected him. He commemorated his martyrdom every year.

Sometimes, our Shaikh would change a word or phrase in an ode to something better. For instance, one poem by caliph Khālid al-Bārūdī (may Allah show mercy to him) started with the phrase "ṣāla ʿalā al-fursān jaddī Ḥaydara" (my grandfather Ḥaydara attacked the knights), where "Ḥaydara (lion)" is a title of Imām ʿAlī Ibn Abī Ṭālib. It is a title that the Imām himself mentioned when he fought and defeated the bravest warriors of Khaybar when Muslims conquered it. The Shaikh pointed out that the word "fursān (knights)" is a flattering description that indicates bravery that should not be used for those who fought Imām ʿAlī. He changed it to the word "kuffār (disbelievers)", so the beginning of the poem became "ṣāla ʿalā al-kuffār jaddī Ḥaydara" (my grandfather Ḥaydara attacked the disbelievers).

In 2015, our Master was gifted by the Shaikhs the following couplet of poetry in Kurdish in praise of the Messenger (PBUH):

Aḥmad Muḥammad har dū yak nāwa
Ṣalawāt ladyār ʾaw jūta chāwa.

It means:

Aḥmad, Muḥammad, the two names are one
Prayers upon the two eyes.

"Aḥmad" and "Muḥammad" are names of the Messenger (PBUH). "Aḥmad" is the superlative of "Ḥāmid", so it means "most-praising", meaning most praising of Allah. As for "Muḥammad", it is the superlative of "Maḥmūd", meaning "much-praised".

Our Shaikh asked caliph ʿAbd al-Salām al-Ḥadīthī to compose a poem in Arabic for which the preceding couplet is used as a refrain when it is sang. This is the poem in full:

Jāhuka Ṭāhā qaṭ lā yuḍāhā,
Majdun Tabāhā, sirru al-naqāwa.
Kahfu al-wujūdi, ʿaynu al-suʿūdi,
Ṣāḥibu al-jūdi, baḥru al-nadāwa.
Sirru al-khalāʾiq, fayḍu al-ḥaqāʾiq,
Nūruhu sābiq wa lā yusāwā.
Kāshifu al-ghumma, rāhimu al-umma,
Sirāju al-ẓulma, māḥī al-shaqāwa.
Durratu Adam, nabʿu al-makārim,
Fa Abū Qāsim ʿaynu al-sakhāwa.
Shaikhī Muḥammad, ghawthun mumajjad,
Wārithu al-asʿad, laysā daʿāwā,
ʿAmidu al-ʿitra, jaddahu asrā,
Wa ʿinda al-haḍra nāla al-hafāwa.
Fakam ʿadīmu, wa kam yatīmu,

Wa kam saqīmu bihi yudāwā.
Al-Kasnazānīyyu badru al-zamāni,
Wa fī lisānī lahu tilāwā.

The poem may be translated as follows:

Your status, Ṭāhā, is ever unparalleled,
Illustrious glory, the secret of purity.
The cave of existence, the essence of happiness,
The source of generosity, the sea of freshness.
The secret of creation, the flow of truths,
His light is the first, with no likeness.
The remover of affliction, the merciful to the nation,
The lamp in the darkness, the eraser of misery.
The pearl of Adam, the spring of gifts,
For Abū Qāsim is the fountain of bounty.
My Shaikh Muḥammad is a glorified Ghawth,
The inheritor of the most fortunate, not a mere claim.
The head of the (Prophetic) progeny, his grandfather journeyed at night,
At the Presence, he was celebrated.
How many a poor person, how many an orphan,
And how many a sick person by him is cured.
The Kasnazānī is the full moon of the time,
And my tongue has a mention of him.

This poem became one of the most often-sung odes. When singers began to perform this poem, our Shaikh would often stand out of respect for the couplet of praise of the Prophet (PBUH) that he received from the Shaikhs. In his last month, he would exclusively ask to listen to this ode.

"Indeed, those who believe and do righteous deeds" (al-Baqara 2:277). Righteous deeds include dhikrs, wirds, repentance, truthfulness, and consuming only what is permissible. It is distancing oneself from lying, that which is prohibited, spying, destruction, killing, stealing, and thievery. Above all, you must be a righteous member of society, "The best of people are those who benefit people".[1] If you hurt people, you are not a seeker. If you commit oppression, treachery, or anything that contradicts the Messenger's Sharia, then you are a contravener and would not benefit from your worship. This is what Allah said to you about prayer through the Messenger, "Indeed, prayer prohibits immorality and wrongdoing" (al-ʿAnkabūt 29:45). O my brother! Even if you are not a seeker, but a believer who prays—whether you are a farmer, an officer, an employee, a merchant, or a believing worker—the sign of ʾĪmān is staying away from violating Sharia. Otherwise, how can you be a believer? How can you have ʾĪmān when you cheat? How can you have ʾĪmān when you consume what is prohibited? You have ʾĪmān and spy on your country? You have ʾĪmān and sabotage your country? You have ʾĪmān and, God forbid, wreak havoc on your country, community, and people? Is this Islam? Islam has conditions, "A Muslim is one whose tongue and hand Muslims are safe from".[2] [You must meet these conditions] for you to call yourself a Muslim, let alone be a seeker.

Shaikh Muḥammad al-Muḥammad al-Kasnazān
(*Sermon*, 12 September 2013)

---

[1] Al-Bayhaqī, *Shuʿab al-ʾĪmān*, VI, no. 7658, p. 117. This ḥadīth also occurs in the form "the best of people are those who are most beneficial to people" (Al-Ṭabarānī, *Al-Muʿjam al-ʾawsaṭ*, VI, no. 5787, p. 58.)

[2] Al-Bukhārī, *Al-Jāmiʿ al-ṣaḥīḥ*, I, no. 10, p. 55.

17

Dealing with Political Persecution

As already mentioned, after becoming Master, Shaikh Muḥammad al-Muḥammad started the building of a grand takya in Baghdad to become the central takya of Ṭarīqa. Construction began in 1980, and he moved from Kirkuk to live there permanently in 1982. He thought that moving the location of the Shaikh's takya to the capital was necessary for Ṭarīqa to spread more and faster inside and outside Iraq.

The new takya not only attracted large numbers of ordinary people, but it also became a place frequented by many famous and learned individuals, including scholars, writers, artists, and media professionals. VIPs, military officials, ambassadors, and diplomats also visited the takya, with many taking the pledge. Foreign TV stations and media visited the takya to document the Ṭarīqa's activities, including dhikr and darbāsha, and air programs about Ṭarīqa. As a result of the increasing popularity of Ṭarīqa, the number of takyas in Baghdad and other cities in Iraq drastically increased.

It is not surprising that the spread of Ṭarīqa aroused suspicion and concern from the government in a one-party country that was controlled by an absolute dictator. Ṭarīqa was always under observation by security agencies, but the central takya, in particular, was under intense and constant surveillance because it was the residence of the Shaikh, hence the takya with the largest gatherings of dervishes. The presence of secret security members was often subtle but it was at times visible. They pretended to be dervishes but their mission was to listen to the Shaikh's sermons, note what dervishes talked about, and observe what took place in the takya in general.

Our Shaikh would respond to the surveillance indirectly by stressing in his sermons that the goal of dervishhood was to draw near to Allah and that the takya was a place for remembering Allah, not for pursuing worldly purposes, including political ones. At times, he would take a completely different stand, exposing spies who had infiltrated the dervishes' community. One day, he interrupted his sermon in the central takya in Baghdad to address someone in the sitting crowd, saying, "My brother, why are you recording what I am saying? What do you hear me talking about? Go to the people who sent you and tell them that all this man speaks about is what Allah (mighty and sublime is He) has said and what His Messenger (PBUH) has said". The person pretended not to realise that the Shaikh was speaking about him, so our Master pointed to him for emphasis, "Yes, you. Go back to whoever sent you". The man stood up and was extremely embarrassed. A couple of caliphs who managed the takya went to him and asked him about the recording device that our Shaikh had referred to, so he took it out of his pocket. Our Shaikh asked them not to harass him, asked him to approach, and he gave him the Ṭarīqa's pledge. He told the spy to return to those who sent him and tell them that he did not find the Shaikh saying or doing anything that would be a cause for concern or suspicion.

The expansion of Ṭarīqa throughout Iraq was the main reason that the security agencies increased their harassment of the Shaikh and the activities of Ṭarīqa. But there was another factor that directly contributed to this escalation. At times, some caliphs and dervishes engaged in talking against the government and the Ba'ath Party. This violated the Shaikh's instructions not to attack the government and to avoid anything that could trigger the fear, anger, and concern of security agencies and cause them to look at dervishes with more suspicion.

One instance of this harassment happened after our Shaikh's return from visiting the holy sites in Najaf and Karbala in 1995. Officials from the leadership of the Ba'ath Party visited him and told him to stop visiting those holy shrines. This perhaps reflected their fear of closer relationships between Ṭarīqa and the centre of Shia religious leadership. Ṭarīqa traces its origin to Imām ʿAlī Ibn Abī Ṭālib after the Prophet Muḥammad (PBUH) and it does not discriminate between the various jurisprudential doctrines, allowing it to attract Shias as well as Sunnīs, which was concerning for the authorities.

Dealing with the growing suspicion, harassment, and restrictions of the government, while simultaneously preserving the Ṭarīqa's ability to preach and the freedom of dervishes, required tremendous wisdom. Our

Shaikh would resort to speaking with and seeking the help of powerful individuals who were on good terms with Ṭarīqa to influence the way the security agencies dealt with it. But, in addition to the harassment of authorities in general, some high-ranking and influential officials also personally harboured enmity for Ṭarīqa, for one reason or another.

Among the decisions of the security authorities that show the escalation of its harassment of Ṭarīqa was in 1998 when the Interior Ministry banned Ṭarīqa from holding its annual celebration of the birth of the Prophet (PBUH), banned army officers who were also dervishes from going to the takya, and stopped Ṭarīqa from sending out dervishes to preach. It also stipulated that there could only be ten takyas in Baghdad and the remaining tens of takyas had to be closed, confining the majority of Ṭarīqa's activities in Baghdad to the central takya. The authorities also banned Ṭarīqa from using drums and tambourines when performing dhikr in the takyas of Baghdad.

Shortly after, our Shaikh saw the Messenger (PBUH) in a dream so he decided to go ahead and celebrate the blessed birthday as usual. He and a few individuals were visiting the Prophet (PBUH), who was sitting in an old-style home in a room whose door was open. In front of the room, there was a courtyard with a column. The Shaikh sat beside the Prophet (PBUH). A man was standing near the Messenger (PBUH), and there was also someone named ʿAlī, who probably represented Imām ʿAlī, sitting in front of the Messenger (PBUH). He was reciting poetry to the Prophet (PBUH) that he hoped would bring joy to his noble heart. The Prophet (PBUH) was looking at him, delighted by what he was hearing. After this lengthy sitting, lunch was brought. The loaves of bread were old-fashioned, red, and in the shape of circles. After they finished having lunch with the Messenger (PBUH), our Shaikh saw the Messenger's (PBUH) noble hand reach into his chest, take out a muṣḥaf (written copy of the Qur'an) with a zipper on it, and place it on the table spread in front of him. He repeated this movement several times, extracting many muṣḥafs from his noble chest. The Prophet (PBUH) wanted to send these muṣḥafs as gifts to people in different parts of the world. This scene reminds us of this noble verse, "There has come to you from Allah a light and a clear Book" (al-Māʾida 4:15). The Messenger (PBUH) is Allah's light through which He sent the clear Book.

The Prophet (PBUH) stood up, so our Shaikh wanted to ask for permission to leave. He looked at the Messenger (PBUH) and implored him, "For Allah's sake, Nahro; for Allah's sake, Nahro". He was asking the Messenger (PBUH) to keep Shaikh Nahro under his care. Asking the Messenger (PBUH) to take care of Shaikh Nahro, but not asking the same for anyone else, including himself, demonstrates our Shaikh's exceptional love for Shaikh Nahro. The Prophet (PBUH) continued to look at our Shaikh without saying anything. The man standing next to the Prophet (PBUH) said that Nahro was the Shaikh's eldest son. The Prophet (PBUH) signalled to our Shaikh and those who came with him to sit so that he could give them something for blessings. He told the standing man to bring a pair of scissors to gift them some hair from the front of his noble head. A towel was placed on the ground so that no hair would fall on the ground and the man began cutting the Prophet's (PBUH) hair. This was so vivid that our Shaikh could hear the sound of the hair being cut. The intense blackness of the hair made it reflect colours. After a tuft of hair was cut, it grew in length. When it was given to our Shaikh, he put it around his neck, held its ends in his hands, began to cry tears of joy, and started saying that he would take it to his children and would not give any of it to anyone else.

The standing man mentioned that ʿAlī, our Shaikh's nephew, who was in Sulaymāniyya, was sick. He was suffering from a heart condition, had lost a lot of weight, and was depressed. The doctors were unable to help him. The Messenger (PBUH) positively responded to the request, and the patient was cured immediately.[1]

A month after the birth celebration, the security authorities arrested Shaikh Nahro. Along with others, he was accused of forging the signature of the Iraqi president, Saddam Hussein, to authorise the granting of rights to export and sell a quantity of Iraqi gas outside the country. They then arrested two of Shaikh Nahro's brothers, first Malās and later Ghāndī. The three stayed in prison for more than eight months before they were put on a sham trial. Shaikh Nahro and Malās were sentenced to ten years in prison while Ghāndī was freed.

The imprisonment of his sons caused our Shaikh deep sadness, one

---

[1] Shaikh Muḥammad al-Muḥammad al-Kasnazān, *sermon*, 26 May 2000; 10 February 2016.

consequence of which was developing diabetes. Two days after the sentencing, his eye bled, marking the beginning of the deterioration of his eyesight and the multiple operations that followed. He trusted that Allah would safely return his sons, especially since the elder of the two was destined to be his successor to the Shaikhdom of Ṭarīqa, but this did not prevent him from grieving. This is similar to how the knowledge of Prophet Jacob that Allah would one day reunite him with his son, Joseph, did not prevent him from grieving over him and temporarily losing his eyesight because of that grief, "[Jacob] said, 'Rather, your souls have enticed you to something, so total patience [is my choice]. May Allah bring them to me altogether. Indeed it is He who is the Knowing, the Wise'. He turned away from them and said, 'Oh, my sorrow over Joseph'; and his eyes became white from grief, for he was [of that] a suppressor" (Yūsuf 83-84).

Our Shaikh's sister, ʿĀʾisha, applied to meet Saddam to ask him to pardon her two nephews. He approved her request and they were released from prison in the middle of January 2000. In April, accompanied by Shaikh Nahro, our Shaikh travelled to London to treat his eyes. He stayed for five months during which he gave many talks to dervishes and lovers of Sufism who visited him. He gave the pledge of Ṭarīqa to a large number of people. He also designated several caliphs to continue preaching and giving the pledge in Britain. Almost every morning, he would spend a few hours in the British Library to review its collection of Sufi manuscripts. I accompanied him on most of these visits.

The following is one incident that shows the extent of the surveillance and the controlling of movement the Iraqi regime had placed Ṭarīqa under. Months before our Shaikh's decision to visit Britain, I had planned to organise a celebration of Shaikh ʿAbd al-Qādir al-Gaylānī in London on 7 May 2000. It was serendipitous that this celebration coincided with our Master's visit to London. I asked Shaikh Nahro to participate by giving a speech. Before the celebration, a security officer visited Shaikh Ghāndī in Baghdad and told him that Shaikh Nahro intended to deliver a speech in a celebration of Shaikh ʿAbd al-Qādir al-Gaylānī and warned him that this would make matters worse for our Shaikh and his family. Our Shaikh decided that Shaikh Nahro would not attend the celebration to avoid any escalation and asked me to deliver Shaikh Nahro's speech on his behalf. Delivering a speech at that religious celebration would not have affected Iraq's security in any way whatsoever, but this attitude of the security authorities reflects their continued and growing suspicion of everything our Shaikh and Shaikh Nahro did and their fear that they were working against the regime in one way or another.

A few days before the celebration, our Shaikh contacted the poet ʿAlī Fāyiz in Baghdad and asked him to compose a poem in praise of Shaikh ʿAbd al-Qādir al-Gaylānī to be read at the celebration. The caliph wrote it in about four hours and sent it to our Shaikh in London by fax on 3 May. This is the poem, and its first two lines explain its genesis:

Write for the people of piety in the farthest of cities,
 about the Quṭb of Baghdad ʿAbd al-Qādir al-Ḥasanī.[2]
A full moon that shone on the two rivers at a time
 When darkness was so long as to almost hid the morning.
Guidance flew to all places no matter how far,
 Like manifestations of the soul flow in the body.
He excelled over all walīs in knowledge and deed,
 He is the Quṭb of karāmas in secret and publicly.
A great Ghawth whose ranks are unattainable,
 No matter how much Allah's servants pay.
Stand in Riṣafa[3] at the Bāz,[4] our master,
 He is the best to answer when you ask him in affliction.
In Karkh[5] I have a progeny from the same lineage,
 My Shaikh Muḥammad, the saviour from temptation.
The Kasnazān are Shaikhs whose seeker wins,
 The cornerstone of Ṭarīqa in obligatory duties and
supererogation.
They are the heirs of the secret of the Shaikhdom of the Bāz,
 The guides to righteousness with the best of advice.

Our Shaikh's extreme caution and prudence did not prevent the

[2] Shaikh ʿAbd al-Qādir was a desendant of Imam Ḥasan.

[3] One of Baghdad's two sides, which is east of the Tigris. This is where the shrine of Shaikh ʿAbd al-Qādir is situated.

[4] One of Shaikh ʿAbd al-Qādir's most renowned titles is "al-Bāz al-Āshhab (the Grey Falcon)".

[5] The side of Baghdad that is west of the Tigris and where the central takya of Ṭarīqa Kasnazāniyya is.

regime from going too far in exposing him, his family, and Ṭarīqa to further persecution and injustice. The official attitude towards him and Ṭarīqa was going from bad to worse. Even the relatively small celebration of the birth of the Prophet (PBUH) organised by Ṭarīqa after our Shaikh's return from the trip for medical treatment in London was a source of concern for the security authorities.

About two months later, ʿIzzat al-Dūrī, the second highest-ranking official in the state, asked our Shaikh to visit him in his on his farm in the city of Dūr. Unlike the rest of the political leadership who harboured enmity for Ṭarīqa, Dūrī had great love and respect for our Shaikh. He had taken the Kasnazānī pledge from Shaikh ʿAbd al-Karīm in the 1950s. He was a patron of Sufi Ṭarīqas in Iraq in general.

Our Shaikh took his two eldest sons, Nahro and Ghāndī, and met Dūrī on 27 November 2000, which coincided with the first day of the blessed month of Ramadan. Dūrī described the release of our Shaikh's sons from prison as "the greatest karāma of Shāh al-Kasnazān". He explained that the Revolutionary Command Council had decided to execute them and that he was surprised when he learned that Saddam had pardoned and released them. He grimly added that it was in Shaikh Nahro's best interests to go somewhere out of reach of the government, as the authorities were planning a new plot against him. The secrecy with which Dūrī spoke and his urging of Shaikh Nahro to quickly flee showed the seriousness of what the government was preparing. Perhaps, the authorities had decided to permanently eliminate Shaikh Nahro this time. The Shaikh decided that his eldest son must leave Baghdad for Sulaymāniyya in secret that night without delay.

About three weeks later, on Monday 18 December 2000, while attending the dhikr circle at night, our Shaikh felt that he was about to fall to the ground had he not leaned on his staff. After the dhikr, he told some of those who were close to him that the regime was planning harm for him and his family, so he decided to leave Baghdad for Sulaymāniyya. Kurdistan had been outside the jurisdiction of the central government since 1991 when the Iraqi army withdrew from it after the first Gulf War. He left Baghdad on 21 December 2000, stayed one night in Kirkuk, and then left for Sulaymāniyya in the morning.

Our Shaikh always showed caution and patience and exercised diplomacy when dealing with the authorities to avoid conflict. His principle was to "sacrifice a part for the sake of the whole" when dealing with the harassment of the security agencies, as any escalation of confrontation came with serious consequences for Ṭarīqa. But this policy had its limitations, as some constraints and encroachments on freedom are unacceptable and cannot be lived under. He had to leave Baghdad.

In 2002, after it became clear that the USA, allied with some countries, had decided to launch a war on Iraq under the pretence of removing its weapons of mass destruction, poet ʿAlī Fāyiz visited our Shaikh in Sulaymāniyya. He read to him this excellent poem:

I love you and that love ignites my longing,
The like of you I had never met and I will never meet.
How many a dear person my heart had in it,
All of them have left and you are still there.
You are as close as my eyes are close to my eyebrows,
Yet I feel your separation despite your closeness.
Far away from you in longitude and latitude,
You reach me so I feel a meeting.
The fire of love burns me in longing to you,
And the fire of my yearning extinguishes my burning.
Reciprocate the love and do not leave me,
Otherwise, love would be bitter-tasted.
Help me against your rejections, O beloved
Who dwelt in the hearts and eyes.
If the heart is broken and I say "Ya Hū",
The lightning of your help comes to me like the Burāq.[6]
If your riding camels have departed my country,
Then Iraq has departed Iraq.

As the poet finished reading the last line, our Shaikh stroke his noble thigh and said "departed", as departing Baghdad was like leaving Iraq. History was to later show that this departure was permanent.

Our Shaikh built a massive takya in Sulaymāniyya and moved to live there when it was ready before the end of 2002. It became the new central takya of Ṭarīqa Kasnazāniyya. It provided accommodation for a

[6] In Islamic tradition, this is the name of the creature that carried the Prophet (PBUH) in his night journey from the Ḥarām Mosque in Mecca to the Aqṣā Mosque in Jerusalem and in his journey to the heavens.

large number of people who had to escape the terror of ISIS after they entered Mosul in the middle of 2014. The takya took over the responsibility of providing for the needs of the immigrants until ISIS was defeated and they could return to their homes.

One karāma of our Shaikh is that in 2004 he sent for a veterinarian to treat cattle of the takya of a certain disease. The vet was accompanied by a talkative old man who questioned Ṭarīqa's need for a takya that large in Sulaymāniyya, referring to a small takya in Chamchamāl. Our Shaikh pointed with his staff to a wall that separated the takya from adjacent land and said that one day this wall would come down because of the number of people. This, indeed, took place during the celebration of the birth of the Prophet (PBUH) on 29 October 2020. His successor, Shaikh Shamsuddin Muḥammad Nahro, demolished the wall to increase the takya's capacity to accommodate all dervishes that were expected to take part in the celebration, who totalled around ten thousand. One amazing aspect of this karāma is that when our Master mentioned demolishing the wall, the adjacent land did not belong to the takya. At some later point, the landlord wanted to sell the land so our Shaikh bought it, which is how it became possible to demolish the wall to extend the takya.

After our Shaikh settled in Sulaymāniyya, Ṭarīqa began to suffer harassment from the local authorities. As the popularity of Ṭarīqa worried the government in Baghdad, the visits of dervishes from inside and outside Iraq to the Shaikh concerned the local security agencies. The harassment of the authorities in Kurdistan continued to escalate until they sent an envoy to a close associate of the Shaikh to inform him of their desire for him to leave Kurdistan. In the second half of 2007, he left Kurdistan and moved to Amman, Jordan.

The seeker wants and Allah (high and exalted is He), the Messenger, and the Shaikhs want from the seeker. They want him to apply the Muḥammadan Sharia, then apply the states, sayings, and actions of the Messenger to himself. If the person would not act in his own interest, how can he act in the interest of others? The seeker must apply Ṭarīqa to himself first, then to his spouse, family, and children. If he can, he may try to apply Ṭarīqa to others, including friends, relatives, and acquaintances. He should talk to them about enjoining what is good and forbidding what is evil.

Shaikh Muḥammad al-Muḥammad al-Kasnazān
(*Sermon*, 5 December 2012)

18

Self-Educating and Admiring Knowledge

Outside of his formal religious and academic studies, our Shaikh never stopped educating himself. For instance, after being forced to leave Karbchna with his father at the beginning of 1959, he studied Farsi in 1959-1960 in Penjwin under Qāḍī Raḥīm, the Qāḍī of Mahābād in Iran and a caliph of Shaikh ʿAbd al-Karīm. His interest in learning Farsi was due to the great number of dervishes in Iran. He was an avid reader and would read as much as he could despite his limited free time. After retiring from politics in the second half of the 1960s, whenever he visited Baghdad, he would frequent the city's bookstores daily looking for books of interest. He was interested in reading about religion, history, politics, and psychology; he had no interest in novels or poetry books.

The following is a karāma that demonstrates his effort to learn and develop his knowledge. In 1972, Shaikh ʿAbd al-Karīm gave caliph Yāsīn Ṣūfī fifteen dinars to buy a copy of Fakhr al-Dīn al-Rāzī's renowned *al-Tafsīr al-Kabīr* (The Great Exegesis). He told him that the commentary consisted of sixteen parts. When the caliph returned to his city of residence in Ramādī, he asked at its two bookshops but they did not have the book. He went to one of Baghdad's biggest bookstores but he did not find it there either. The store owner told him that it was unlikely that he would find it. When he asked for it in a small bookstore nearby, he found what he was looking for. The shopkeeper brought the book, but it turned out that it was written in eight volumes. Yāsīn said that he had been told that it would consist of sixteen parts, but the shopkeeper assured him that every volume contained two parts, so that was sixteen in total. The commentary was an old lithograph edition dating back eighty-three years. Caliph Yāsīn asked about the price, and the seller said that it was fifteen dinars—the exact amount Shaikh ʿAbd al-Karīm had given him! He agreed to purchase it on the condition that he could return it if it turned out not to be the same commentary that the person who sent him wanted. The commentary originally belonged to a deceased Sufi Shaikh whose family had asked the shopkeeper to sell it for them. He agreed to a ten-day return period after which he would give the money to the selling family.

When the caliph went into Shaikh ʿAbd al-Karīm's assembly in Kirkuk carrying the commentary, the Shaikh stood out of reverence for the magnificent Qur'an and signalled to him to place the commentary on a table. The caliph explained that even though the eighty-three-year-old edition was in eight volumes, it consisted of sixteen parts. Shaikh ʿAbd al-Karīm leafed through the book, confirming that it was what he was looking for. Yāsīn was wondering why the Shaikh would need this specific commentary when Shaikh ʿAbd al-Karīm looked at him and said, "My son, I do not need this commentary. Kāka Muḥammad (meaning our Shaikh) has read twenty-two Qur'anic exegeses, which is something no one knows, including his wife and mother. I want him to read this one as well".

Shaikh Muḥammad al-Muḥammad was interested in education and culture in general. After he retired from politics, his assembly in Kirkuk became a daily forum for scholars and intellectuals. Various religious and philosophical issues and books were discussed and debated. These discussions included critiquing anti-religious philosophies that were popular among intellectuals, such as atheism and materialism, and defending Islamic and Sufi thought. He would purchase various newly published books that he and his assembly would read and discuss.

This intellectual assembly continued after he became the Master of Ṭarīqa and moved to Baghdad, with prominent intellectuals, academics, writers, and artists frequenting it. These included sociologist ʿAlī al-Wardī, linguist Ḥusayn ʿAlī Maḥfūẓ, historian Ḥusayn Amīn, historian and archaeologist Sālim al-ʾĀlūsī, Sufi history and literature specialist Kāmil Muṣṭafā al-Shībī, archaeologist Bahnām Abū al-Ṣūf, astronomer Ḥamid Mijwil al-Niʿaymī, preacher of Sulaymāniyya and president of the Scholars of Northern Iraq Association Muḥammad al-Qaradāghī, and expert and reciter of the Iraqi maqam Hāshim al-Rajab. His daily assembly attracted great minds and hosted diverse and detailed discussions. ʿAbd Allah Sallūm al-Sāmurrāʾī, a prominent thinker of the then-ruling Ba'ath Party who frequented our Shaikh's assembly, described it as a place where "one could breathe intellectually and be spiritually enriched". At times, these intellectual assemblies lasted well past midnight, possibly as late as 2 a.m. Our Shaikh's interest in all sciences reflected his immense respect for scientists.

After assuming the Shaikhdom, he continued reading and self-educating, focusing primarily on Sufi books. When he lived in Baghdad in 1982-2000, he visited the large bookshops in Bāb al-Sharqī nearly every day. He would familiarise himself with what they had on their shelves and check out new releases, picking up titles that interested him. On Fridays, he would visit al-Mutanabbī Street bookstores, where books from personal libraries were sold. It was possible to acquire rare and very old books this way. He would also check to see what mobile vendors were offering from the books they displayed on the ground.

After assuming the Shaikhdom, he added ancient Sufi manuscripts, including those that specialised in dhikrs and supplications, to the list of books he took interest in. From the early 1980s until he migrated from Baghdad in 2000, he would spend most of the morning, usually two to five hours, visiting libraries housing manuscripts and books on subjects that were of interest to him. These included the Iraqi House of Manuscripts, formerly Saddam's House of Manuscripts, which contained more than 45,000 manuscripts; the al-Awqāf Library; and the al-Ḥaḍra al-Gaylāniyya Library. He did not limit his visits to the manuscript libraries in Baghdad, also visiting libraries in Mosul and Sulaymāniyya.

Even the deterioration of his eyesight and his need to use a magnifying glass did not diminish his interest in manuscripts and reading. For example, in April 2000, he had to wait for two weeks in Istanbul for the completion of his travel arrangements to London, where he would receive treatment for his eyes. Instead of resting his eyes and taking a break from reading, he would visit the famous Süleymaniye Library daily. The library contains more than 67,000 manuscripts. He would review certain manuscripts from the library's four indexes. He would also visit the Atatürk Library in the same city. He kept this practice up during his five-month stay in London, from April to September 2000, during which time he underwent two eye operations. Almost every day, he would go to the British Library, which contains a large number of ancient Arabic manuscripts. I had the honour of accompanying him on those visits. He would choose specific manuscripts from the indexes and scan through them. When he found something of interest, he would mark the pages he wanted to photocopy, but he would sometimes ask for the entire manuscript to be photocopied.

These efforts contributed to his massive work *Mawsūʿat al-Kasnazān*, the only extensive Sufi encyclopaedia, which we discussed in §11.4. When he came to London, he had already compiled more than 5,000 entries, which is more than half of its contents. This unique encyclopaedia was completed and published less than five years after his return from Britain.

He also made multiple visits to the Library of Congress, Washington DC, as he travelled to the USA several times. He went there for medical examinations and treatment in 2003 and 2004, and in early August 2010, he underwent a kidney transplant there. He returned in 2014, 2016, and 2019 for periodic evaluations and treatment.

In the Shaikh's last years, when he was living in Amman, his body could no longer stand walking through bookshops, so bookstore owners would send new arrivals in areas of interest to the takya. He would look them over and decide whether he would like to purchase or return them. The severe weakening of his eyesight made it difficult for him to read, except when the writing was very large. A personal assistant, which was usually his office manager, caliph Muḥammad al-Kātib, would read the index, and at times specific topics of our Shaikh's choosing, of any new book so that he could choose whether to keep the book. Most days, he would ask his assistant to read for him topics from certain books. His deteriorating health in general, and his weakening eyesight in particular, did not affect his interest in reading books. Not a day would go by without him reading through some books.

One example that shows his interest in reading and manuscripts despite his poor health is that on his last trip to the USA, he visited the Library of Congress to review its Sufi and prayer manuscripts. This, which I think was his last visit to the Library, was on 13 August 2019. I was one of those who accompanied him. This visit took place over 19 years after his many visits to the British Library, most of which I was with him for. The two decades in between had exhausted him physically, but time had not weakened his determination and love for knowledge and work.

I, and at times caliph Majīd Ḥamīd, would read out the catalogue for him and he would identify any manuscript he was interested in. As we could not work through the entire catalogue in that visit, our Master wanted to revisit the Library. Caliph Majīd suggested that he and I would do that on his behalf, given his poor health, which he agreed to. No better indication of his determination and intention to continue to read regardless of the state of his health is that he asked for forty-five manuscripts to be photocopied! The tenth-century poet al-Mutanabbī was spot on when he described this sublime state as follows:

> When souls are ambitious and demanding,
> Their bodies tire in keeping up with their objectives.

In addition to reading books and manuscripts, our Shaikh was also interested in collecting them. His invaluable personal library contained numerous printed books and many Sufi, prayer, and dhikr manuscripts. Some of these manuscripts were very old and rare. It also contained photocopies of manuscripts.

He would constantly stress the need to acquire knowledge and that it is a door to faith and approaching Allah. He also mentioned that knowledge is a form of power, citing the noble Prophetic ḥadīth, "A strong believer is better and more loved by Allah than a weak believer".[1] Just as he respected, opened his assembly to, and praised the efforts of thinkers and intellectuals, he constantly reminded disciples of the necessity to acquire as much knowledge as possible:

> We do not instruct the seeker to abandon knowledge, because it is through knowledge he worships his Lord. Knowledge makes the person understand the act of worship because knowledge is light, "Are those who know equal to those who do not know?" (al-Zumar 39:9). We instruct the disciple to perform righteous deeds. We instruct the disciple to study, to read, to go to school, to learn, to become educated, and to worship. How beautiful it is when a seeker is well-educated![2]

He would reiterate the saying "knowledge is light". He would urge

---

[1] Muslim, *Ṣaḥīḥ*, IV, no. 2664, p. 2052.

[2] Shaikh Muḥammad al-Muḥammad al-Kasnazān, *sermon*, 29 January 2010.

disciples to seek as much education as possible and to obtain the highest academic degrees. He also allowed students to temporarily stop reading the Ṭarīqa's dhikrs during exams, while continuing to perform the obligatory prayers, and to try to make up for what they missed once on holiday. Just as he encouraged disciples to acquire the highest academic qualifications, he urged his children to excel in their studies and to obtain at least a basic university degree. All of his sons completed their undergraduate studies and some completed postgraduate studies. His daughter graduated from a teachers' college.

One manifestation of his support for education and his urging of disciples and people, in general, to obtain the greatest amount of it was his establishment in 2003 of a private university-level educational institution in Baghdad. It was first called "Shaikh Muḥammad al-Kasnazān University College" but was later renamed the "al-Salām University College".

The university opened in 2004 with four departments: Computer Science, Law, English, and Interfaith and Intercivilization Dialogue. To encourage students to enter the latter, tuition in this department was free for several years. The university now includes science and humanities departments. Specifically, it has the following departments: Computer Engineering, Computer Science, Law, English, Banking and Finance, Pathology, Islamic Studies, and Interfaith and Intercivilization Dialogue. It grants baccalaureate degrees in these subjects. The Shaikh wanted it to ultimately develop to teach various disciplines and award postgraduate degrees.

He exerted much effort into increasing the dervishes' degree of awareness and understanding of the thought and practice of Ṭarīqa. He pursued this through the publication of books and literature dealing with various aspects of Ṭarīqa, delivering sermons regularly, urging dervishes to study and acquire different types of knowledge that were easily available to them, and attracting many intellectuals and academics to Ṭarīqa. The educational development of the Kasnazānī seeker was one of his permanent concerns.

In May 2006, he was awarded the Arab Historian Medal and the Arab History Certificate by the Union of Arab Historians, in recognition of the large role he played in enriching Islamic and Arabic culture.

The Kasnazānī person must have zeal, gallantry. Bravery is one of the attributes of the Messenger. A person who is not brave is not Kasnazānī, because a Kasnazānī person has to apply and have the attributes of the Messenger (PBUH). These are the attributes of the Messenger (PBUH), as well as trustworthiness, truthfulness, and bravery, as you must have heard. You have to have all those attributes. The Kasnazānī person has the attributes of the Messenger (PBUH).

Shaikh Muḥammad al-Muḥammad al-Kasnazān
(*Sermon*, 1 July 1990)

19

Appointing the Next Shaikh

As mentioned in Chapters seven and eight, the Shaikh of Ṭarīqa must name his successor before his death. Selecting someone for the Shaikhdom of Ṭarīqa is a spiritual decision, not a reasoning exercise, so the present Shaikh cannot leave it for people after him to decide. Shaikh Muḥammad al-Muḥammad followed this tradition by naming his eldest son, Nahro, as his successor.

Our Shaikh knew the identity of his successor long before announcing it publicly. For example, one morning in late 1981 or early 1982, when Shaikh Nahro was around twelve years old, our Shaikh was having breakfast with his brother-in-law, Shaikh Sāmān. He was filled with joy as he shared with him a dream he had the night before. He saw Sultan Ḥusayn al-Kasnazān take someone off a chair and put Shaikh Nahro in his place. The chair here refers to the position of Shaikhdom. This visionary dream illustrates that the Shaikhs of Ṭarīqa chose Shaikh Nahro as our Shaikh's successor as early as a few years after Shaikh Muḥammad al-Muḥammad assumed the Shaikhdom.

From the end of the 1990s, our Shaikh indicated from time to time that Shaikh Nahro was his Deputy and has treated him with distinction. In 2005, he called a large number of caliphs and dervishes for a meeting in the central takya in Sulaymāniyya. In that meeting, named the "Meeting of the Lovers", our Shaikh said about "caliph Nahro", "Allah willing, he is the future Shaikh; your Shaikh, your brother, your servant, and the Ṭarīqa's servant".[1]

The official public announcement of appointing Shaikh Nahro to the deputyship of the Shaikhdom of Ṭarīqa Kasnazāniyya was made in 2006 in the central takya. In a sermon to hundreds of caliphs and dervishes called the "Address of the Pledge", our Master said the following:

---

[1] Shaikh Muḥammad al-Muḥammad al-Kasnazān, *sermon*, 22 December 2005.

The Shaikh has a General Deputy, and caliphs are deputies among you. However, the General Deputy is Shaikh Nahro. Any instruction from Shaikh Nahro is an instruction from the Shaikh. He is the Shaikh's eldest son and deputy. No one besides Nahro represents Ṭarīqa after Shaikh Muḥammad al-Muḥammad. He is the one who represents Ṭarīqa after the Shaikh. Be mindful of this. He is your little brother, but he is also the Shaikh's deputy. When the Shaikh is present, he is a small dervish in your midst, but when the Shaikh is absent, he is the Shaikh's deputy. Protect yourselves from anyone who wants to deceive you in the name of Ṭarīqa, in the Shaikh's name, or in the Kasnazāniyya name. Be ready and see what your little brother Shaikh Nahro needs from you. Help him, Allah willing, because he is my successor, the Shaikh after me. As of now, no one represents me other than Nahro, because he is the Shaikh's General Deputy. His instructions are the Shaikh's instructions, so it is obligatory to obey him. Allah willing, all he wants is what is best for you. He works for your best interests, and he is sincere with you, sincere with your Ṭarīqa.

The Shaikhs do not designate an unqualified person to preside as Shaikh. The Shaikh does not choose by himself but, it is rather, they—from the Messenger (PBUH) to sayyid 'Abd al-Karīm—who choose. They are the ones who appoint the Shaikh's General Deputy. The Shaikh needs deputies. After Shaikh Nahro comes the caliphs, who are the Ṭarīqa's deputies. Shaikh Nahro does not command you to do wrong. He commands you to do good. He commands you to do what is right and forbids you from doing what is wrong. Obeying Shaikh Nahro derives from obeying the Shaikh, and obeying the Shaikh derives from obeying the Messenger (PBUH), "Obey Allah and obey the Messenger and those in authority among you" (al-Nisā' 5:59).

You must not follow any words besides those of the trustworthy caliphs who have taken these words from the Shaikh or Shaikh Nahro. There may be someone who comes and claims that he was told such and such a thing in a vision. You must not rely on him. There is the Shaikh and there are the caliphs. The present is not like the past. Wherever you are, you can inquire about any matter from the Shaikh's office or from Shaikh Nahro, as he represents Ṭarīqa after the Shaikh. Protect yourselves from hypocrites who claim that Shaikh Nahro is one thing and the Shaikh is another. This is not true. Shaikh Nahro is my heart; he is my liver. He is your servant and a servant of your Ṭarīqa.[2]

Our Shaikh continued to remind people of Shaikh Nahro's

---

[2] Shaikh Muḥammad al-Muḥammad al-Kasnazān, *sermon*, 2006. The video recording of the sermon shows the date 14 November 2008, but this is its production date.

succession now and then, as in this sermon in 2012 in Amman:

> I would like you to be dear brothers for Shaikh Nahro because Nahro represents me after I am gone. He is your Shaikh, the future Shaikh, he is your brother. Keeping to Nahro means keeping to the Shaikhs. He was chosen from his childhood. A righteous person once told me that one night he saw Sultan Ḥusayn had put his tongue in Nahro's mouth.
>
> A few days ago, I saw some people trying so hard to take Nahro out of the chain (of Shaikhs) but, by Allah, they could not do that. He stayed in the chain of Ṭarīqa. They could not remove him from the chain. Allah willing, this is no lie, it is the truth. I must tell the dervishes only what is true. They (the Shaikhs) are people of the truth. Speaking the truth to dervishes is obligatory on the Shaikh. He must not cancel from the seeker something that draws him near to Allah, something that is beneficial to the seeker.[3]

He had immense love for Shaikh Nahro and showed exceptional care for him because he was destined to carry the Ṭarīqa's responsibilities after him. Our Shaikh had a special place in Shaikh ʿAbd al-Karīm's heart, and so Shaikh Nahro had a unique status with our Shaikh. As a testimony for history, I witnessed our Shaikh's love for Shaikh Nahro only exceeded by his love for the Prophet Muḥammad (PBUH). In my last two visits to him, in August and October 2019 in Virginia, he looked to have increasingly more love for Shaikh Nahro and more attachment to him. It seems this was because his departure, hence Shaikh Nahro's succession, was imminent, as our Shaikh left this world early in July 2020.

---

[3] Shaikh Muḥammad al-Muḥammad al-Kasnazān, *sermon*, possibly September 2012.

The dervish must have the manners, etiquette, and behaviours of the Messenger (PBUH). The dervish must emulate the honourable Messenger (PBUH). Anyone who hurts his family, his kin, or people in general is not a dervish. The dervish must apply the noble ḥadīth to himself, "The best of people are those who benefit others".[1] He must be among the best of people.

Shaikh Muḥammad al-Muḥammad al-Kasnazān
(*Sermon*, 22 January 2010)

---

[1] Al-Bayhaqī, *Shu'ab al-'Īmān*, VI, no. 7658, p. 117. This ḥadīth also occurs in the form "the best of people are those who are most beneficial to people" (Al-Ṭabarānī, *Al-Mu'jam al-'awsaṭ*, VI, no. 5787, p. 58.)

20

Muḥammadan Traits

A prophet's muʿjizas (miracles) are necessary for people to believe in his message. Prophethood is a call related to the unseen, so for those who live in the visible world to believe in it, evidence of its belonging to the unseen world is needed. Miracles are proofs of the reality of the unseen world that prophethood speaks of, as they are a window in the natural world into the supernatural world. Originating from a prophet, they prove that that particular prophet has been sent by Allah Almighty, the Knower of the seen and unseen. Muʿjizas humble the intellect and assure it of the messenger's truthfulness in speaking on behalf of the Sender. Religion presents a unique, consistent interpretation of life and the universe, both its visible and hidden aspects. Supernatural occurrences are proofs of this revelation.

Yet, faith is more than just an intellectual conviction. It is also a state of the heart. Faith is a combination of conviction of the intellect and love in the heart. A person's actions are not solely driven by their intellectual convictions. In fact, the role of rational arguments and logic is limited relative to the role of emotions. Emotions play a bigger role in a person's actions, even if people are tempted to believe that their actions are more rational than emotional. This false belief makes them feel that their actions are closer to being right. A person often justifies their actions, including their mistakes, using rational arguments and logic, when it is clear to others that their actions were emotionally driven. Hence, rational conviction does not suffice as a method to mend a person's actions to align them with the requirements of faith. A person needs to have love in their heart that inclines them towards good deeds and diverts them from doing bad. If mental conviction comes from the logic of prophethood and its miracles, then what is this love in the heart and what is its source?

This love is love for Allah (mighty and sublime is He). Its origin is love for the one whom Allah sent as a guide to Him. Humans know the

Sender (mighty and sublime is He) by way of a messenger from Him. The messenger must reflect the beautiful attributes of the Sender so that love for the messenger and, consequently, love for the Sender can grow in the hearts of the people to whom the messenger was sent. Allah blessed our Master Muḥammad (PBUH) by showering him with the most beautiful of traits. He addressed him in His noble Book, praising his noble qualities, "Indeed, you are of a great moral character" (al-Qalam 68:4). One of those great character traits was his mercy and compassion for believers:

> Among them are those who abuse the Prophet and say, "He is an ear". Say, "[It is] an ear of goodness for you that believes in Allah, believes the believers, and is a mercy to those who believe among you". Those who hurt the Messenger of Allah—for them is a painful punishment. (Al-Tawba 9:61)
>
> There has certainly come to you a Messenger from among yourselves, grievous to him is what you suffer, concerned over you is he, to the believers he is kind and merciful. (Al-Tawba 9:128)

The noble Qur'an shows that the Prophet Muḥammad's (PBUH) mercy and softheartedness were necessary for the success of his mission:

> So by mercy from Allah [O Muḥammad!] you have been lenient with them. Had you been rude, harsh in heart, they would have disbanded from about you. So pardon them, ask forgiveness for them and consult them in the matter. When you have decided, then rely upon Allah. Indeed, Allah loves those who are reliant. (Āl 'Imrān 3:159)

It is evident that this noble verse is referring to those who were physically close to the Messenger (PBUH), that is, "the Companions". If the Prophet (PBUH) did not show mercy, softheartedness, and tenderness, which are the opposites of harshness, coarseness, and incivility, even his closest Companions would have left him. It is clear from the command to the Prophet (PBUH) to pardon and forgive them that he treated them with mercy and softheartedness, rather than rudeness or harshness, even when they made mistakes.

There is great wisdom in this divine revelation. Over the years, the Companions had been first-hand witnesses to the revelation of the Qur'an and directly and continuously witnessed an abundance of miracles of the Prophet (PBUH). Yet these alone would not have been enough to prevent the Companions from deserting him, had Allah not combined them with putting exceptional mercy and deep tenderness in his heart. Indeed, this mercy was behind many of his miracles that helped people with their needs, aiding them in both religious and worldly matters. The secret behind Islam's continuous spreading is not solely the Qur'an, as those who wish to belittle or limit the role of the Messenger (PBUH) claim, nor is it even the Qur'an and miracles together. The secret is a combination of the Qur'an, the miracles of the Qur'an's possessor (PBUH), and his wholesome traits of mercy, softness, and compassion, in particular, and his fine character in general.[1]

Wholesome character traits are a necessity of prophethood. A prophet must be an exemplary role model, as Allah (exalted and high is He) has described our noble prophet, "There has certainly been for you in the Messenger of Allah an excellent example for anyone whose hope is in Allah and the Last Day and [who] remembers Allah often" (al-Āḥzāb 33:21). Following a prophet means taking him as an exemplar, so he must exemplify the qualities that Allah wants people to have. Admirable traits also attract the heart, the same way loathsome traits repel it. It is incumbent upon every prophet to be of an elevated moral character. Hence, Allah Almighty commends our Master Muḥammad's (PBUH) moral character beyond all praise, "Indeed, you are of a tremendous moral character" (al-Qalam 68:4). The Messenger (PBUH) said, "I have not been sent except to perfect the best of conduct".[2] He also directly linked 'Īmān with moral character, "The most perfect of believers are those who are best in character".[3]

An elevated moral character is like karāmas in being fruits and signs of a person's righteousness and spiritual advancement and in being a requirement for reforming others. People proactively seek a righteous person because they see him as a source of blessings and good that they can freely avail themselves of. Yet they stay away from a righteous reformer and often even take him for an enemy because he reminds them of the difference between their condition and the state that they should be in and urges them to work and change. Reforming others

---

[1] Fatoohi, "Leadership qualities".

[2] Al-Bayhaqī, *Al-Sunan al-kubrā*, X, no. 20782, p. 323; Aḥmad b. Ḥanbal, *Musnad al-Imām Aḥmad b. Ḥanbal*, XIV, no. 8952, p. 513.

[3] Al-Ṭabarānī, *Al-Mu'jam Al-Ṣaghīr*, I, no. 605, p. 362.

requires from the spiritual reformer fine traits, miracles, and various visible and subtle skills so that he can influence people.

Since the Shaikhs of Ṭarīqa are representatives of the Prophet (PBUH), whom He selected, Allah has bequeathed his states to them. The same way karāmas happen at the hands of a Shaikh of Ṭarīqa because they are an extension of the Prophetic muʿjizas and ceaseless proof of these miracles, the Shaikh also inherits the Prophet's (PBUH) moral character. There are countless karāmas of Shaikh Muḥammad al-Muḥammad that show his inheritance of the way and blessing of the Messenger (PBUH). Similarly, he had Muḥammadan traits that would attract the heart and assure it that he was an inheritor of the Prophet (PBUH).

Allah inculcates in the person He chooses as a Shaikh of Ṭarīqa an instinctive inclination for good traits and provides the circumstances and upbringing that make him acquire those attributes. When he assumes the Shaikhdom, the Shaikh's internal state, conduct, and qualities begin to transform and evolve, rapidly and tremendously, to reflect the requirements and responsibilities of representing the Messenger (PBUH) among people. We will now review some of the Muḥammadan traits of Shaikh Muḥammad al-Muḥammad al-Kasnazān.

20.1 Modesty

Modesty showed in our Shaikh's actions and words. A sign of this deep modesty was that he would avoid attributing any karāmas to himself, ascribing them instead to the Prophet (PBUH) or the Shaikhs. Even when the karāma included clear evidence of his involvement, such as being seen by the person who experienced the karāma, our Shaikh would avoid relating it to himself.

He used to describe himself as a "Servant of the Poor"—a title that the Kasnazānī Shaikhs have proudly bestowed upon themselves. The sanctity with which disciples regarded him and their great reverence for him, being the Master of Ṭarīqa, did not stop him from using this title and repeating the adage "a people's master is their servant". He gave disciples a striking lesson in humility, obeying Allah's command, "Lower your wing to the believers" (al-Ḥijr 15:88). We find an explanation of the saying "a people's master is their servant" in the

Messenger's (PBUH) ḥadīth, "Most beloved to Allah (exalted is He) are those who benefit people most".[4] Our Shaikh had many beautiful, moving words in this regard, as in this example:

> I would cherish that I every day clean the takya myself, wash the takya, and clean the dervishes' shoes. It is an honour for me to clean the shoes of the dervishes who come to the takya seeking Allah's Face because the takya is Allah's house (exalted and high is He): "In homes that Allah has ordered to be raised and that His name to be mentioned therein" (al-Nūr 24:36). I am a Shaikh, but I am a servant; I am a Shaikh, but I am the smallest person in Ṭarīqa. The Shaikh must be a servant, and he must teach his brothers, the caliphs, and his sons, the dervishes, about service.[5]

A sign of our Shaikh's modesty and his service to disciples was his concern for every seeker that visited him and how he allocated time for them, regardless of their social, economic, or cultural standing. Many people of high social standing loved to visit him and spend time with him, so had he wanted, he could have spent most of his time allocated for visitors with them. While dedicating some attention to society's elite, he spent the majority of his time with ordinary people, discussing matters related to dervishes, preaching to them, asking about them, and listening to their needs. A moving situation that his visitors often saw was how he patiently and attentively listened to the details of the needs of the simplest dervishes, some of whom had just taken the pledge. In addition to praying for the one in need, he would, depending on the need, prescribe a specific dhikr for him, advise him, or direct one of his assistants to give him what he needed, such as preparing herbal medicine for an illness he had, providing him with information he was unaware of, directing him to someone he needed to connect with, or helping him financially. The number of visitors with needs did not dissuade him from demonstrating such concern.

One night, when I was visiting the Shaikh in Amman, he was in a lot of pain due to some health issues. The following night, the takya was going to hold the annual celebration of the birthday of the Prophet (PBUH). During those celebrations, our Shaikh would stay in his assembly continuously for about eight hours, which would leave him

---

[4] Al-Ṭabarānī, *Al-Muʿjam al-kabīr*, XII, no. 13646, p. 453.

[5] Shaikh Muḥammad al-Muḥammad al-Kasnazān, *sermon*, 22 December 2005.

exhausted. With seekers waiting to visit him, I politely suggested that it might be better for him to rest in his private room early that night and not receive visitors. He replied with the love of a father for his children on his face that he could not do that to dervishes who had come to see their Shaikh, some from another country or far city, who had left their business and family, and spent their time and money to see him. In his last years, he was in continuous pain, yet he would ignore the pain every night and day to meet dervishes and visitors and discharge his Shaikhdom duties.

20.2 Loyalty

Shaikh Muḥammad al-Muḥammad had tremendous loyalty to anyone who served and aided Ṭarīqa. He would not forget a person's help, no matter how small a gesture or how long ago, and he would not hesitate to lend a helping hand to him when he was in need. He would often inquire about the families of deceased dervishes, their condition, and whether they needed any assistance. These words of the Prophet (PBUH) were personified in our Shaikh, "The person who does not thank people does not thank Allah".[6] Loyalty is one of the most beautiful forms of thankfulness.

Once he spoke about loyalty, saying, "See how loyal Allah (high is He) is to His servants!" He then quoted the following noble verse that does not contain the word "wafā' (loyalty)" but demonstrates most beautifully Allah's loyalty towards his believing servants, "As for the wall, it belonged to two orphan boys in the city, and there was a treasure for them beneath it, and their father had been righteous. So your Lord wanted that they reach maturity and extract their treasure, as a mercy from your Lord. I did it not of my own accord" (al-Kahf 18:82). Because of the righteousness of the orphans' father, Allah made Khaḍir fortify the wall, which was on the verge of crumbling, to hide their treasure until they grew up and found it and could make use of it. He went on to stress that loyalty is an attribute of Allah (exalted and high is He), hence "al-Wafī (The Loyal One)" is one of his beautiful names.[7] Scholars have identified noble verses that contain derivatives of

---

[6] Abū Dāwūd, *Sunan*, VII, no. 4811, p. 188.

[7] Al-Qurṭubī, *Al-Asnā fī-sharḥ asmā' Allah al-ḥusnā*, I, pp. 422-423.

the word *wafā'* related to Allah, such as, "That Day, Allah will pay them (*yuwaffīhim*) in full their deserved recompense" (al-Nūr 24:25). But I have not come across anyone noting the attribute of loyalty in verse 82 of al-Kahf, so the Shaikh's was a new contribution to the interpretation of this verse. He went on to add that loyalty is a trait of the person who is "a believer, religious, and sagacious".

One beauty of the company of our Shaikh was witnessing his actions embody his words. I heard his above words about loyalty in a private assembly that was attended by another caliph. Shortly afterwards, it was the time for the dervishes' night visit to our Shaikh. Among the visitors was one of the sons of caliph Yūsuf Ḥasan Ṣāliḥ (may Allah show mercy to him) who served Ṭarīqa a lot before he was martyred in 2013. Our Shaikh received him with much generosity in loyalty to his father. He kissed him, sat him next to him, called him now and then "my son" and "my beloved", and described his father as a "hero".[8]

Even though there was a large number of people—dervishes and others—who have served Ṭarīqa, our Shaikh would remember all of them, which was a testament to his powerful memory before it was weakened by illness towards the end of his life. At times, someone who was not well known would visit him after a long absence, but he would surprise his assembly's attendees by remembering that person and a service they did decades ago, including details from the distant past about that service that no one thought were possible to remember. He would often take the initiative of remembering those who had distanced themselves from Ṭarīqa and would send someone to call and ask about them, perhaps because of some help that person had once given. Shaikh Muḥammad al-Muḥammad's loyalty was exceptional and not limited to those who were close to him. It included those who helped him or Ṭarīqa in a small way.

I should also mention that the strength of his memory was also seen when he was forced to cut his conversation with someone as a result of receiving an urgent phone call or dealing with an emergency, which might have taken several minutes to resolve. As soon as he would finish dealing with the issue, he would resume his conversation with that person from where they stopped as if he had been reading a book and

[8] Shaikh Muḥammad al-Muḥammad al-Kasnazān, *sermon*, 16 June 2018.

had marked where he had left off!

20.3 Forbearance and Forgiveness

Shaikh Muḥammad al-Muḥammad controlled his anger and loved forgiving people. If something upset him, his anger would be fleeting, "Those who spend [in the cause of Allah] during ease and hardship and who restrain anger and who pardon the people. Allah loves the doers of good" (Āl ʿImrān 134). A beautiful facet of this Qur'anic verse is that it commands us to be charitable and forgiving towards everyone, without discrimination, meaning not only towards Muslims. There were many instances of people hurting our Shaikh in one way or another—because of a grudge, envy, or enmity towards Ṭarīqa—and him responding to that harm with patience, restraining anger, and even forgiveness and generosity. These are noble Prophetic attributes that Allah instilled in his honourable Prophet (PBUH), as in this command, "Repel [evil] by that [deed] which is better; and thereupon the one whom between you and him is enmity will become as though he was a devoted friend" (Fuṣṣilat 34). Allah goes on to reveal that this immensely refined moral character can only be attained through much patience, but it is also a door to great good, "But none are granted it except those who are patient, and none are granted it except one having a great portion [of good]" (Fuṣṣilat 35). For instance, in the Ba'ath Party era in Iraq, there were many individuals whom government agencies charged with spying on our Shaikh and Ṭarīqa. They wrote confidential reports that sometimes harmed and led to problems for the Shaikh, Ṭarīqa, and dervishes. When that regime came to an end, our Shaikh did not try to take revenge on those spies, even when he knew who they were. Some of them even started to consistently frequent the takya and at times visit our Shaikh, who would not blame them for the past and would not even mention it.

Alongside his forgiving nature and tolerance towards those who harmed him and his family, as well as towards those who attacked Ṭarīqa from the outside, he was firm with any disciple that harmed it, by word or by deed, and brought its name into disrepute. Enemies of Ṭarīqa would particularly use whatever disciples did to attack it. Its reputation and image are a responsibility the Messenger (PBUH) and its

Shaikhs entrust the Shaikh of the time with. It is incumbent upon him to protect and defend its purity. Our Shaikh would forgive the erring disciple when he repented, apologised, and reformed his ways.

20.4 Softheartedness

Shaikh Muḥammad al-Muḥammad had an extremely soft and sensitive heart and was inclined to weeping. He would burst into tears when he heard the remembrance of Allah or when the Messenger (PBUH) and Shaikhs were mentioned. He was particularly sensitive to any mention of Imām Ḥusayn (peace be upon him) and the injustice he and his family suffered.

This softness of his heart was also seen in his interactions with disciples and people in general, and in his response to the hardships and difficult circumstances they faced, individually or as groups. As a Servant of the Poor, he was extremely generous with the poor and needy. Many families depended entirely on his assistance.

During the time of the difficult circumstances in Iraq caused by ISIS terrorist activities, which led to the displacement of many people, he cared for thousands of those families. He charged Shaikh Nahro with the responsibility of housing and feeding them, in addition to looking after their health and the rest of their needs. He converted his farm in Dora, Baghdad, into a massive camp to shelter displaced people, whether followers of Ṭarīqa or not. The number of people in the camp reached 35,000. The central takya in Sulaymāniyya also received large numbers of those refugees and assumed responsibility for their accommodation and living needs.

20.5 A Cheerful Countenance

Our Shaikh had a cheerful disposition, always welcoming people with a smile on his handsome face. You could see on his illuminated face this description of the Prophet (PBUH) by the Companion ʿAbd Allah Ibn al-Ḥārith Ibn Jazʾ, "I never saw anyone smile more than the Messenger of Allah (PBUH)".[9] This description embodies the Messenger's advice (PBUH), "Smiling at your brother is an act of charity".[10] Many an

[9] Al-Tirmidhī, *Al-Jāmiʿ al-kabīr*, VI, no. 3641, p. 30.

[10] Ibid., III, no. 1956, p. 506.

individual met our Shaikh with inward or outward enmity but his smile and cheerful disposition cleansed their hearts of all feelings of malice and enmity, filling it instead with amity and goodwill.

20.6 Helping the Poor and Needy

Not only was he generous with those who helped Ṭarīqa or him but the Shaikh also loved to help anyone in need. Ṭarīqa Kasnazāniyya has always been a destination for the poor, needy, and orphans, Muslims and non-Muslims alike. Even when experiencing financial difficulties, our Shaikh did not stop helping those who asked the takya for help. He considered poverty and destitution as holding serious consequences for the individual and society as a whole. He would always remind dervishes that every Muslim is obligated to help the poor and needy:

> When people are poor, they turn to impermissible deeds. But if I, you, and others help them, then they will not resort to what is forbidden. Then, the poor person will say: "Allah has provided for me. My Muslim brothers, my dervish brothers, my good brothers help me; why should I turn to what is forbidden?"[11]

He would cite the noble verse, "Cooperate in righteousness and piety" (al-Mā'ida 4:2), as a reminder that helping the poor and needy is one form of righteous collaboration that this noble verse obligates. He would also stress that this help is one of the responsibilities of the Muslims that the Prophet (PBUH) commanded in his ḥadīth, "Every one of you is a guardian, and every one of you is responsible for his subjects".[12] This responsibility is also a manifestation of the love, compassion, and sympathy that the following honourable ḥadīth mentions, "In their mutual love, compassion, and sympathy, the believers are like a body. When a part of it suffers, the whole body responds to it with wakefulness and fever".[13]

Our Master would often mention the noble verse "spend out of what We have provided for them". The fact that it is mentioned in Allah's Book six times (al-Baqara 2:3, al-Ānfāl 8:3, al-Ḥajj 22:35, al-Qaṣaṣ 28:54, al-Sajda 32:16, al-Shūrā 42:38) is a testament to the importance

---

[11] Shaikh Muḥammad al-Muḥammad al-Kasnazān, *sermon*, 16 September 2013.

[12] Al-Bukhārī, *Al-Jāmi' al-ṣaḥīḥ*, I, no. 872, p. 261.

[13] Muslim, *Ṣaḥīḥ*, IV, no. 2586, p. 1999-2000.

of what it commands. He stressed that the majority of people have misunderstood this noble verse, thinking that it means to provide help to the poor and needy with what exceeds one's need for sustenance. He explained that it urges the Muslim to spend from his daily sustenance, from what he eats and drinks, thus helping the needy from what he spends on himself and his family, "This way he is rewarded. You attain the reward when you think of the poor and orphan children as you think of your children".[14]

The following beautiful incident shows how our Shaikh used to seek ways to help people. While walking in the markets of Amman, he saw something and wanted to buy it even though it seemed like he did not need it. He asked one of his assistants to enquire about its price. The seller demanded a price that was way above market value. The Shaikh asked his assistant to offer the seller a lower price, but the assistant told him that the price he was offering was still very high, only to be surprised by the reply, "I know, but I want to help this seller out!" At times, he would buy things that were overpriced to benefit the seller, perhaps because the seller was low on income or someone who helped the needy.

20.7 Charitableness towards Orphans

Our Master had special tenderness towards orphans, whom Allah Almighty singled out for mention in many noble verses. This is another trait that all Kasnazānī Shaikhs have. In one incident that demonstrates the extent of their love and care for orphans, Sultan ʿAbd al-Qādir al-Kasnazān was walking from Shāh al-Kasnazān's reservoir to Karbchna's mosque when he saw two orphans. He reached into his pocket to give them some money, but he did not find any. He asked the dervishes that were with him whether they were carrying money, but they also did not have any. The Shaikh lifted the orphans onto his shoulders and walked until they laughed, then they hopped off him. When people asked why he had done so, he replied that the displeasure of these two orphans would lead to Allah Almighty being displeased with him. He wanted to give them something to make them happy, and since he did not have any money, he carried them on his shoulders to please them.

[14] Shaikh Muḥammad al-Muḥammad al-Kasnazān, *sermon*, 11 August 2013.

Shaikh ʿAbd al-Qādir al-Kasnazān would also set aside food from the takya and go out at night to distribute it to orphans himself.

In another exploit of our Shaikhs in this regard, a woman came to meet Sultan Ḥusayn al-Kasnazān, but his attendants told her that he was preoccupied with worship. She insisted that they tell the Shaikh that a widow with orphans wanted to see him, and he agreed to see her. She told him that she was taking care of orphans and did not want to beg people for money, so she was asking for his help. The ascetic Shaikh did not have any money that he could give her, but he did not want to send her back empty-handed either. He pulled a golden tooth he had out of his mouth and gave it to her so that she could sell it and support herself and her orphans.

20.8 Giving Gifts

Our Shaikh liked to present gifts to people. He would not hesitate to gift rare or expensive things that he owned. His love for giving gifts to people was not only a feature of his generosity but also an application of the Prophet's (PBUH) ḥadīth, "Exchange gifts, for it causes you to love one another".[15]

One peculiarity of his behaviour was that at times he would buy a thing that he did not need and it seemed that there was no reason for him to purchase it. Later, it would turn out that he knew it would be of benefit in the future, often as a gift for someone. In early 2015, he was visiting a shop in Amman that sold prayer rugs when he asked his companion to purchase a prayer rug that had a picture of the Prophet Jesus on it and another that had the picture of his mother, Mary (peace be upon them both). The companion wondered why the Shaikh wanted these sorts of prayer rugs that Christians usually bought. He was visibly confused, so our Shaikh told him to get the prayer rugs and not to worry himself about the matter. About two months later, in early March, the Vatican ambassador to Jordan, Archbishop Giorgio Lingua, visited him in the takya, so the Shaikh sent for the prayer rugs and gifted them to the visitor!

---

[15] Mālik b. Anas, *Muwaṭṭa'*, V, no. 3368, p. 1334.

20.9 Love for Children

Our Shaikh was fond of children. He loved playing with his grandchildren and devoted attention to the children of dervishes when they visited him with their families and spoke to them with tenderness and prayed for them. When he went to the marketplace, he would sometimes ask his assistants to bring some chocolates or treats to give to children whom they met in the market. He was even affected by the sight of children going to school on foot, saying that he wished he could provide a car for every child to take them to and from school.

As his house in Karbchna was located on a small hill and the number of houses in the small village did not exceed sixty, the nights there were perfectly quiet and he could hear any relatively loud sound. While worshipping at night, the sound of a crying child sometimes reached and pained him until he would find it difficult to continue his dhikrs or worship. He would ask one of his aids to go to the child's house, enquire why the child was crying, and ask the family to try and satisfy the child's need to stop the crying. If they could not, the aid would try to help them in fulfilling that need.

In 2010, the Shaikh used to go for a daily walk in an area on the way to the airport in Amman. One day, he saw young brothers, the oldest of whom was about seven years old and the other one year younger. They were from a very poor family that was living in a tent there. He asked his personal assistant, ʿĪsā, to help each with an amount of money. From then on, every day, the small children would wait at the point where the car would park and the Shaikh would start his walk. He would greet and joke with them and would give them whatever Allah had for them through him in money and sweets. This continued for four years and stopped only after the Shaikh changed the route of his daily walk.

Three years later, in 2017, he went back to his old daily walking route. When the car got close to its stopping place, the passengers noticed that someone on the back of a camel was following them. The driver parked the car facing the Qibla for our Shaikh to perform the sunset prayer. The camel rider disembarked at a distance and approached the car on foot while leading the camel. He greeted the disembarked passengers and asked ʿĪsā whether he recognised him. When ʿĪsā apologised and said that he did not, the rider told him that he was one of the two young brothers that the Shaikh helped for years.

They had saved some of that money and bought a camel, which they had been using to support their family. He threw the leash and said in gratitude that the camel was actually theirs. ʿĪsā took him and the camel to the front passenger side of the car where our Shaikh was sitting. He was still doing his post-prayer dhikrs during which he would not speak, so he signalled with his hand enquiringly. ʿĪsā explained what the youth had told him. The Shaikh's eyes welled up, and after finishing his dhikrs, he prayed for the youth and his family.

In the middle of 2015, I mentioned to our Shaikh that my brother had initiated the process to divorce his wife, and I asked for his prayer. His first reaction was to ask me whether they had children. When I confirmed that they had one ten-year-old son and another that was eight years old, he looked at me in sadness and expressed his pain for the effect of the divorce on the children. He asked whether there was any possibility of mending the relationship and avoiding the divorce. I said that the disagreement and conflict were too much for the marriage to continue and that divorce had become inevitable. He started asking me to look after my nephews as if he were talking about his grandsons, so much so that I found myself having to repeatedly reassure him that my brother and I would take good care of them!

20.10 Caring for the Mentally Ill

Our Shaikh had exceptional concern for the vulnerable in society, including the mentally and psychologically ill and those with special needs. Decades ago, when society lacked the awareness to treat these people with dignity and respect, he would care for them, look after their needs, and ask that they were treated well. When Iraq was under harsh economic embargoes after its occupation of Kuwait, someone told the Shaikh that there were cases of deaths among inpatients of the al-Rashād hospital for mental health due to a shortage of food. These patients suffered from a scarcity of food more than others because they were from vulnerable groups of society that received the least attention from the government and society in general. Our Shaikh had the main takya in Baghdad send food to the hospital daily. Happiness would pervade the hospital's patients as soon as they saw the Kasnazānī emergency aid vehicle. After a while, the government, which treated

Ṭarīqa and everything it did with caution and suspicion, told the Shaikh to stop this humanitarian initiative.

Mentally and psychologically ill patients and those with special needs would sometimes come or be brought to the takya seeking blessings and a cure. Our Master's instruction was to treat even those who suffered from behavioural problems well and to be generous in feeding them.

In the 1980s and 1990s, a retired policeman named ʿAbd Allah (may Allah have mercy on him) with special needs frequented the central takya in Baghdad daily, often for long hours. He had no family to care for him. Our Shaikh ensured that he was looked after well, treated him with special kindness, and chatted with him now and then to teach dervishes to treat this vulnerable group of people with dignity and leniency. When ʿAbd Allah was afflicted with a severe illness, the Shaikh asked a caliph to accompany him for as long as he stayed in the hospital and to donate blood to him. When ʿAbd Allah passed away, our Master instructed dervishes to bury him as his family would have done.

20.11 Compassion towards Animals

Our Shaikh's wholesome nature, compassion and softheartedness were not limited to people only. They encompassed all creation, including animals and plants. This is the disposition of every Shaikh of Ṭarīqa, having inherited softheartedness and compassion from their Master (PBUH). The greatest teacher (PBUH) told his Companions the following story:

> A man was walking when he became thirsty. He went down a well and drank from it. As soon as he came out, he came upon a panting dog eating mud out of thirst. He said: "This dog is suffering from the same thirst I was suffering from". He [went back down into the well], filled his shoe [with water], gripped it with his teeth, climbed back out, and gave the dog water. Allah thanked and forgave him.

The Companions asked him, "O Messenger of Allah, is there a reward for us in serving animals?" He said, "There is a reward in serving any living thing".[16]

---

[16] Al-Bukhārī, *Al-Jāmiʿ al-ṣaḥīḥ*, II, no. 2292, p. 16.

This ḥadīth reminds us of a touching incident that took place one afternoon in the summer of 2016. While on his daily walk in the Jabal area in Amman, the Shaikh heard a faint sound coming from the shrubs and thorny plants on the side of the road. He asked his personal assistant, ʿĪsā, to investigate. It turned out that there was a very young puppy that was seriously thirsty and hungry. It looked like, for some reason, its mother had abandoned it, so it was left unfed for days.

When he saw the puppy, the Shaikh broke down in tears, as if he had lost someone dear to him! He asked ʿĪsā to quickly bring to the puppy water and any food they had in the car. ʿĪsā gave the Shaikh a bottle of water and a container. He poured water into the container and gave it back to ʿĪsā who put it in front of the puppy. The way the little animal began to drink the water showed that he was extremely thirsty, in particular as the weather had been very hot. The Shaikh then threw biscuits to the puppy, which was the only food they had. The impact of this situation on our Shaikh's assistants was further increased by seeing him raise his hands to the sky while crying and praying, "My Lord, forgive me for the sake of this dog!" He would come to the same spot every day and bring water and food from the takya for the puppy until its health was restored. Up until his last visit to America, now and then our Shaikh would take food to the dogs in that area. The dogs started to gather around the car as soon as they spotted it!

There are many events and karāmas that demonstrate the sympathy of the Shaikhs towards animals and their care for them. We will recount some of these. In the 1990s, the Shaikhs informed our Shaikh that the fish in his farm in Dora were hungry. After enquiring from the people in charge of the farm, he learned that the fish had been left without food for three days. He personally went to the farm and fed them. The way the fish competed for the food showed how hungry they were.[17]

In 2006, he phoned, from Amman, a caretaker of the Sulaymāniyya takya and told him that this night, the Shaikhs had informed him that the takya's dogs were hungry and asked him to look after them. When a dervish called Ḥājj Laṭīf went out looking for the dogs, he found them all gathered in one place as if they were waiting for him! He signalled to

[17] Shaikh Muḥammad al-Muḥammad al-Kasnazān, *sermon*, 29 October 2019.

them and they followed him to where he had the food.[18] Our Shaikh would also remind the takya's caretakers now and then of the necessity of feeding the takya's dogs.

A similar karāma occurred one morning in 2014 or 2015. He contacted from Amman a caretaker of his farm in Sulaymāniyya and told him that the Shaikhs had informed him that the dogs were hungry and asked him to feed them. It turned out that those in charge of the farm had not fed the dogs for four days.

Having compassion for every creature was one of the noble traits of the Prophet, "We have not sent you [O Muhammad!] except as a mercy to the worlds" (21:107). Mercy and softheartedness were characteristics that our Shaikh particularly acquired a great deal of after he assumed the Shaikhdom.

20.12 Joking

Alongside his seriousness and firmness in managing the affairs of Ṭarīqa and its dervishes and his keenness on adhering to the commands and prohibitions of Sharia and Ṭarīqa, the Shaikh liked to joke when the time was right. At times, he would make light, humorous conversation with a dervish who was clever and witty, and he also enjoyed listening to stories of funny pranks. Managing the Ṭarīqa's affairs and challenges that arise place the Shaikh under stress, so laughter plays a healthy role in relieving it. The Companion ʿIkrima described the Prophet (PBUH) as follows, "The Prophet was a bit of a jokester".[19] When Ibn ʿAbbās was asked whether the Prophet (PBUH) joked, he replied, "The Prophet (PBUH) would joke".[20] The Companion Nuʿaymān Ibn ʿAmrū al-Ānṣārī often joked and laughed, and the Prophet (PBUH) enjoyed his jokes and humour.[21]

Here is a lovely story about our Shaikh. Caliph Yāsīn Sūfī was joking with some dervishes in the central takya in Baghdad when a caliph named Ṭāhā called him and advised him to stop joking in the takya. Even though Yāsīn knew there was no harm in joking with

---

[18] Shaikh Muḥammad al-Muḥammad al-Kasnazān, *sermon*, 2006; 29 October 2019.

[19] Al-Āṣbahānī, *Akhlāq al-nabī wa-ʾādābuh*, I, p. 495.

[20] Ibid., I, p. 487.

[21] Ibn ʿAbd al-Barr, *Al-Istīʿāb fī-maʿrifat al-aṣḥāb*, 1526-1530.

dervishes, he stopped out of respect for this older caliph. The topic of the conversation between the two had changed by the time our Shaikh's assistant came to inform Yāsīn that the Shaikh wanted to see him in his lounge. Yāsīn was surprised when the Shaikh told him that earlier that day he obtained a book that compiled all reports of the Messenger's (PBUH) jokes! Then he called his wife and asked her to bring the book and lend it to the caliph to read. Before the latter left, our Master related a joke from the book.

After leaving, caliph Yāsīn went to Ḥajj Ṭāhā and asked him, smiling, what he had said to him before he went to see our Shaikh. Ṭāhā replied that he had advised him not to joke in the takya. Yāsīn told him that our Master had sent for him to give him a book that compiled the Prophet's (PBUH) jokes and banter! Ḥajj Ṭāhā was stunned by the Shaikh's precisely timed intervention and realised that his objection to joking had no basis in the Prophetic Sunna. One detail about this karāma is that the book was not in our Shaikh's hands at the time of the incident, but he had to send for it. It is evident that he knew what had happened between Yāsīn and Ṭāhā, so he called the former and then sent for the book to lend it to him.

The person in whose heart there is no love for the Messenger is not a Muslim, "Say [O Muhammad] 'If you should love Allah, then follow me, [so] Allah will love you and forgive you your sins. And Allah is Forgiving and Merciful'" (Āl 'Imrān 31). The faith of the person who does not follow in the footsteps of the Messenger, the affairs of the Messenger (PBUH), is incomplete. Complete faith means love for the Messenger (PBUH) which pulls you towards love for Allah (exalted and high is He). You love the Messenger (PBUH) for Allah's sake. The complete seeker is faithful, loving.

Shaikh Muḥammad al-Muḥammad al-Kasnazān
(*Sermon*, 21 June 1990)

21

Leadership Qualities

As we saw in the previous chapter, having Prophetic traits is both a result and a sign of righteousness. Every righteous person has a noble character. Good manners are a requirement for a person to reform others. A righteous person cannot help others unless he has good manners that make him a good role model to them, so they would listen to what he says, observe how he behaves, and emulate him. In addition to fine character, there are abilities and gifts required for any role of leadership, including spiritual leadership. Noble manners and leadership qualities were both present in the Messenger (PBUH), making him the best of the messengers and people.

The Shaikh of Ṭarīqa is a spiritual reformist leadership role that leads seekers, both visibly and spiritually, on their journey to Allah. The person whom the Prophet (PBUH) and the Shaikhs choose for this great reformist role must have leadership skills to discharge the huge responsibilities of this role, in the same way that he has to have the manners of the Prophet (PBUH). Allah looks with care at the person whom He has chosen for the Shaikhdom of Ṭarīqa, instilling in him an instinctive ability to acquire leadership skills and providing for him the upbringing and circumstances that help him turn that disposition into reality. These skills and capabilities continue to develop and are polished by spiritual progress, experience, and intellectual growth, both before becoming a Shaikh and while in this position.

In this chapter, we will review some of the leadership attributes that our Shaikh possessed.

21.1 Attractive Personality

Allah graced our Shaikh with an attractive, wholesome personality that endeared him to people since his childhood. This personality was one of Allah's gifts that was related to his future role as the Master of Ṭarīqa, "I bestowed love upon you from Me" (Ṭāhā 20:39). The blessing of the

Shaikhdom multiplied this wholesomeness, causing love for him to spontaneously and quickly enter the hearts of all who saw him. This effect was not something that only dervishes felt, but it extended to people in general. Often, people who had met him for the first time would mention his endearing personality. This helped him to establish a wide range of social relationships with different people, old and young, rich and poor. This attractiveness made him sociable by nature. He was always surrounded by people and his assembly was never free of visitors. When going out, he would always have others accompany him. He enjoyed having people around him and enjoyed helping and serving people.

His attractive personality and leadership qualities, which made people trust him, gave him, from his youth, great social standing among tribal chieftains and community elders. They would listen to what he had to say and often turned to him to resolve their problems and disputes. They started to treat him like a clan chieftain when he was still just a young man.

His love for defending the oppressed made him a mecca for the weak. Many who escaped oppression and persecution turned to him and lived in his village under his protection. The protection of the law was limited, if at all present, in some remote areas. He was brave and unyielding when confronting any oppressor, and he was not afraid of blame when standing up for what is right.

21.2 Establishing Relationships with Various People

Our Shaikh had a tremendous ability to develop successful relationships with people from different social, cultural, and religious backgrounds. He had strong relationships with a large number of intellectuals, academics, politicians, artists, scientists, clerics, tribal chieftains, and others. He was helped in this regard by his interest in and awareness of different kinds of knowledge, an exceptional ability to engage with people and exchange views on various scientific, cultural, and political subjects, and his respect for different opinions.

His relationship with someone would not be confined to their mutual interests. He was genuinely interested in people's personal circumstances and the well-being of their families. He was always ready to help.

Personal traits that made him extremely successful in developing social relationships included general courteousness, generosity in addressing others, and purity of heart when treating people. By nature, he loved people in general. He loved to spread amity and cordiality, reiterating and applying this Prophetic tradition, "When a man loves his brother, let him tell him that he loves him".[1]

21.3 Strategic Thinking

Leadership requires a strategic outlook that enables the leader to see into the future and perceive what most people would fail to see. Sometimes our Shaikh would plan or do something that others did not understand or appreciate at the time and whose benefits would be clear only years later. He also would make decisions and do things that involved a fair amount of risk, but these were calculated risks and far from being reckless or inconsiderate. One example was his historic decision after he became Master to move the central takya from Kirkuk in northern Iraq to the capital of Baghdad, despite the sensitivity of government authorities at the time to religious movements and organizations in general. Besides, he was seen as a Kurd, despite descending from the Prophet (PBUH), at a time when the state and the Kurdish nationalist movement were in uneasy peace. Without this change, Ṭarīqa Kasnazāniyya would have remained of limited presence, mainly existing in the north of Iraq and some other Iraqi cities.

21.4 Multitasking

Shaikhdom comes with responsibilities that are completely different from one another. Leading Ṭarīqa requires the ability to manage all those responsibilities simultaneously and with clear vision and efficiency. Within a very short period, our Shaikh might have discussed details of building a takya in a certain city, proposed solutions to certain agricultural problems on his farm, prescribed dhikrs and herbal remedies to diseased dervishes who had come to visit him, checked out new book

[1] Abū Dāwūd, *Sunan*, VII, no. 5124, p. 444.

releases to choose what he would like to read, discussed sending a preaching delegation to some country, and other tasks that completely differed from one another. Managing these responsibilities not only required understanding the details of each case adequately and making the right decisions but also being able to do all this very quickly. A large number of responsibilities means that there is limited time to manage each. Managing different responsibilities efficiently requires special talent that is a necessity of a position of leadership.

21.5 Working Hard

Managing multiple responsibilities at the same time requires the person to be hardworking and willing to dedicate as much time and effort as the different tasks need. Since his childhood, our Shaikh was diligent and assiduous and disliked laziness. When he was at school, he enjoyed his studies and was a hardworking student. He was only eighteen years old when his older brother, Ḥusayn, died, so from then he started to deputise his father regarding his tribal and social responsibilities. He also managed his father's agricultural lands. He would often drive the harvesting machine until he felt tired and would then ask a farmer to continue the work. Had he not had an excellent work ethic and been able to bear difficult circumstances, he would not have joined the Kurdish movement and lived six years in extreme hardship and austerity.

Throughout his life, out Shaikh continued to work hard. He always urged dervishes to work hard and diligently. He would often repeat the well-known saying, "There is a blessing in moving". One of his sayings in this regard was, "Work is blessed and renews life".[2] As he advanced in age and his health deteriorated, this increasingly limited what he could do but he continued to practise as many activities as he could. We have already seen, for example, that in his last months, when his health had seriously deteriorated, he asked for photocopies of forty-five Sufi manuscripts in the collection of the Library of Congress.

Shaikh Muḥammad al-Muḥammad would urge people to work hard for the good of this world and the hereafter, often quoting this famous

[2] Shaikh Muḥammad al-Muḥammad al-Kasnazān, *sermon*, 21 October 2019.

ḥadīth,[3] "Work for this world as if you would live forever, and work for the hereafter as if you would die tomorrow". He would also reiterate it as a reminder that Islam does not call on Muslims to shun this world and its pleasures, but it instructs them to remember that the hereafter is the permanent abode and that they should give it its due in this world.

21.6 Religious Tolerance

The Prophet Muḥammad (PBUH) used to welcome People of the Book, debate with them in a friendly manner, and honour them, in an era when religious tolerance was unheard of.[4] Indeed, one of the first things he did after he migrated to Medina was to create what would later become known as the "Constitution of Medina". It laid out the bases of peaceful coexistence, and even cooperation, between Muslims and the People of the Book and recognized their religious and civil rights.[5] This document, also known as the "Charter of Medina", is considered the first civil constitution of its kind in history.

The Shaikhs of Ṭarīqa follow in the footsteps of the Prophet (PBUH) in respecting other faiths and urging their followers, and people in general, to not ridicule the beliefs of others. This makes people of other faiths look at Sufi Shaikhs with love and respect. For instance, there was a Jewish cleric named Saʿīd who loved visiting Shaikh Ḥusayn al-Kasnazān. Out of his respect for the Shaikh, he would not sit in his assembly, despite the Shaikh's repeated request to him to take a seat. His typical reply was that seeing the Shaikh was enough to make him happy. Khawaja Saʿīd even asked for a letter that he had from Shaikh Ḥusayn to be placed under his head when he died as a source of blessings.

Also, when Shaikh ʿAbd al-Karīm was in Iran, some Jews frequented

[3] Ibn Qutayba, *Gharīb al-Ḥadīth*, vol. 1, p. 286; Ibn al-Āthīr, *Al-Nihāya fī gharīb al-ḥadīth*, vol. 1, 359. This ḥadīth is also mentioned by Bayhaqī, "Work like a person who thinks he would never die, and be cautious like a person who is fearful that he would die tomorrow" (Al-Bayhaqī, *Al-Sunan al-kubrā*, vol. 3, no. 4744, p. 28.) It is mentioned by Kulaynī in this form, "Work like a person who thinks he would die an old man, and be cautious like a person who is fearful that he would die tomorrow" (Al-Kulaynī, *Uṣūl al-kāfī*, vol. 2, p. 57.).

[4] Ibn Hishām, *Sīrat al-nabī*, I, pp. 489-490.

[5] Ibid., I, pp. 126-130.

his assembly. When our Shaikh was in the Kurdish movement, he would from time to time send to his father in Iran a list of medications that he needed. The Jews who frequented Shaikh ʿAbd al-Karīm's assembly were the ones who sourced those medications.[6]

Shaikh Muḥammad al-Muḥammad was keen on bringing different faiths closer and he encouraged respecting different beliefs and cultures. He opened the doors of the Kasnazānī takyas to those of other faiths who would like to learn about Islam and observe how Muslims worship. In addition to his refusal to make a distinction between Muslim schools of thought, he was doubly keen on cultivating a spirit of cordiality, respect, and constructive dialogue between Muslims and those of other faiths.

Muslim clerics who criticised Sufism or were not inclined towards it did not attend Shaikh ʿAbd al-Karīm's assembly. Our Shaikh strived to establish relationships with them, showing generosity towards them when they visited the takya or when he met them anywhere else. At times, he would send delegations of caliphs to religious clerics who attacked Ṭarīqa in their assemblies or from pulpits, to show them, through respect and dialogue, the error in what they said and in creating an unjustified schism between Muslims. His efforts succeeded in reducing the hostility of such clerics towards Ṭarīqa Kasnazāniyya, in particular, and Sufism, in general. He has also reduced tensions between Sufi and non-Sufi groups. This also reflects his extraordinary ability to successfully establish cordial ties with various people, including those of different beliefs.

These are brief descriptions of the leadership qualities of Shaikh Muḥammad al-Muḥammad, which he combined with exceptionally good manners, as we saw in the previous chapter. This made him an educator, reformer, and spiritual leader through whom Allah showered benefits on millions of people.

[6] Shaikh Muḥammad al-Muḥammad al-Kasnazān, *sermon*, 26 October 2019.

Allah (exalted and high is He) says, “Indeed, I will make upon the earth a successive authority (caliph)” (al-Baqara 2:30). Allah’s caliph is a Shaikh who enjoins good and forbids evil. You pledged, you promised the Shaikh of Ṭarīqa that you would be a seeker, meaning a righteous person, a believer, one who has faith in Allah (exalted and high is He). [You promised] that you would be the best person in society; that you would be a just person, an honest person, avoid lying; [that you would] consume what is permissible, speak according to what is permissible, walk towards what is permissible, expel what is forbidden, not consume what is forbidden, not speak of forbidden things, eschew lying, and be a good member of society, so that anyone who looks at you knows that you are a person who has taken the pledge, meaning that you are a human being signed to Allah (exalted and high is He) to be good in society so that people point to you [and say], “this is a caliph or dervish”.

Shaikh Muḥammad al-Muḥammad al-Kasnazān
(*Sermon*, 28 September 2012)

22

Hobbies and Interests

As we have seen, reading was our Shaikh's main hobby. Yet his diverse talents and curiosity for learning meant that he had several hobbies and interests.

He was fascinated by agriculture, which was also his profession. From his youth, he was in charge of his father's agricultural lands, often directly overseeing the planting and harvesting work. After moving to Kirkuk, he established a farm in Bānī Maqān, which is five kilometres away from Chamchamāl in Sulaymāniyya. We referred earlier to his 180-acres farm in Dora in Baghdad where the 1998 celebration of the birth of the Prophet (PBUH) was held after the main takya could not accommodate the large number of attendees.

His talent and creativity in agriculture were especially evident from the farm he set up in Qopī in Sulaymāniyya. When construction began at the end of 2003, the 650-acre land was completely bereft of trees, and it seemed very difficult to use this rocky, high-altitude land that was located between two mountains in a successful commercial agricultural project. The project required overcoming challenges such as identifying a close natural water source and designing water storage and transport methods, in addition to the preparation of roads for the transport of agricultural equipment. When our Shaikh lived in Sulaymāniyya, he personally supervised the work done on the farm and discussed details, big and small, with the engineer in charge. After moving to Amman, he continued to constantly follow up on news of the farm, sometimes daily.

A manifestation of our Shaikh's acumen and intelligence was that he would often alert those in charge of the farm to details they missed, despite his physical distance from the farm and the limited time that he could devote to it due to his many responsibilities. This was another exhibition of his efficient multitasking. One of his karāmas in this regard was that he once called from Amman the farm engineer in

Sulaymāniyya to ask him whether an insect had attacked the Euphrates poplar trees, known locally as *qogh*. The engineer had not noticed this but promised to check and make sure. In a later telephone call, he asked him the same question. The engineer confirmed that when the Shaikh previously asked him, he examined the trees and found no trace of any insect. The following day, the engineer was walking between some Euphrates poplar trees when he noticed that an insect, locally known as *ḥaffār*, had spread on those trees.

The farm grew to have about 40,000 trees, including 25,000 trees of various kinds of pistachios, in addition to other kinds of plants, including walnuts, almonds, oak, chestnuts, pomegranates, apricots, grapes, quinces, tomatoes, okra, laurels, and persimmons, which were new to that area. Our Shaikh also installed artesian wells to supply water when it was scarce. A commentator was spot on when he praised the farm's role in serving the environment, noting that "the Shaikh has built an oxygen factory that suffices all the cities of Sulaymāniyya", noting the role of plants in the process of photosynthesis, where they absorb carbon dioxide from the atmosphere and release oxygen.

The Shaikh's focus on plant quality was no less than his interest in its types and quantities, planting the best cuttings and seeds. His tendency to be creative would particularly shine in his interest in introducing new agricultural products that did not exist in the region, many of which were brought from outside Iraq. To this end, he built a special nursery on the farm for the cultivation of experimental new plants. After successfully cultivating a new species in the nursery, it was planted on the farm. He would generously gift about half of what the nursery succeeded in planting to other farmers so that they could benefit from growing these new crops in their fields. For example, he succeeded in cultivating a type of Indian berry that was not available in Iraq but is now found in many farms in the north of the country.

He was also interested in herbal medicine and had herbal treatments for various diseases. He used honey in many of his medical prescriptions. At times, he would prescribe certain herbal remedies along with a special dhikr for a patient, although he would often prescribe patients only dhikrs. It is important to stress that he did not use these treatments as an alternative to conventional medical treatment. He respected all sciences that serve people, so much so that he would urge dervishes to obtain the most academic education that they could, as discussed in Chapter eighteen.

He had an experimental approach to herbal medicine. When he discovered a certain treatment for a particular disease and prescribed it to an individual who suffered from that disease, he would follow up on the patient's condition to ascertain the effectiveness of the drug. Reading and talking to people with experience and expertise in this area were sources of our Shaikh's information about herbal remedies. There were also remedies that previous Shaikhs used to prescribe and others that they spiritually informed him of.

One hobby that he used to practise before old age stopped him was hunting animals on prairies and in the mountains using a shotgun. He was a skilled huntsman whose skills with various kinds of weapons were polished by the years he spent in the Kurdish movement. Even when he moved to Baghdad, he would often go to the wilderness to hunt rabbits. This was where his interest in hound dogs came from.

It is not surprising that he kept ancestral heirlooms of Ṭarīqa Kasnazāniyya Shaikhs, from Shāh al-Kasnazān to Shaikh ʿAbd al-Karīm, such as dhikr beads, staffs, swords, and daggers. He was also interested in collecting the belongings of Shaikhs of Ṭarīqa in general. He had an ablution water jug that belonged to Shaikh ʿAbd al-Qādir al-Gaylānī, a staff of Kāka Aḥmad al-Shaikh, Shaikh Ḥasan al-Qarachwārī's ring, and other blessed belongings of great walīs. His estate contained a belt of the Prophet (PBUH) that he gifted to Imām ʿAlī Ibn Abī Ṭālib.

He had a special love for dhikr beads, precious stones, and rings decorated with Qur'anic verses and dhikrs. He would regularly buy and gift them, which was one aspect of his generosity and love for presenting gifts. He also cared for antiques and had a longstanding interest in horses.

This world is temporary, a short period. Look at those who lived before us, is there anyone who lived two hundred years, two hundred and fifty years, three hundred years, four hundred years? “Every soul will taste death” (Āl ʿImrān 3:185), “Everyone upon the earth will perish (26) And there will remain the Face of your Lord, Owner of Majesty and Honour” (al-Raḥmān 55:26-27). Death is the destiny of every human being. No matter how much you escape from it, it continues to chase you. When your time comes, when your appointed time is here, there would be no bringing forwards or pushing backwards. You will surrender your soul, even if you amass billions after billions, even if you had all the armies of the world. Where are the pharaohs? Where are the most powerful presidents and kings, wealthy people, billionaires? They are all dust now. The person who is one of the people of worship, the people of prayer, his soul, Allah willing, will be in Paradise. As for the person who is one of the people of corruption will be in the fire. Who will save him from Allah (exalted and high is He)? His creator is the one who can harm him and save him.

Shaikh Muḥammad al-Muḥammad al-Kasnazān
(*Sermon*, 4 March 2013)

23

The Absent Yet Present Full Moon of Kasnazān

Our Master saw the Prophet (PBUH) on the night of his trip to the USA in 2014. He kissed his blessed hand and said to him, "Thanks be to Allah that I did not die so I have touched your hand again".

In a later vision, our Master was told that there was a message for him from the Messenger (PBUH) inside the Karbchna shrines. When he entered the hall of the shrines, he found a message in the form of a framed plaque mounted on the wall. The message was written in raised golden letters. He and his companion in the vision, Shaikh Sāman, took the message outside the shrines and started to read it. A third man from Jordan was reading it with them. The message contained the following, "Accordingly, leave him alone".

Our Shaikh recounted another vision of encounter with the Prophet (PBUH), which seems to have been at the end of 2015 or early 2016. He saw a unique huge dome. There were people outside surrounding it but inside there was only the Messenger (PBUH) lying down. Our Shaikh was told that he was required to visit the Prophet (PBUH). An opening was made for him at the top of the dome so he entered through it. He found the Messenger (PBUH) lying on a very beautiful bed in the middle of the hall, facing the qibla. The Shaikh moved towards him, put his head on his chest, and held his hand, kissing it, asking for his help, and crying. The Prophet (PBUH) put his right-hand index finger, which is used when reading the shahāda, in our Shaikh's mouth. He continued to move his noble finger in the mouth of our Shaikh, who was crying out of love. Then our Shaikh was told that this was sufficient, so he withdrew.[1]

When I visited the Shaikh in Virginia, USA, on Eid al-ʾAḍḥā in August 2019, he mentioned this vision to me briefly, describing it as the

---

[1] Shaikh Muḥammad al-Muḥammad al-Kasnazān, *sermon*, 10 February 2016.

last time that he saw the Prophet (PBUH). I do not know whether he saw the Prophet (PBUH) again before his death. Two months after his passing, our present Shaikh, Shamsuddin Mohammad Nahro, also recounted this meeting in a public assembly and called it "a meeting before the meeting".[2] This indicates that the vision was a temporary meeting in this world before the permanent meeting in the spirit world that took place after the Shaikh departed from this world.

Strangely, all previous Kasnazānī Shaikhs died of a heart attack, departing this world shortly after it. Shāh al-Kasnazān survived only one night, Sultan ʿAbd al-Qādir one hour, Sultan Ḥusayn three days, whereas Sultan ʿAbd al-Karīm lived for three days.[3] Shaikh Muḥammad al-Muḥammad passed away in the same way.

He travelled to Virginia, USA, at the end of June 2019 for treatment for an abdominal condition that caused him severe pains and forced him to continuously be on strong painkillers, as well as for a general medical checkup. He had had heart problems for years before then, but in March 2020 he suffered a heart attack followed by a cardiac arrest. His younger son, Dr ʿAbd al-Karīm, was with him and gave him first aid before he was admitted into intensive care. Despite leaving the hospital after a while, the Shaikh's health was poor and unstable because his heart had been severely weakened.

During the period of his final illness, which left him bedridden, our Shaikh loved to listen to an ode of praise called "Aḥmad Muḥammad". It would be sung by caliph Majīd Ḥamīd, who accompanied our Master throughout his medical trip. He says that one day he visited the Shaikh in the intensive care unit where he was almost in a coma, yet he found him reading al-Burda of al-Buṣīrī, the timeless poem of praise of the Prophet (PBUH).

On 24 June 2020, the condition of our Shaikh dangerously deteriorated, so he was admitted into intensive care in The Johns Hopkins Hospital. Shortly after midnight on Saturday 4 July 2020, his heart stopped and doctors could not restart it, and he departed this world to the mercy of Allah (mighty and glorified is He).

Long in the past, our Shaikh had asked caliph Majīd Ḥamīd to read

---

[2] Shaikh Shamsuddin Mohammad Nahro al-Kasnazān, *sermon*, 10 September 2020.

[3] Shaikh Muḥammad al-Muḥammad al-Kasnazān, *sermon*, 8 May 2000.

the Qur'anic chapter of Yāsīn over him when he died. He said that he had benefited from its blessings and witnessed some of its secrets. The caliph went to the hospital to carry out our Shaikh's wish even though he did not have permission to enter it, which was one of the necessary precautions enforced by the hospital at the time against coronavirus. No one stopped him as he went to our Shaikh's room, although usually even permission holders would be carefully checked before being allowed inside. The wish of our Shaikh was thus fulfilled.

The noble body was washed and prayed over on Thursday 9 July in Virginia in the presence of our Shaikh's elder son and successor, Shaikh Shamsuddin Mohammad Nahro, who accompanied his father throughout his stay in the USA. Our Shaikh was also accompanied throughout that entire trip by his youngest son Shaikh, 'Abd al-Karīm, and caliph Majīd Ḥamīd. On the following day, Shaikh Shamsuddin Mohammad Nahro brought back the noble body of his father to Sulaymāniyya where thousands of dervishes and those who loved the Shaikh were in waiting. All were engulfed in deep sadness for the loss of a rare spiritual father and teacher and a human being whose manners embodied the best of qualities. Before burying the noble body in the shrine that was quickly built in the central takya in Sulaymāniyya, caliph Majīd recited the pledge to Shaikh Shamsuddin Mohammad Nahro as his father's successor, the Shaikh of Ṭarīqa Kasnazāniyya, with all those present repeating it. This was in fulfilment of the instruction of our Master, the full moon of Kasnazān (may Allah sanctify his secret).

May Allah shower mercy on our Shaikh who is absent from our eyes but present in our hearts. May Allah grant him a dwelling with those whom He most favoured of the prophets, the truthful, the martyrs and the righteous. May Allah show mercy to the educator of seekers who spent his life in the service of the noble Qur'an and the Sunna of the Prophet (PBUH) and in spreading the love for the beloved of Allah (PBUH) until he became all love. May Allah show His mercy to a teacher of the noblest and most sacrosanct love and reward him on our behalf.

The Shaikh is a medium for good. The Shaikh enjoins good and forbids evil. The Shaikh directs you towards Allah, so he is a medium for good. You do not worship the Shaikh, I seek forgiveness from Allah. No! You worship Allah (exalted and high is He) with knowledge through the Shaikh's words, through the Shaikh's orders. The Shaikh enjoins good and forbids evil: good as described in the Book and the Sunna; good as described in Islamic texts. The Shaikh orders you to follow Ṭarīqa, Ṭarīqa that the Shaikhs have decreed. This way is not an innovation of Shaikh Muḥammad. This way is decreed from Allah (exalted and high is He), "Hold firmly to the rope of Allah all together and do not become divided" (Āl 'Imrān 103), "Indeed, those who pledge allegiance to you [O Muḥammad] are pledging allegiance to Allah. The hand of Allah is over their hands" (al-Fatḥ 48:10).

Shaikh Muḥammad al-Muḥammad al-Kasnazān
(*Sermon*, 30 January 2013)

Biographical Timeline

I have compiled in the following table major events in the life of Shaikh Muḥammad al-Muḥammad al-Kasnazān in chronological order.

Event	Date
Born in the village of Karbchna in Sulaymāniyya	Friday 15 April 1938
His first marriage	Late 1957
Leaving Karbchna to live in the village of Būbān in the province of Penjwin	February 1959
Divorce from his first wife	1961
Retiring from political and military involvement with the Kurdish revolution	1966
His second marriage, to sayyida Kažāl	Early 1969
The birth of his first son, Nahro	12 December 1969
Shaikh ʿAbd al-Karīm's announcement that Shaikh Muḥammad al-Muḥammad was his General Deputy	January 1971
Settling in Kirkuk until moving to Baghdad in 1982	1971
Performing pilgrimage to Mecca	January 1973
Travelling to Cairo to enrol at al-Āzhar University	Late 1977
Assuming the Shaikhdom of Ṭarīqa	4 February 1978
Performing ʿumrah	The first half of 1978
Starting his first seclusion in Karbchna	26 July 1978
Increasing the number of perennial dhikrs to 100,000	The second half of 1978
Starting his second seclusion in Karbchna	15 July 1979
Starting his third seclusion in Karbchna	4 July 1980
Completion of the construction of the main takya in Baghdad and moving to live there	1982
Renovation of the shrines in Karbchna	Middle of 1982
Replacing the crown of the shrine of Shaikh ʿAbd al-Qādir al-Gaylānī	1983
Publication of his first book *Al-Anwār al-Raḥmāniyya fīl-Ṭarīqa al-ʿAliyya al-Qādiriyya al-Kasnazāniyya*	The first half of 1988
Publication of the book *Jilāʾ al-khāṭir*	1989
Publication of the book *Al-Ṣalawāt al-Kasnazāniyya*	1990

Proposing the Muḥammadī calendar and starting its implementation	19 September 1991
Sending the first caliph to India to preach	1994
Proposing the Muḥammadī Shamsī calendar and starting its implementation	2 May 1994
Adding al-Ṣalāt al-Waṣfiyya to the dhikrs of Ṭarīqa	July 1996
Publication of the book *Al-Ṭarīqa al-ʿAliyya al-Qādiriyya al-Kasnazāniyya*	1998
Arrival in London, UK, for medical treatment	26 April 2000
Migration from Baghdad to Sulaymāniyya	21 December 2000
Travelling to the USA for medical treatment	2003
Founding the Shaikh Muḥammad al-Kasnazān University College (al-Salām University College)	2003
Travelling to the USA for medical treatment	2004
Pulication of *Mawsūʿat al-Kasnazān fīmā aṣṭalaḥa ʿalayhi ahlu al-taṣṣawuf wal-ʿirfān*	2005
Renovation of the shrine of Shaikh Ismāʿīl al-Wilyānī in ʿAqra and clothing it in a gold shroud	9 May 2006
Being awarded the "Arab Historian Medal" and the "Arab History Certificate" by the Union of Arab Historians	May 2006
Migration from Sulaymāniyya to Amman, Jordan	2 August 2007
Having a kidney transplant in the USA	2010
Receiving the Ḥizb al-Wāw	2013
Travelling to the USA for medical treatment	2014
Adding this dhikr to the daily wirds: *Astaghfiru Allah al-ladhī Lā ilāha illā Huwa ar-Raḥmān ar-Raḥīm al-Ḥayyu al-Qayyūm al-ladhī lā yamūt wa-atūbu ʿilayhi Rabbī ighfir lī*	March 2016
Being called Muḥammad al-Muḥammad by the Prophet (PBUH)	18 May 2016
Being awarded the title of "caliph" by the Shaikhs of Ṭarīqa	22 June 2016
Travelling to the USA for medical treatment	22 July 2016
Adding one hundred repetitions of *lā ilāha illā Allah* to Wird al-ʿAṣr	28 January 2018
Travelling to the USA for medical treatment	24 June 2019
Departing this world to Allah's mercy	4 July 2020

References

ʿAbd al-Raḥmān, Saʿīd. *Shuyūkh al-azhar.* Vol. 5, Cairo: Al-Sharika al-ʿArabiyya lil-Nashr wal-Tawzīʿ, Undated.

Abū al-Fidāʾ, ʿImād al-Dīn Ismāʿīl. *Al-Mukhtaṣar fī akhbār al-bashar.* 4 vols. Egypt: Al-Maṭbaʿa al-Ḥusayniyya, 1907.

Abū Dāwūd, Sulaymān b. al-Ashʿath. *Sunan Abī Dāwūd.* Edited by Shuʿayb al-Arnaʾūṭ and Muḥammad Qaraballī. 7 vols. Damascus: Dār al-Risāla al-ʿĀlamiyya, 2009.

Aḥmad b. Ḥanbal. *Musnad al-Imām Aḥmad b. Ḥanbal.* Edited by Shuʿayb al-Arnaʾūṭ et al. 50 vols. Beirut: Muʾassasat al-Risāla, 1995-2001.

Al-Bakrī, Abū Bakr. *Iʿānat al-ṭālibīn.* 4 vols. Egypt: Dār Iḥyāa al-Kutub al-ʿArabiyya, H 1300.

Al-Bayhaqī, Aḥmad b. Al-Ḥusain. *Al-Sunan al-kubrā.* Edited by Muḥammad ʿAṭāʾ. 11 vols. Beirut: Dār al-Kutub al-ʿIlmiyya, 2003.

Al-Bayhaqī, Aḥmad Ibn al-Ḥusayn. *Shuʿab al-ʾīmān.* 7 vols. Beirut: Dār al-Kutub al-ʿIlmiyya, 2000.

Al-Bukhārī, Muḥammad. *Al-Jāmiʿ al-ṣaḥīḥ.* Edited by ʿAbd al-Qādir al-Ḥamad. 3 vols. Riyadh: ʿAbd al-Qādir al-Ḥamad, 2008.

Al-Dārimī, ʿAbd Allāh. *Musnad Al-Dārimī.* Edited by Ḥusain al-Dārānī. 4 vols. Riyadh: Dār al-Maghnī lil-Nashr wal-Tawzīʿ, 2000.

Al-Gaylānī, ʿAbd Al-Qādir. *Purification of the Mind (Jila' al-khatir) – Third Edition: Sermons on Drawing Near to God.* Translated by Louay Fatoohi and Shetha Al-Dargazelli. 3 ed. Birmingham, UK: Safis Publishing, 2021.

Al-Gaylānī, ʿAbd al-Razzāq. *Al-Shaikh ʿAbd al-Qādir: al-imām al-zāhid al-qudwa.* Damascus: Dār al-Qalam, 1994.

Al-Gaylānī, Mājid ʿArsān. *Hākathā ẓahara jīl ṣalāḥ al-dīn wa-hākathā ʿādat al-quds.* Virginia: Al-Maʿhad Al-ʿĀlamī Lil-Fikr Al-Islāmī, 1981.

Al-Gaylānī, Shaikh ʿAbd al-Qādir. *Dīwān ʿAbd al-Qādir al-Jīlānī.* Edited by Yūsuf Zaydān. Beirut: Dār al-Jīl, Undated.

Al-Haytamī, Aḥmad Shihā al-Dīn Ibn Ḥajar. *Al-Fatāwā al-ḥadīthiyya.* Beirut: Dār al-Maʿrifa, Undated.

Al-Iṣbahānī, Faḍl Allah Ibn Rūzbhān. *Sharḥ ṣalawāt chharda maʿṣūm – wasīlat al-khādim ʾilā al-makhdūm.*.

Al-Kasnazān, Alī Ḥusayn. "Al-Mujāhid al-Akbar al-shaikh ʿAbd al-Qādir al-Kasnazān". *Unpublished article shared by the author* (2017).

Al-Kasnazān, Shaikh Muḥammad Al-Muḥammad. *Al-Anwār al-raḥmāniyya fīl-ṭarīqa al-ʿaliyya al-qādiriyya al-kasnazāniyya.* Baghdad: Sharikat ʿIshtār Lil-Ṭibāʿa wal-Nashr, 1988.

———. *Al-Ṭarīqa al-ʿaliyya al-qādiriyya al-kasnazāniyya.* Baghdad: Al-Ṭarīqa Al-Kasnazāniyya, 1998.

———. *Mawsūʿat al-kasnazān fīmā aṣṭalaḥa ʿalayhi ahl al-taṣṣawuf wal-ʿirfān.* Damascus: Dār al-Maḥabba, 2005.

Al-Kasnazān, Shaikh Muḥammad Al-Muḥammad, Shetha Al-Dargazelli, Louay Fatoohi, and Hāmīd M. Al-Niʿīmī. "Nahjun jadīdun naḥwa taʾrīkhin daqīqin lil-sīra al-nabawiyya wal-ʿaṣr al-islāmī al-awwal". *Dirāsat ʿArābiyya* 1, no. 2 (1994).

Al-Kulaynī, Muḥammad Yaʿqūb. *Uṣūl al-kāfī.* Beirut: Manshūrāt al-Fajr, 2007.

Al-Marʿashī, Shihāb al-Dīn. *Mulḥaqāt al-ʾihqāq.* Edited by Maḥmūd Al-Marʿashī. Vol. 33, Qom: Manshurāt Maktabat ʾĀyat Allah al-ʿUẓmā Al-Marʿashī al-Najafī, 1957.

Al-Mudarris, ʿAbd al-Karīm. *ʿUlamāʾunā fī-khidmat al-ʿilm wal-dīn.* Baghdad: Dār al-Ḥurriya Lil-Ṭibāʿa, 1983.

Al-Muttaqī Al-Hindī, ʿAlāʾ al-Dīn. *Kanz al-ʿummāl fī sinan al-aqwāl wal-afʿāl.* Beirut: Muʾassasat al-Risāla.

Al-Nabhānī, Yūsuf Ismāʿīl. *Daʿwat tashrīfāt maʿā al-malaʾ al-aʿlā li-afḍali al-salawāt ʿalā sayyid al-sādāt.* Edited by Bashshār Al-Dimashqī. Damascus: Dār Qabāʾ, 2017.

———. *Saʿādat al-dārayn fī al-ṣalāt ʻalā sayyid al-kawnayn.* Beirut: Dār Al-Fikr, 2012.

Al-Najafī, Muḥammad. *Baḥr al-ansāb (al-mushajjar al-kashshāf li-uṣūl al-sāda al-ashrāf).* Edited by Anas al-Ḥasanī. Medina: Dār Al-Mujtabā Lil-Nashr wal-Tawzīʿ, 1999.

Al-Nazilī, Muḥammad. *Khazīnat al-asrār jalīlat al-adhkār.* Egypt: Al-Maṭbaʿaal-Khayriyya, 1891.

Al-Qurṭubī, Muḥammad. *Al-Asnā fī-sharḥ asmāʾ Allah al-ḥusnā.* Edited by Muḥammad Ḥasan Jabal and Ṭāriq Aḥmad Muḥammad. 2 vols. Tanta: Dār al-Ṣaḥaba Lil-Turāth bi-Ṭanta, 1995.

Al-Qushayrī, Abū al-Qāsim. *Al-Risāla al-qushayriyya.* Edited by ʿAbd al-Ḥalīm Maḥmūd and Maḥmūd bin Al-Sharīf. Cairo: Muʾassasat Dār al-Shaʿb, 1989.

Al-Rāzī, Fakhr al-Dīn. *Al-Tafsīr al-kabīr (mafātiḥ al-ghayb).* 32 vols. Beirut: Dār al-Fikr lil-Ṭibāʿa wal-Nashr wal-Tawzīʿ, 1981.

Al-Ṣallābī, ʿAlī Muḥammad. *Al-Dawla al-zangiyya wa-najāḥ al-mashrūʿ al-islāmī biqiyādat Nūr al-Dīn Maḥmūd al-Shahīd fi-muqawamt al-taghalghul al-bāṭinī wal-ghazū al-ṣalībī.* Beirut: Dār al-Maʿrifa, 2007.

Al-Ṭabarānī, Sulaymān Ibn Aḥmad. *Al-Muʿjam al-ʾawsaṭ.* Edited by Ṭ. ʿAwaḍ Allah and ʿA. Ibrāhīm. Cairo: Dār Al-Ḥaramyn lil-Ṭibāʿa wal-Nashr, 1995.

———. *Al-Muʿjam al-kabīr.* Edited by Ḥamdī al-Salafī. Cairo: Maktabat Ibn Taymiyya, Undated.

———. *Al-Muʿjam Al-Ṣaghīr.* Edited by Muḥammad Amrīr. Beirut: Al-Maktab al-Islāmī, 1985.

Al-Tādifī, Muḥammad Ibn Yaḥyā. *Qalāʾid al-jawāhir.* Cairo: Al-Maṭbaʿa Al-Ḥamīdiyya, 1356 H.

Al-Tirmidhī, Muḥammad. *Al-Jāmiʿ al-kabīr.* Edited by Bashshār Maʿrūf. 6 vols. Beirut: Dār al-Gharb al-Islāmī, 1996.

Al-Āṣbahānī, Abū Naʿīm. *Akhlāq al-nabī wa-ʾādābuh.* Edited by Ṣāliḥ al-Wanyān. 4 vols. Riyadh: Dār al-Muslim, 1998.

———. *Dalāʾil al-nubuwwa.* Edited by Muḥammad Rawās Qalʿa Jī and ʿAbd al-Barr ʿAbbas. 2 vols. Beirut: Dār al-Nafāʾis, 1986.

ʿAlī Ibn Abī Ṭālib, Imām. *Dīwān al-imām ʿAlī.* Edited by Muḥammad Khafājī. Beirut: Dār Ibn Zaydūn, Undated.

Bell, Gertrude. *Review of the civil administration of Mesopotamia.* His Majesty's Stationery Office, 1920.

Edmonds, C. J. *Kurds, Turks and Arabs: politics, travel and research in North-Eastern Iraq 1919-1925.* London: Oxford University Press, 1957.

Fatoohi, Louay. *Al-Taṣawwuf fil-ṭarīqa al-ʿalīyya al-qādiriyya al-kasnazāniyya: manjahjun taʿbīqī lil-jānib al-rūḥī lil-Islām.* Birmingham: Dār al-Ṭarīqa, 2020.

———, "Leadership qualities of Prophet Muhammad," *Louay Fatoohi's Blog*, 10/10, 2014, https://tinyurl.com/4sjn84dr.

———. *Shaikh Muhammad al-Muhammad al-Kasnazan al-Husayni: a life in the footsteps of the best of lives.* Birmingham: Safis Publishing, 2020.

———. *The wonders of Ṭarīqa Kasnazāniyya brought to India.* Birmingham: The Way Publishing, 2015.

Ḥamdā, Wālīd. *Al-Kurd wa Kurdistan fi al-wathā'iq al-biriṭāniyya: dirāsa tārīkhiyya wathā'iqiyya.* Mu'assasat Mukuryānī lil-buhū wal-nashr, 2008.

Ibn 'Abd al-Barr, Yūsuf. *Al-Istī'āb fī-ma'rifat al-aṣḥāb.* Edited by 'Alī al-Bijjāwī. Beirut: Dār al-Jīl, 1992.

Ibn al-Āthīr, Majd al-Dīn. *Al-Nihāya fī gharīb al-ḥadīth.* Edited by Ṭāhir Al-Rāwī and Maḥmūd Al-Ṭināḥī. Cairo: Al-Maktaba al-Islāmiyya, 1963.

Ibn Hishām, 'Abd al-Malik. *Sīrat al-nabī.* Edited by Fatḥī al-Dābūllī. 4 vols. Tanta: Dār al-Ṣaḥāba lil-Turāth, 1995.

Ibn Qutayba, Abū Muḥammad 'Abd Allāh. *Gharīb al-Ḥadīth.* Edited by 'Abd Allah al-Jubūrī. Baghdad: Wazarat al-Awāf, 1977.

Ibn Sa'ad, Muḥammad. *Kitāb al-ṭabaqāt al-kabīr.* Edited by 'Alī Muḥammad 'Umar. Cairo: Maktabat al-Khānijī, 2001.

Khafājī, Muḥammad. "Introduction". In *Dīwān al-imām 'Alī,* edited by Muḥammad Khafājī. Beirut: Dār Ibn Zaydūn, Undated.

Mālik b. Anas, Abū 'Abd Allāh. *Muwaṭṭa' al-imām Mālik (narrated by Yaḥyā b. Yaḥyā al-Laithī).* Edited by Muḥammad al-A'ẓamī. 6 vols. Abu Dhabi: Mu'assasat Zāyid b. Sulṭān 'Āl Nhayyān al-Khairiyya, 2004.

Muslim, Abū al-Ḥusain. *Ṣaḥīḥ Muslim.* Edited by Muḥammad 'Abd al-Bāqī. 5 vols. Cairo: Dār al-Ḥadīth, 1991.

www.ingramcontent.com/pod-product-compliance
Lightning Source LLC
Chambersburg PA
CBHW031544040426
42452CB00006B/180
9781906342418